First World War
and Army of Occupation
War Diary
France, Belgium and Germany

17 DIVISION
Divisional Troops
Royal Army Medical Corps
51 Field Ambulance
12 July 1915 - 6 May 1919

WO95/1996/1

The Naval & Military Press Ltd
www.nmarchive.com
Published in association with The National Archives

Published by

The Naval & Military Press Ltd

Unit 10 Ridgewood Industrial Park,

Uckfield, East Sussex,

TN22 5QE England

Tel: +44 (0) 1825 749494

www.naval-military-press.com

www.nmarchive.com

This diary has been reprinted in facsimile from the original. Any imperfections are inevitably reproduced and the quality may fall short of modern type and cartographic standards.

© **Crown Copyright**
Images reproduced by permission of The National Archives, London, England, 2015.

Contents

Document type	Place/Title	Date From	Date To
Heading	WO95/1996/1		
Heading	17th Division Troops 51st Field Ambulance Jly 1915-May 1919		
Heading	17th Division 51st 57th Field Ambulance Vol: I. Jly & August 15		
War Diary	Warminster Enc.	12/07/1915	12/07/1915
War Diary	Southampton	12/07/1915	12/07/1915
War Diary	Havre	13/07/1915	14/07/1915
War Diary	Sant Omer	15/07/1915	15/07/1915
War Diary	Cormette	15/07/1915	18/07/1915
War Diary	Eblingham	18/07/1915	19/07/1915
War Diary	Eecke	19/07/1915	25/07/1915
War Diary	Reninghelst	26/07/1915	31/08/1915
Heading	17th Division 51st Field Ambulance Vol 2 Sept 15		
War Diary	Reninghelst	27/08/1915	24/09/1915
War Diary	Reninghelst.	18/09/1915	30/09/1915
Heading	17th Division 57th. Field Amb. Part Of 2 Oct 15		
War Diary	Reninghelst	01/10/1915	06/10/1915
War Diary	Eecke	07/10/1915	20/10/1915
War Diary	Rest Camp	21/10/1915	23/10/1915
War Diary	Poperinghe	24/10/1915	31/10/1915
Heading	17th Division 51st. F.A. Vol: 3 Nov 15		
War Diary	Poperinghe	01/11/1915	30/11/1915
Heading	17th Div 51st F.A. Vol 4. Dec 1915		
War Diary	Poperinghe	01/12/1915	31/12/1915
Heading	17th Div F/152/2. 51st F.A. Vol: 5. Jan 1916		
War Diary	Poperinghe	01/01/1916	06/01/1916
War Diary	Houlle	07/01/1916	31/01/1916
Heading	51st Field Amb. Feb 1916		
Heading	51st F.A. Vol: 6		
War Diary	Houlle	01/02/1916	06/02/1916
War Diary	Reninghelst	06/02/1916	06/02/1916
War Diary	Houlle Reninghelst	07/02/1916	07/02/1916
War Diary	Houlle	08/02/1916	08/02/1916
War Diary	Reninghelst	08/02/1916	29/02/1916
Heading	51 F. Amb Vol 6. March 1916		
War Diary	Reninghelst	01/03/1916	01/03/1916
War Diary	Additional For	01/03/1916	01/03/1916
War Diary	Reninghelst	02/03/1916	08/03/1916
War Diary	Steenevoorde	09/03/1916	10/03/1916
War Diary	Outtersteene	11/03/1916	18/03/1916
War Diary	Armentieres	18/03/1916	31/03/1916
Heading	17th Div. No. 51 F. Amb. April 1916		
War Diary	In The Field	01/04/1916	16/04/1916
War Diary	Armentieres	24/04/1916	28/04/1916
War Diary	Armentieres	17/04/1916	30/04/1916
Heading	17th Div. No. 51 F. Amb. May 1916		
War Diary	In The Field	01/05/1916	10/05/1916
War Diary	Armentieres	10/05/1916	15/05/1916
War Diary	Estaires	15/05/1916	15/05/1916

War Diary	Morbecques	15/05/1916	16/05/1916
War Diary	Wardrecques.	16/05/1916	17/05/1916
War Diary	Houlle	17/05/1916	31/05/1916
Heading	No. 51st F.A. June 1916		
War Diary	Houlle	01/06/1916	12/06/1916
War Diary	In The Train	12/06/1916	12/06/1916
War Diary	Longeau	12/06/1916	12/06/1916
War Diary	Allonville.	12/06/1916	30/06/1916
War Diary	Morlancourt	30/06/1916	01/07/1916
Heading	War Diary Of 51st Field Ambulance From 1.7.16. To 31.7.16. Vol 10		
War Diary	Morlancourt.	01/07/1916	03/07/1916
War Diary	Meaulte	03/07/1916	11/07/1916
War Diary	Saisseval.	11/07/1916	13/07/1916
War Diary	Allonville	13/07/1916	15/07/1916
War Diary	Famechon	15/07/1916	23/07/1916
War Diary	Near Buire. (Sheet. 62.d. N.E. D.18. b. 8.2.)	24/07/1916	31/07/1916
Heading	War Diary of 51st Field Ambulance From Aug 1st 1916 to Aug 31st 1916. Vol III.		
War Diary	Becordel-Becourt P.7.d.9.9	01/08/1916	02/08/1916
War Diary	Becordel-Becourt	03/08/1916	12/08/1916
War Diary	Dernancourt	13/08/1916	15/08/1916
War Diary	Bretel.	16/08/1916	16/08/1916
War Diary	Neuvillette	17/08/1916	18/08/1916
War Diary	Gaudiempre	19/08/1916	31/08/1916
Heading	17th Div. War Diary of 51st Field Ambulance From Sept 1st 1916. To Sept 30th 1916		
Heading	Detached Gassed Cases Heated during Sept 1916 Field Medicine "9"		
War Diary	Gaudiempre	01/09/1916	10/09/1916
War Diary	St Amand	11/09/1916	22/09/1916
War Diary	Mondicourt	23/09/1916	23/09/1916
War Diary	Barly	23/09/1916	24/09/1916
War Diary	Auxi-Le-Chateau	24/09/1916	30/09/1916
Heading	War Diary of 51st Field Ambulance 17th Div From October 1st 1916 to October 31st 1916 (Volume 3).		
War Diary	Auxi Le Chateau	01/10/1916	02/10/1916
War Diary	Barly	03/10/1916	03/10/1916
War Diary	Halloy	04/10/1916	08/10/1916
War Diary	Map Ref. 57D 1.40000 D. 26. Central	06/10/1916	10/10/1916
War Diary	D. 26 Central W. Couin	11/10/1916	19/10/1916
War Diary	Luchuel	20/10/1916	22/10/1916
War Diary	Ville	23/10/1916	31/10/1916
Heading	17th Div. War Diary of 51st Field Ambulance R.A.M.C. From November 1st 1916 to November 30th 1916 Volume 3		
War Diary	Bernafay	01/11/1916	15/11/1916
War Diary	Hengest	16/11/1916	30/11/1916
Heading	17th Div. War Diary of 51st Field Ambulance From. December 1st 1916 to. December 31st 1916 Volume. 3		
War Diary	Hengest	01/12/1916	12/12/1916
War Diary	Corbie	13/12/1916	23/12/1916
War Diary	Meaulte	24/12/1916	24/12/1916
War Diary	A.2.d.5.5. (Albert Confirmed 1/40000)	25/12/1916	28/12/1916
War Diary	A.2.d.5.5. Carnoy Montauban Road	29/12/1916	31/12/1916

Heading	17th Div. War Diary of 51st Field Ambulance From 1-1-17 to 31-1-17 (Volume 4).		
War Diary	Carnoy Montauban Rd A.2.d.5.5	01/01/1917	17/01/1917
War Diary	Meaulte	17/01/1916	25/01/1916
War Diary	Carnoy	26/01/1917	31/01/1917
Heading	17th Div. War Diary of 51st Field Ambulance From Febry 1st 1917 to. Febry 28th 1917. Volume (IV).		
War Diary	Carnoy	01/02/1917	17/02/1917
War Diary	Meaulte	18/02/1917	18/02/1917
War Diary	Bonnay	19/02/1917	28/02/1917
Heading	War Diary of 51st Field Ambulance 17th Div From March 1st 1917 to March 31st 1917 (Volume IV).		
War Diary	Bonnay	01/03/1917	02/03/1917
War Diary	Herrisart	03/03/1917	12/03/1917
War Diary	Bretel	13/03/1917	13/03/1917
War Diary	Bernatre	14/03/1917	14/03/1917
War Diary	Hauteville	15/03/1917	21/03/1917
War Diary	Boffles	22/03/1917	22/03/1917
War Diary	Brevillers	23/03/1917	31/03/1917
Heading	No. 51 Field Amb. April 1917		
Heading	###		
Miscellaneous	51st. F.A., 17th Division, O.C. Lt. Col. E.L. Gowlland. 18th Corps, 3rd Army. Phase "B"-Battle Of Arras. "April-May 1917." 1st Period, April 1917. Attack On Vimy Ridge.	00/04/1917	00/04/1917
War Diary	Brevillers	01/04/1917	04/04/1917
War Diary	Monts Ternois	05/04/1917	06/04/1917
War Diary	Givenchy Le Noble	07/04/1917	07/04/1917
War Diary	Habarcq	08/04/1917	08/04/1917
War Diary	Arras Habarcq Road	09/04/1917	09/04/1917
War Diary	Arras	10/04/1917	30/04/1917
Heading	No 51. F.A. 140/2161 May 1917		
Miscellaneous	B.E.F. Summary of Medical War Diaries of 51st Field Ambulance. 17th Division.		
Miscellaneous	B.E.F. 51st F.A., 17th Division, O.C. Lt. Col. E.L. Gowlland. 17th Corps, 3rd Army. Phase "B"-Battle Of Arras. "April-May 1917." 2nd Period, May 1917. Capture Of Siegfried Line.		
War Diary	Arras	01/05/1917	02/05/1917
War Diary	St Nicholas	03/05/1917	09/05/1917
War Diary	Hervin Farm	10/05/1917	31/05/1917
Heading	Mondicourt	31/05/1917	31/05/1917
Heading	Medical 17 War Diary of 51st Field Ambulance From June 1st 1917 to June 30th 1917 (Volume IV)		
War Diary	Mondicourt	01/06/1917	21/06/1917
War Diary	St Nicholas	22/06/1917	30/06/1917
Miscellaneous	Re-Inoculation With T.A.B. Vaccine	27/05/1917	27/05/1917
Miscellaneous	Inoculation	01/06/1917	01/06/1917
Heading	17th Div. War Diary of 51st Field Ambulance From 1st July to 31st July 1917. Volume VI.		
War Diary	St. Nicholas	01/07/1917	31/07/1917
Heading	Medical 3. War Diary of 51st Field Ambulance From 1-8-17 to 31-8-17 Volume VII		
War Diary	St Nicholas	01/08/1917	31/08/1917
Heading	War Diary of 51st Field Ambulance. From September 1st-17 to. September 30th 1917. Volume 8		

War Diary	St Nicholas	01/09/1917	24/09/1917
War Diary	Simencourt	24/09/1917	30/09/1917
Heading	War Diary of 51st Field Ambulance October 1st 1917 October 31st 1917 Volume. 9		
Miscellaneous	B.E.F. Summary Of Medical War Diaries For 51st F.A., 17th Divn. 14th Corps, 5th Army.		
Miscellaneous	B.E.F. 51st F.A., 17th Div. 14th Corps, 5th Army. Western Front O.C. Lt. Col. E. Gowlland. 19th Corps From 20/10/17	20/10/1917	20/10/1917
Miscellaneous	B.E.F. 51st F.A., 17th Div. 19th Corps. Western Front. O.C. Lt. Col. E. Gowlland. 5th Army. 2nd Corps From 29/10/17	29/10/1917	29/10/1917
Miscellaneous	B.E.F. 51st F.A., 17th Divn. 2nd Corps. Western Front. O.C. Lt. Col. E. Gowlland. 5th Army. 18th Corps From 2/11/17	02/11/1917	02/11/1917
Miscellaneous	B.E.F. 51st F.A., 17th Divn. 14th Corps, 5th Army. Western Front. O.C. Lt. Col. E. Gowlland. 19th Corps From 20/10/17	20/10/1917	20/10/1917
Miscellaneous	B.E.F. 51st F.A., 17th Divn. 19th Corps. Western Front. O.C. Lt. Col. E. Gowlland. 5th Army. 2nd Corps From 29/10/17	29/10/1917	29/10/1917
War Diary	Gr. Rullicourt	01/10/1917	04/10/1917
War Diary	Proven	05/10/1917	07/10/1917
War Diary	Canada Farm	08/10/1917	12/10/1917
War Diary	Solferino Farm	13/10/1917	31/10/1917
Heading	War Diary Of 51st Field Ambulance From Nov. 1st To. Nov. 30th Volume 10		
Miscellaneous	B.E.F. Summary Of Medical War Diaries For 51st F.A., 17th Divn. 14th Corps, 5th Army.		
Miscellaneous	B.E.F. 51st F.A., 17th Divn. 18th Corps. O.C. Lt. Col. E. Gowlland. 5th Army. 19th Corps From 8/11/17. Western Front. Nov. 1917	08/11/1917	08/11/1917
Miscellaneous	B.E.F. 51st F.A., 17th Divn. 19th Corps. O.C. Lt. Col. E. Gowlland. 5th Army. 2nd Army From 14/11/17. Western Front. Nov. 1917	14/11/1917	14/11/1917
Miscellaneous	B.E.F. 51st F.A., 17th Divn. 18th Corps. O.C. Lt. Col. E. Gowlland. 5th Army. 19th Corps From 8/11/17. Western Front. Nov. 1917	08/11/1917	08/11/1917
Miscellaneous	B.E.F. 51st F.A., 17th Divn. 19th Corps. O.C. Lt. Col. E. Gowlland. 5th Army. 2nd Army From 14/11/17. Western Front. Nov. 1917	14/11/1917	14/11/1917
War Diary	Solferino Farm	01/11/1917	07/11/1917
War Diary	Proven	08/11/1917	30/11/1917
Heading	War Diary Of 51st Field Ambulance From Decbr 1st To Decbr 31st Volume 11		
War Diary	Proven	01/12/1917	11/12/1917
War Diary	Monnecove	12/12/1917	15/12/1917
War Diary	Barastre	16/12/1917	21/12/1917
War Diary	Metz	22/12/1917	31/12/1917
Heading	War Diary Of 51st Field Ambulance From January, 1st 1918 To January 31st 1918. Volume 12		
War Diary	Metz	01/01/1918	05/01/1918
War Diary	Velu	06/01/1918	31/01/1918
Heading	War Diary Of 51st Field Ambulance From February 1st 1918 To February 28th 1918. Volume 13 Medical.		
War Diary	Velu	01/02/1918	28/02/1918

Heading	War Diary Of 51st Field Ambulance From March 1st 1918 To March 31st 1918 Volume 14. Medical			
War Diary	Velu		01/03/1918	31/03/1918
Heading	War Diary Of 51st Field Ambulance From April. 1st To April 30th 1918. Volume 15. Medical			
War Diary	Warloy		01/04/1918	02/04/1918
War Diary	Villers-Bocage		03/04/1918	03/04/1918
War Diary	Flesselles		04/04/1918	06/04/1918
War Diary	Franqueville		07/04/1918	10/04/1918
War Diary	Lavicogne		11/04/1918	11/04/1918
War Diary	Clairfaye		12/04/1918	26/04/1918
War Diary	Halloy-L-Pernois		27/04/1918	30/04/1918
Heading	War Diary Of 51st Field Ambulance From May 1st 1918 To May 31st 1918 Volume 16. Medical.			
War Diary	Halloy-L-Pernois		01/05/1918	17/05/1918
War Diary	Beauquesne		18/05/1918	25/05/1918
War Diary	Arqueves		26/05/1918	31/05/1918
Heading	War Diary Of 51st Field Ambulance From June 1st To June 30th 1918 Volume 17. Medical.			
War Diary	Arqueves		01/06/1918	16/06/1918
War Diary	Raincheval N18d Map 57d.		17/06/1918	17/06/1918
War Diary	Raincheval		17/06/1918	22/06/1918
War Diary	Herissart		23/06/1918	30/06/1918
Heading	War Diary of 51st Field Ambulance From July 1st 1918 To July 31st 1918. Volume 18. Medical.			
War Diary	Herissart		01/07/1918	09/07/1918
War Diary	Clairfaye O.30.a.9.9. (Sheet 57 D)		10/07/1918	31/07/1918
Heading	War Diary Of 51st Field Ambulance From August 1st 1918 To August 31st 1918. Volume 19			
War Diary	Clairfaye O.30.a.9.9. (Sheet 57 D)		01/08/1918	05/08/1918
War Diary	Talmas		06/08/1918	07/08/1918
War Diary	O.25. Central (Sheet 62 D)		08/08/1918	08/08/1918
War Diary	Corbie		09/08/1918	11/08/1918
War Diary	Fouilloy. (Hospice).		12/08/1918	16/08/1918
War Diary	Vecquemont.		17/08/1918	18/08/1918
War Diary	Talmas		19/08/1918	31/08/1918
Heading	War Diary Of 51st Field Ambulance From September 1st 1918 To September 30th 1918 Volume 20 Medical.			
War Diary	Talmas.		01/09/1918	05/09/1918
War Diary	Millencourt (Near Albert)		06/09/1918	06/09/1918
War Diary	N.10.c.4.2. (Sheet 57 C)		07/09/1918	10/09/1918
War Diary	N.10.c.4.2. (Sheet 57 D)		11/09/1918	16/09/1918
War Diary	O.34 Central (Sheet 57C)		17/09/1918	25/09/1918
War Diary	V.13.c.6.2. (Sheet 57C)		26/09/1918	26/09/1918
War Diary	Manancourt		27/09/1918	30/09/1918
Heading	War Diary Of 51st Field Ambulance From October 1st 1918 To October 31st 1918 Volume 21 Medical.			
War Diary	Manancourt		01/10/1918	04/10/1918
War Diary	W.11.b. Sheet 57c.		05/10/1918	07/10/1918
War Diary	M 33 Central Sheet 57b.		08/10/1918	08/10/1918
War Diary	Selvigny		09/10/1918	09/10/1918
War Diary	Audencourt		10/10/1918	11/10/1918
War Diary	Inchy		12/10/1918	12/10/1918
War Diary	Audencourt		13/10/1918	31/10/1918
Heading	War Diary Of 51st Field Ambulance From November 1st 1918 To November 30th 1918 Volume. 22. Medical.			

War Diary	Audencourt	01/11/1918	01/11/1918
War Diary	Inchy	02/11/1918	06/11/1918
War Diary	Forest.	07/11/1918	08/11/1918
War Diary	Locquignol	09/11/1918	12/11/1918
War Diary	Troisvilles	13/11/1918	30/11/1918
Heading	War Diary (Medical) Of 51st Field Ambulance From December 1st 1918 To December 31st 1918 Volume 23		
War Diary	Troisvilles	01/12/1918	06/12/1918
War Diary	Masnieres	07/12/1918	07/12/1918
War Diary	Hermies	08/12/1918	08/12/1918
War Diary	Favreuil	09/12/1918	09/12/1918
War Diary	Albert	10/12/1918	10/12/1918
War Diary	Pont Noyelles	11/12/1918	11/12/1918
War Diary	St Pierre A Gouy	12/12/1918	12/12/1918
War Diary	Hocquincourt	13/12/1918	16/12/1918
War Diary	Fontaine-Sur-Somme	17/12/1918	31/12/1918
Heading	War Diary Of 51st Field Ambulance From 1.1.19 To 31.1.19 Volume 24		
War Diary	Fontaine-Sur-Somme	01/01/1919	31/01/1919
Heading	War Diary Of 51st Field Ambulance From 1.2.19 To 28.2.19 Volume 25		
War Diary	Fontaine-Sur-Somme	01/02/1919	28/02/1919
Heading	War Diary Of 51st Field Ambulance From 1.3.19 To 31.3.19 Volume 26		
War Diary	Fontaine-Sur-Somme	01/03/1919	31/03/1919
Heading	War Diary Of 51st Field Ambulance From 1.4.19 To 30.4.19 Volume 27		
War Diary	Fontaine Sur Somme	01/04/1919	30/04/1919
Heading	No 51 Field Ambulance May 1919		
War Diary	Harfleur	01/05/1919	06/05/1919

00995/1996/1

17TH DIVISION TROOPS

51ST FIELD AMBULANCE
JLY 1915 - ~~DEC 1918~~
MAY 1919

151/6754

17th Division

51st
57th Field Ambulance
Vol. I
July & August 15.

July 1915
Aug "

Army Form C. 2118

WAR DIARY
or
INTELLIGENCE SUMMARY
(Erase heading not required.)

Instructions regarding War Diaries and Intelligence Summaries are contained in F.S. Regs., Part II. and the Staff Manual respectively. Title Pages will be prepared in manuscript.

Place	Date	Hour	Summary of Events and Information	Remarks and references to Appendices
WARMINSTER ENG.	12/4/15	8.20 a.m	Half of the 51st Field Ambulance left WARMINSTER for SOUTHAMPTON DOCKS	
		10.20 am	Remainder left for SOUTHAMPTON DOCKS. Arrangements were well carried out and the movement was made without accident.	
SOUTHAMPTON		12.10 pm	First train arrived SOUTHAMPTON DOCKS	
		2. pm	Second train arrived SOUTHAMPTON DOCKS. Transport was unloaded from trains and on board S.S. INVENTOR by 4 p.m.	
		6 pm	5 Officers, 5 N.C.O's, 34 A.S.C (attached to 51 F.A.), 1 W.O., 53 horses and mules and transport and ambulance wagons left SOUTHAMPTON DOCKS on board S.S. INVENTOR.	W. Barclay
		9.15 pm	5 Officers and 146 other Ranks left SOUTHAMPTON DOCKS on board S.S. EMPRESS QUEEN.	
HAVRE	13/4/15	6.30 a.m	EMPRESS QUEEN arrived HAVRE, without any casualties.	
		9.0 a.m	INVENTOR arrived HAVRE. No casualties were incurred during the voyage	
		5.0 p.m	Unit arrived at a rest camp on the outskirts of HAVRE for a few hours rest under canvas.	W. Barclay
		12 midnight	Reveille	

Army Form C. 2118

WAR DIARY
or
INTELLIGENCE SUMMARY
(Erase heading not required.)

Instructions regarding War Diaries and Intelligence Summaries are contained in F.S. Regs., Part II. and the Staff Manual respectively. Title Pages will be prepared in manuscript.

Place	Date	Hour	Summary of Events and Information	Remarks and references to Appendices
HAVRE	14/7/15	1-0 a.m	Unit left rest camp and marched to HAVRE STATION.	
		1-45 a.m	Arrived HAVRE STATION and immediately commenced to load the transports on to the wagons, which was carried out satisfactorily.	W.F.Bagnall
		5.30 a.m	Train left HAVRE for an unknown destination	
SAINT OMER	15/7/15	1.30 a.m	Arrived SAINT OMER. Unloaded transports and also helped to unload transports of YORKS & LANCS Regiment which was an expenditure of time.	
		3.30 a.m	Marched from SAINT OMER to Farmhouse	
CORMETTE		6.0 a.m	Arrived CORMETTE. Officers billeted in a farmhouse, other ranks billeted in barns.	W.F.Bagnall
	16/7/15		Sanitation bad. Water supply fairly good. Men employed on sanitation of camp.	W.F.Bagnall
	17/7/15		Received notification of movement, which was to take place 18/7/15	W.F.Bagnall
	18/7/15	12.30 a.m	Commenced march from CORMETTE to starting point	
EBLINGHAM		3 p.m	Arrived EBLINGHAM. No men fell out en route. Wagon fell out with one of other. Unit picked up en route. Billets at a farm, officers in farm house, other ranks in barns. Sanitation bad. Water supply inadequate. Received notification that Unit had to move 19/7/15	W.F.Bagnall

Army Form C. 2118

WAR DIARY
or
INTELLIGENCE SUMMARY
(Erase heading not required.)

Instructions regarding War Diaries and Intelligence Summaries are contained in F.S. Regs., Part II. and the Staff Manual respectively. Title Pages will be prepared in manuscript.

Place	Date	Hour	Summary of Events and Information	Remarks and references to Appendices
EBLINGHAM	19/4/15	9 am	Marched from EBLINGHAM. Roads rough. Disposition of all ranks good, none falling out on march. Carried sick and lame of other Units in Ambulance wagons.	W.Barclay
ECKE		2 pm	Reached ECKE and found water supply bad and sanitation affairs to contend with. Good billeting found in barns.	W.Barclay
	20/4/15		The A.D.M.S & D.A.D.M.S visited the camps. Officers and men not otherwise engaged.	W.Barclay
	21/4/15		Opened Field Hospital to receive sick cases from other Units of the Brigade	W.Barclay
	22/4/15		Adjutant visited Field Cashier and men were paid	W.Barclay
	23/4/15		Received notification of movement, which has to take place before daybreak 25th/26th. to RENINGHELST.	XVII Div Order No 5(e) W.Barclay
	24/4/15		Nothing to record	W.Barclay

WAR DIARY
or
INTELLIGENCE SUMMARY
(Erase heading not required.)

Army Form C. 2118

Place	Date	Hour	Summary of Events and Information	Remarks and references to Appendices
Staffe ECKE	26/7/15	9·45 p.m.	"A" & "B" Sections commenced march to RENINGHELST, leaving "C" Section to carry on a Queen Hospital for part of Brigade remaining. Disposition of troops on march good, none falling out. W.Barclay	
RENINGHELST	26/7/15	2 a.m.	Arrived RENINGHELST, parties wagons and transport. Water supply inadequate, Camp having been left in filthy condition. Officers and Senior N.C.O's motored to H.Qrs 9th Field Ambulance for lectures. Officers & other Ranks bivouacked 32m Field Ambulance in adjacent camp, being Officers & Hospital and Battn. W.Barclay	
RENINGHELST	24/9/15		Sections "A" & "B" employees in making camp habitable. Had to close unnecessary latrine pits, & build incinerators, ablution benches, cookhouse etc.	
		7.30 pm	3 Officers and self motored to advanced dressing station 9th F.A. and Regimental Aid Post. W.Barclay	

Army Form C. 2118

WAR DIARY
or
INTELLIGENCE SUMMARY
(Erase heading not required.)

Instructions regarding War Diaries and Intelligence Summaries are contained in F.S. Regs., Part II. and the Staff Manual respectively. Title Pages will be prepared in manuscript.

Place	Date	Hour	Summary of Events and Information	Remarks and references to Appendices
RENINGHELST	28/7/15	7.50 p.m.	2 Officers and 4 N.C.O's proceeded by motor ambulance via OUDERDOM and DICKEBUSCH to advance dressing of 9th Fd Amb and Regimental Aid Post for instructional purposes	W S B as be day
RENINGHELST	29/7/15	2 a.m.	Officers & N.C.O's arrived back at camp	
		3 a.m.	Received message from A.D.M.S. that ambulance wagons and horses have to turn out which was promptly done. When ready for departure was advised that movement was cancelled	
		7.45 p.m.	Remainder of Officers and Senior N.C.O's took similar journey as that taken on 28/7/15	W S B as be day
RENINGHELST	30/7/15	7.0 p.m.	Received notification that bearer division had to be ready to move at a moment's notice	W S B as be day
RENINGHELST	31/7/15		Nothing to record	W S B as be day

Place	Date	Hour	Summary of Events and Information	Remarks and references to Appendices
RENINGHELST	1/8/15	7.30 p.	5 ambulance wagons containing officers and wagon orderlies set out to learn the geography of the particular area taken on by XVII Div. Through DICKEBUSCH, VERMOCELLE, KEMMEL and LA CLYTTE. Rifle shots whistled near the cars. One car drove into wire stretched across a road the result of which no officer (LT BLOCKLEY) received superficial wound from neck to ear. On returning the car was ditched, this eventually being man handled on to the road safely, and no damage am to the car. W. Bage Day	
RENINGHELST	2/8/15	2.45 am	Party arrived back at camp. Nothing to record during the day.	
		9 P.	Two motor ambulance wagons accompanied by 2 wagons from 52nd Field Ambulance, started to clear the regimental aid posts established at the Brasserie and at Vormezeele (Map no 28 no.000. N 5/B9.1 and 1.31/B3.7 respectively) The senior officer present was Capt W. Barclay R.amc. Two journeys were found to be necessary. Patients were in each case handed over to the 52nd Fd. Amb. at Reninghelst	

WAR DIARY
or
INTELLIGENCE SUMMARY
(Erase heading not required.)

Place	Date	Hour	Summary of Events and Information	Remarks and references to Appendices
RENINGHELST	3.6.15	10.15 a.m.	At 10.15 a.m. the leading car of convoy (see war diary date 2.6.15) collided with a motor despatch rider on the La Clytte – RENINGHELST road. First aid was rendered and the patient brought into the 57th F.A. D.S. at RENINGHELST. (Officers present were Capt. W. Barclay and Lieut. J.P. Black).	
		9 a.m.	Nothing to record during the day. The motor amb. wagon under charge of Lt W.M Barclay of No 5 S/A FA despatched to clear caus. regimental aid posts at Brasserie and Voormezeele. On arrival at Voormezeele it was ascertained that one patient from H.Q 1st Yorkshire Regt. had been sent to SCOTTISH WOOD (H.35. B.5.4). One car was sent to clear same. All cars arrived at RENINGHELST without further incident and patients were handed over to 57th F.A.	
do	4.6.15 20--		Nothing to record during the day.	

WAR DIARY
or
INTELLIGENCE SUMMARY
(Erase heading not required.)

Army Form C. 2118

Place	Date	Hour	Summary of Events and Information	Remarks and references to Appendices
RENINGHELST	4.8.15	9 p.m.	Nothing to record during day. The usual convoy was despatched at night and performed their duties without incident. W.M.Barcla	
—do—	5.8.15		2750 francs drawn from Field Cashier and advance payments were paid. The usual convoy was despatched and performed their duties without incident. W.M.Barcla	
—do—	6.8.15		Capt. Barclay visited Cameron at Eecke and paid the men. Convoy despatched at night. W.M.Barcla	
—do—	7.8.15		1 N.C.O. and no men despatched to H.Q. 50th Brigade 52nd —do— —do— for duty in care of emergency. The despatch and convoy were carried on as usual. W.M.Barcla	

Army Form C. 2118

WAR DIARY
or
INTELLIGENCE SUMMARY
(Erase heading not required.)

Instructions regarding War Diaries and Intelligence Summaries are contained in F.S. Regs., Part II. and the Staff Manual respectively. Title Pages will be prepared in manuscript.

Place	Date	Hour	Summary of Events and Information	Remarks and references to Appendices
RENINGHELST	8.8.15	9 a.m.	1 Corporal and his men with one motor amb. wagon despatched to Kr Kartoria Diekebusch (H33.B77) to be in readiness to Convey urgent cases from the regimental aid post to RENINGHELST during daylight. The motor convoy was despatched at night. W.T. Basada	
–do–	9.8.15		Acting to recommendation Sgt. J. Ganet A.S.C. admitted to 52nd F.A. with hernia.	
		6.15 p.m.	1 heavy draught horse died at 6.15 p.m. for purpura.	
		9 p.m.	The motor convoy was despatched at night and reported that they collided with telegraph wires at Kruisstraethoek. W.T. Basada	
–do–	10.8.15	9 a.m.	Report of O.C. Convoy (9.8.15) delivered to A.D.M.S. 17th Div.	

Army Form C. 2118

WAR DIARY
or
INTELLIGENCE SUMMARY
(Erase heading not required.)

Instructions regarding War Diaries and Intelligence Summaries are contained in F.S. Regs., Part II. and the Staff Manual respectively. Title Pages will be prepared in manuscript.

Place	Date	Hour	Summary of Events and Information	Remarks and references to Appendices
RENINGHELST	10.6.15	9 p.m.	Usual convoy despatched at night. W.P.Barclay	
-do-	11.6.15	9 a.m.	One refractory and unbroken mule handed over to Mobile Vet. Section. One riding horse for chaplain taken on strength.	
		8 p.m.	O.C. C Section reported that all 7th Div. troops that had left his district. He was instructed to report here with his section on the following day. Usual convoy despatched. W.P.Barclay	
		9 p.m.		
-do-	12.6.15	9 a.m.	Two more men despatched to Lantiere - Discharged 1 N.C.O. and 1 man attached to 51st Bgde.Brigade for duty. C Section under Lt. Lewis arrived and reported and was despatched. Usual convoy departed. No casualties. W.P.Barclay	
		5.30 p.m.		
		6 p.m.		
		9 p.m.		

Army Form C. 2118

WAR DIARY
or
INTELLIGENCE SUMMARY
(Erase heading not required.)

Instructions regarding War Diaries and Intelligence Summaries are contained in F. S. Regs., Part II. and the Staff Manual respectively. Title Pages will be prepared in manuscript.

Place	Date	Hour	Summary of Events and Information	Remarks and references to Appendices
RENINGHELST	13.8.15	9 p.m.	Nothing to report during day. Usual convoy despatched	
		7 p.m.	Order of A.D.M.S. to send a section in readiness to proceed to La Clytte. W. Barclay	
-do-	14.8.15	9 a.m.	Capt. Barclay and St. T.P. Harriss proceeded to inspect the 53rd F.A.D.S. at La Clytte.	
		4 p.m.	Orders by A.D.M.S. to send a section to La Clytte early on 15.8.15. Ernest Renshaw	
			B Section detailed	
		9 p.m.	Usual convoy for Collection of Sick & wounded despatched	
	15.8.15	9 a.m.	B Section into two Daimler motor Ambulances Tappins proceed to La Clytte and take over the Advanced Dressing Station from 53rd Field Ambulance.	
		9.30 a.m.	Report from Off i/c Details at Collecting Station DICKEBUSCH that the town was shelled on 14th inst. that trim ?iary Casualties Edward Renshaw	
		9 p.m.	Usual convoy despatched	

Army Form C. 2118

WAR DIARY
or
INTELLIGENCE SUMMARY
(Erase heading not required.)

Instructions regarding War Diaries and Intelligence Summaries are contained in F.S. Regs., Part II. and the Staff Manual respectively. Title Pages will be prepared in manuscript.

Place	Date	Hour	Summary of Events and Information	Remarks and references to Appendices
RENINGHELST	16.8.15 to 22.8.15		No.7/A/20/262/87 A.S.C. Lenon attaches the unit who reported sick on 14th inst, bacteriologically diagnosed as suffering from Enteric. All Officers N.C.O's & men who have at any period suffered from Enteric ordered to proceed to No.7 Mobile Laboratory to be tested as "Carriers". A satisfactory report obtained on all there. — E. Dom[illegible]	
		9 a.m.	No events of importance. Convoy Dispatched Daily as usual.	
	23.8.15	12 noon	Lieut H.J. Cotter R.A.M.C. returned from leave. Nothing to report. B[illegible]	
	24.8.15		Nothing to report.	
	25.8.15	1 p.m.	Ordered to establish baths at La Clytte. Lieut. Murdoch R.A.M.C. ordered to arrange.	
	26.8.15 ? p.m.		Ordered to send 2 men to collecting Station at DICKEBUSCH. Sent in charge Sergt. Page. Instructed to collect wounded from VERMEZEELE & A. BRISSERIE. A motor ambulance wagon was sent to the Chateau ROSENTHAL which is in the R.A.P. at I.32.B (sheet 28) at 9.30 p.m. that night. The Evacuating station for this station. Sich & wounded from Station in future collected. Major E.L. Gosland's Roth the R.A.R.M.S. contracted a bout anterior examination or Privates 7th Border Regt, who died from pectoralis in formalin contents of the internal organs and a specimen of Bogsed things sent to No.7 Mobile Laboratory for investigation. Ed[illegible]	

Army Form C. 2118

WAR DIARY
or
INTELLIGENCE SUMMARY
(Erase heading not required.)

Instructions regarding War Diaries and Intelligence Summaries are contained in F.S. Regs., Part II. and the Staff Manual respectively. Title Pages will be prepared in manuscript.

Place	Date	Hour	Summary of Events and Information	Remarks and references to Appendices
RENINGHELST	28/8/15	noon	Report re examination of organs in case noted under Date 26/8/15 negative. ? Cerebro Spinal meningitis. Edw J Rowland	
	28.8.15 to 30.8.15		nothing to report.	
	31.8.15		Field Ambulance workshop tent moved to fresh encampment at G.33.8.2 from 28 to 0.0 Edw J Rowland	

2/7517

17th Known

51st Field Ambulance
vol 2
SEPT
Oct 15.

Aug 1915
Sept "
Oct '15

Place	Date	Hour	Summary of Events and Information	Remarks and references to Appendices
RENINGHELST	27.8.15	noon	Report re examination of others in case noted under Date 26/8/15 negative. ? Cerebro Spinal meningitis. *Edward Rowland*	
-do-	28.8.15 to 30.8.15		Nothing to report.	
	31.8.15		Field Ambulance Workshop Hut moved to fresh Encampment at G.33.8.2 from 28 to -do- *Edward Rowland*	
-do-	1.9.15		Nothing to report. Men paid by Lt. Leoin *W. Barclay*	
-do-	2.9.15 3p		Capt. Barclay returned to RENINGHELST from LA CLYTTE Lt Gona went to LA CLYTTE for dinner Adv. Dress. Station. *W. Barclay*	
-do-	3.9.15		Nothing to report. *W. Barclay*	

WAR DIARY
or
INTELLIGENCE SUMMARY
(Erase heading not required.)

Army Form C. 2118

Instructions regarding War Diaries and Intelligence Summaries are contained in F.S. Regs., Part II. and the Staff Manual respectively. Title Pages will be prepared in manuscript.

Place	Date	Hour	Summary of Events and Information	Remarks and references to Appendices
RENINGHELST W.Sec.	5/5	9am	Nothing to report.	
-do-		2.15pm	Pte Hams sent to LACLYTTE AD from off duty. There are now 10 to 10⁵ Pers Priviken for casualties	W.Barela W.Barela
-do-	6/5		Nothing to report.	
-do-	7/5	2pm	Water cart (captured pattern) sent to A.D.S. to refit. Broken cart will now repair.	W.Barela W.Barela
-do-	8/5		Nothing to report.	W.Barela W.Barela
	9/5			W.Barela
	10/5			W.Barela
	11/5	2pm	A. Thackrah w.a.a. 10 ap. place despatches for duty at the Divisional Hqrs Office.	W.Barela

Place	Date	Hour	Summary of Events and Information	Remarks and references to Appendices
REMINGHURST			Nothing to report	W. Barda
—do—	13/5/17	6pm	Orders received to A.O.N.S.D to turn out sufft of Maxim Coy to relieve H.Q Coy's 70% of Jocks temporarily in H.Q Coys made to tea for the day.	
			Reserve notification for T.O.M	W Barda
		16.15 am		
		7pm	Lieut Cooper departed to rejoin 1st E. Yorks. Lieut Gaunt W Barda	
		15/5 9a	Wether can't returned from brigade worked with defensive schemes. Wells Gaunts Jr.	W Barda
		11pm	Lt Cooper returned	
		10.55	Nothing to report.	
		11	Brigade of Bn. for funeral and staff for welk.	C.S.J Barda

WAR DIARY or INTELLIGENCE SUMMARY

Army Form C. 2118

Place	Date	Hour	Summary of Events and Information	Remarks and references to Appendices
REMINGHELST	18/9/15	—	Nothing to report	
	19/9/15	—	— do —	W. Barclay D.A.D.M.S.
	20/9/15	—	— do —	W. Barclay
	21/9/15	—	9 cases of Chocolate, a gift for Wet & dries Colonies, received for distribution amongst the personnel of the 3 F.Ambs. 3 cases passed to 52nd F.A. and 3 to 53rd. Chocolate supplies to staff of A.D.M.S. office.	W. Barclay D.A.D.M.S.
	22/9/15	—	Nothing to report	W. Barclay D.A.D.M.S.
	23/9/15	—	Nothing to report. Interview with	W. Barclay
	24/9/15	—	The A.D.M.S. inspected the M.D.S. at the Asylum, and ordered it to be cleaned; patients were removed to the Rest Station at Boeschepe by the 53rd F.Amb. Lt H.J. Cotter today assumed temporary duty as O.C. No 3 Sanitary Section, and 9th Division Sanitary Officer.	

WAR DIARY or INTELLIGENCE SUMMARY

Army Form C. 2118

Place	Date	Hour	Summary of Events and Information	Remarks and references to Appendices
RENINGHELST	25/5/15	9am	Authority granted by C.R.E. Eng. grafs to procure materials for hutting and to keep.	
			Horse some watchmen for the LAITERIE, DICKIEBUSCH and prepared to general dump at RENINGHELST and the A.D.M.S. issued orders for all RENINGHELST bearers.	
		11.5pm	to proceed to BRAND HOEK to assist the 3rd Division. 28 men paraded and went off under Lt. Gouland and Lt Eyre to 97 K 57 J 7A. 2 Dismounted orderlies went on foot in two dixies as far as 97 K 57 J 7A. The horse ambulance wagons went off under Lt Berkeley carrying some of the personnel of the 57 J 7A.	
				W. Barclay
-do-	26/5/15	7am	All bearer officers returned safely	
		9.30pm	Lt R.W. Wilson proceeded to the 9th Northumbs Fusiliers for temporary duty vice Lt W.K. Murphy.	
				W. Barclay
-do-	27/5/15		nothing to note	
				W. Barclay

Army Form C. 2118

WAR DIARY
or
INTELLIGENCE SUMMARY
(Erase heading not required.)

Place	Date	Hour	Summary of Events and Information	Remarks and references to Appendices
RENINGHELST	28/4/15	—	Nothing to note — W. Barclay Capt.	
do	29/4/15	9 am	2nd Lieut James & Major Reid reported at this unit for duty.	
		Noon	The men were paid by Capt Barclay.	
		3 pm	B section and the men at La Clytte bath were paid.	
		9 pm	2 Daimler cars under Major Sutherland proceeded to Kruistraat to aid the 10th Sherwood Foresters who are out of the trenches. The Col and one man Dr Barclay	
do	30/4/15	5 pm	Lieut J.F. Levis, one N.C.O. and one man proceeded to ROSENTHAL Chateau (BEDFORD HOUSE) as advance party to take over from 7d. Ambulance 7d Div. W. Barclay	

Oct. 1915.

57th/Burma 121/4593

121/7593

57
57th Field Amb:
Part of 2

Oct 15

Army Form C. 2118

WAR DIARY
or
INTELLIGENCE SUMMARY
(Erase heading not required.)

Instructions regarding War Diaries and Intelligence Summaries are contained in F.S. Regs., Part II. and the Staff Manual respectively. Title Pages will be prepared in manuscript.

Place	Date	Hour	Summary of Events and Information	Remarks and references to Appendices
RENINGHELST	1/10/15	10 a.m.	Lieut J.H. Reid assumed duty as 2nd i/c 34 Sanitary Section. Lt. H.G. Cother returned to duty with this unit.	
			20 N.C.O.s and men under S. Sgt Pike proceeded to BEDFORD HOUSE Advanced Dressing Station.	
		6 p.m.	Lt Cother and 19 men proceeded to BEDFORD House with Stores to complete Advanced Dressing Station.	
			Lt. McGorman annual reporting duty with No 7 Barrie & Wimbarra Car Section to report.	W.H Barclay
-do-	2/10/15		Nothing to report	W.H Barclay
-do-	3/10/15		Nothing to report	W.H Barclay
-do-	4/10/15	8.30 a.m.	One officer and twenty men of No 28 & 30 Ambulance were taken to BEDFORD HOUSE as advance party to relieve this unit. His unit returned to RENINGHELST.	W.H Barclay
-do-	5/10/15	5 p.m.	Lt Herriot & Lt Gorman with Bearers were relieved by a Pa Amb of 9th Division and returned to RENINGHELST. Lt Gorman 20 N.C.Os and men of 9th Division returned to LA CLYTTE.	
		6 p.m.	The detachment at DICKEBUSCH returned to RENINGHELST after being relieved by 9th Division.	
		9 p.m.	Lt LEVIS and Lt Cother returned to RENINGHELST with their detachment. W.H Barclay	

Army Form C. 2118

WAR DIARY
or
INTELLIGENCE SUMMARY
(Erase heading not required.)

Instructions regarding War Diaries and Intelligence Summaries are contained in F. S. Regs., Part II. and the Staff Manual respectively. Title Pages will be prepared in manuscript.

Place	Date	Hour	Summary of Events and Information	Remarks and references to Appendices
RENINGHELST	6/5		Camp closed during day.	
		6.45 pm	Proceed to rendezvous for 51st Inf. Brigade transit parade and marched off in column of sections; advance via EECKE: route WESTOUTRE — BOESCHEPE — GOEDEWERSWELDE.	
		9 pm	The motor ambulance wagons under Lt GORMAN of RENINGHELST Convoy Park day transpired by 1 am.	
EECKE	7/5	12.30 am	The unit arrived in EECKE and was billeted by 1 am. A new motor field ambulance picked up by Km motor wagons were returned to parent unit. A camp captured for 51st Inf. Brig. was shared.	W.S. Barclay
-do-	8/5	pm	Orders received from A.D.M.S. to deal with French parade to deal with several hundred cases.	W.S. Barclay
-do-	9/5 10/5 11/5		Nothing to report	W.S. Barclay

WAR DIARY
or
INTELLIGENCE SUMMARY
(Erase heading not required.)

Army Form C. 2118

Place	Date	Hour	Summary of Events and Information	Remarks and references to Appendices
EECKE	12/5		Pte J Nagle admitted to No 15 C.C.S.	W.Barclay
- do -	13/5		Nothing to report	W.Barclay
- do -	14/5		- do -	W.Barclay
- do -	15/5	9 p.m.	Pte Chomlice departed for England on leave	W.Barclay
- do -	16/5		Capt. J.S. Keevil granted no fortnight's leave. Capt Holland this day to report.	W.Barclay
- do -	17/5		Nothing to report	W.Barclay
- do -	18/5		- do -	W.Barclay
- do -	19/5		2 A.S.C. drivers arrived from B's drain transp.	W.Barclay
- do -	20/5		Orders received from 51st Brigade to proceed. Less one section, to rest camp at Onderdom. A and C sections marched at 4 p.m. B section under Capt Barclay and Lieut. McNot remained at Eecke.	W.Barclay
RESTCAMP	21/5	9 a.m.	Lieut Gorman and "B" MCOs and men proceeded to Maple Cotton (Collecting post) from	W.Barclay

WAR DIARY or INTELLIGENCE SUMMARY

Place	Date	Hour	Summary of Events and Information	Remarks and references to Appendices
REST CAMP	22/10/15	12 noon	8th Fd. Ambulance. Lt. Murdock went round collecting area with 8th Fd. Amb. W.J. Barclay	
		7.30 p.m.	C section under Lt Cotter and Lt Murdoch took over advanced dressing station at BRANDHOEK from 8th Fd. Amb. Proceed to orders for A.D.M.S. 17th Division from EECKE and joined headquarters unit. Pte Kondell returned to motor ambulance under the O.C. 51st F.A. soon round collecting area. W.J. Barclay	
		9 p.m.	No 38802 Q/KCp Johnston P. was killed at the crossing station at MARIE COPSE by a shell. W.J. Barclay	
do	23/10/15	11 a.m.	A and C sections marched to POPERINGHE and took over Dressing Station at 65 Rue de Roosebeke from 6 Field Ambulance at 5 p.m. W.J. Barclay	
		3 p.m.	No 38802 Q/KCp Johnston P was buried in cemetery at BRANDHOEK. W.J. Barclay	
POPERINGHE	24/10/15		Day occupied in arranging the hospital at headquarters. W.J. Barclay	

Army Form C. 2118

WAR DIARY
or
INTELLIGENCE SUMMARY
(Erase heading not required.)

Instructions regarding War Diaries and Intelligence Summaries are contained in F.S. Regs., Part II. and the Staff Manual respectively. Title Pages will be prepared in manuscript.

Place	Date	Hour	Summary of Events and Information	Remarks and references to Appendices
POPERINGHE	25/10/15	4 pm	Capt W Morton proceeded to Brandhoek to take over command of A.D.S. Lieut Murdoch returned to Headquarters the same day.	J M Blockley
"	26/10/15	12 noon / 1.50 PM	A.D.M.S paid a visit to the Headquarters. Men were paid by Lt Blockley. Staff Sergt Mackey proceeded on a weeks leave. Lt Blockley reported a dangerous piece of road on the road leading from the Ypres-Menen road to Zillebeke	J M Blockley
"	27/4	8 AM / 10 pm	One N.C.O. and 4 men went to represent the ambulance at the inspection of troops by the King at Reninghelst. The A.D.M.S. accompanied the motor convoy at night and visited the A.D.S. at Maple Copse.	J M Blockley
"	28/10	10 pm	Nothing to report. Lieut Cotter proceeded from Brandhoek to Maple Copse to relieve Lieut Gorman who returned to Headquarters.	J M Blockley

WAR DIARY
or
INTELLIGENCE SUMMARY
(Erase heading not required.)

Place	Date	Hour	Summary of Events and Information	Remarks and references to Appendices
Poperinghe	29/10/15		Lieut Gorman left headquarters for duty at Brandhoek. DADMS 5th Corps visited Headquarters and A.D.S. Brandhoek. J.M.Lockley	
"	30/10/15	8 AM	Capt Luns returned from leave.	
		2 pm	7 reinforcements R.A.M.C. arrived from the Base for duty. Lieut Reid was attached to this unit for duty. J.M.Lockley	
"	31/10/15			

Army Form C. 2118

Army Form C. 2118

WAR DIARY
or
INTELLIGENCE SUMMARY
(Erase heading not required.)

Instructions regarding War Diaries and Intelligence Summaries are contained in F. S. Regs., Part II. and the Staff Manual respectively. Title Pages will be prepared in manuscript.

Place	Date	Hour	Summary of Events and Information	Remarks and references to Appendices
Poperinghe	31/10/15	2pm	Two RAMC private reinforcements were attached to the 51st Field Ambulance from this date.	

61qk 7A.
Tel. 3
12
7678

17th Division

Nov 15.

Nov 1915

Army Form C. 2118

WAR DIARY
or
INTELLIGENCE SUMMARY
(Erase heading not required.)

Instructions regarding War Diaries and Intelligence Summaries are contained in F.S. Regs., Part II. and the Staff Manual respectively. Title Pages will be prepared in manuscript.

Place	Date	Hour	Summary of Events and Information	Remarks and references to Appendices
Poperinghe	1/4/15	2 pm	The A.D.M.S. and the O.C. paid a visit to Maple Copse and Sanctuary Wood visiting the Advanced Dressing Stations and the Regimental Aid posts.	J.P.Stockley
"	2/4/15		Sergt. Ray proceeded on leave. Two Daimler cars were borrowed from the 52nd Field Ambulance. 1000 francs were drawn from the Field Cashier.	J.P.Stockley
"	3/4/15		Staff Sergt Mackay returned from leave. Sgt Pugh with 9 men proceeded to Maple Copse to relieve half the detachment there.	J.P.Stockley
"	4/4/15	4 pm	Last letter returned to Headquarters from Maple Copse and Sgt Pugh assumed command, the remainder of the detachment was relieved by another 8 bearers. Pt Acton was wounded on the Menin road by a bullet. Pt Norris proceeded on leave.	J.P.Stockley
"	5/4/15	11 AM	Q.M.S. Crossley and Pt proceeded on leave. Lieut Murdoch took up duty as M.O. to the 7th Inniskns relieving Lieut H.V. White who is proceeding on leave.	J.P.Stockley

Army Form C. 2118

WAR DIARY
or
INTELLIGENCE SUMMARY
(Erase heading not required.)

Instructions regarding War Diaries and Intelligence Summaries are contained in F.S. Regs., Part II. and the Staff Manual respectively. Title Pages will be prepared in manuscript.

Place	Date	Hour	Summary of Events and Information	Remarks and references to Appendices
Poperinghe	6/4/15		Surgeon General Porter and the ADMS paid a visit to Headquarters. Capt. Barclay returned to Branduick. Capt. Harris & Lieut. Lister proceeded to Branduick.	JPBlackley
"	7/4/15		Pt. Ringer W.H. proceeded on leave. Capt. Kingston R.A.M.C. became attached to this Field Ambulance for duty from this date. Poperinghe was shelled a little.	JPBlackley
"	8/4/15		O.C. proceeded on leave. Capt. Barclay took over command of unit.	JPBlackley
"	9/4/15		Visited Field Cashier and drew £400 for men at Headquarters were paid. Staff Sergt. Pike proceeded on leave. Detachment was removed from Maple Copse which was taken over by 28th F. Amb.	JPBlackley
"	10/4/15		Men at Brandhoek were paid. Capt. Barclay visited the regimental aid post N. of Menin Road.	JPBlackley
"	11/4/15		Lieut. Harriot proceeded with 16 men to take over A.D.S. in the Asylum at Ypres.	JPBlackley

Army Form C. 2118

WAR DIARY
or
INTELLIGENCE SUMMARY

(Erase heading not required.)

Instructions regarding War Diaries and Intelligence Summaries are contained in F.S. Regs., Part II. and the Staff Manual respectively. Title Pages will be prepared in manuscript.

Place	Date	Hour	Summary of Events and Information	Remarks and references to Appendices
Poperinghe	12/1/15		Nothing to note.	J.P.Blackley
"	13/1/15		Nothing to note; Pt Renier returned from leave	J.P.Blackley
"	14/1/15		Nothing to note	J.P.Blackley
"	15/1/15		Capt H.V. White returned from leave and proceeded to join his regiment the 7th Lincolns.	J.P.Blackley
"	16/1/15		Major Gourland returned from leave and resumed command of the unit. Capt Wallace RAMC. returned from leave and was attached to this unit for duty.	J.P.Blackley
"	17/1/15		Capt Barclay proceeded on leave and Staff Sergt Pike returned from leave. Lt Elsworth and Dr Whitney. A.S.C.M.T. were evacuated to L.L.S.	J.P.Blackley

WAR DIARY
or
INTELLIGENCE SUMMARY
(Erase heading not required.)

Army Form C. 2118

Place	Date	Hour	Summary of Events and Information	Remarks and references to Appendices
Poperinghe	18/9/15		Lt Lee and Sgt Major Neil proceeded on leave. Three hostile aircraft dropped bombs around the hospital and the Town. About noon 5 enemy's aeroplanes were observed. The ADMS visited the hospital in the morning.	
		2.30	The D.C. and 4 other officers attended a lecture on 'abdominal injuries' at Boeschepe delivered by Sir Anthony Bowlby, Surgeon General.	
		11AM.	Lieut Gorman, one N.C.O. and 6 men proceeded to Ypres to relieve Lieut Morriot, 1 NCO and 6 men who returned to Headquarters. The OC and Lieut Herriot attended a lecture by an officer R.F.C. on aerial photography. J.M.Blackley	
	19/9/15		Sgt Page R.A.M.C. and Dr Forlin proceeded on leave. Sgt Taylor RAMC proceeded to the A.D.S. Ypres and 7 men to relieve Serjt Doulton and 6 men who returned to Headquarters. Cpl Harman RAMC was evacuated to the CCS.	

Army Form C. 2118

WAR DIARY
or
INTELLIGENCE SUMMARY
(Erase heading not required.)

Instructions regarding War Diaries and Intelligence Summaries are contained in F.S. Regs., Part II. and the Staff Manual respectively. Title Pages will be prepared in manuscript.

Place	Date	Hour	Summary of Events and Information	Remarks and references to Appendices
Poperinghe	20/8/15	8 AM	Nine hostile aeroplanes were observed over the town. Several bombs were dropped. J M Blakeley	
"		8.30	One motor ambulance and one driver Pte Brown proceeded to the base. J M Blakeley	
"	21/8/15	9 pm	One Daimler motor ambulance and one driver reported at Headquarters for duty in place of the one evacuated. Pte Whale A.S.C. H.T. returned from leave. J M Blakeley	
"	22/8/15		Sgt Blake A.S.C. and Pte Nelson and Smith A.H. (wounded on leave). Capt Kingston R.A.M.C. left the unit to take up duty as M.O. 6th Dorset. Lieut Coatsworth R.A.M.C. was attached to this unit for duty. J M Blakeley	
"	23/8/15		Drew rations from Field Cashier. Men at Headquarters were paid. J M Blakeley	

WAR DIARY
or
INTELLIGENCE SUMMARY
(Erase heading not required.)

Army Form C. 2118

Instructions regarding War Diaries and Intelligence Summaries are contained in F.S. Regs., Part II. and the Staff Manual respectively. Title Pages will be prepared in manuscript.

Place	Date	Hour	Summary of Events and Information	Remarks and references to Appendices
Poperinghe	24/11/15		Men at Brandhoek were paid. Arrangements were made to send our car each night to the Hill at Vlamertinghe to take all cases of the 17th Division to Brandhoek.	
"	25/11/15		Lieut. Reid RAMC returned from leave and proceeded to YPRES to take up duty as M.O. to the 80th Bdy RFA. Lieut Aumist proceeded to take up duty at Brandhoek and took over duty as proceeded to the Asylum at YPRES with a detachment of 7 men to relieve Lieut Gorman who returned to Headquarters. J M Blockley J M Blockley	
"	26/11/15		Capt Barclay RAMC returned from leave and assumed duty at Headquarters. B. Section proceeded to relieve C section at Brandhoek. C section then the clerks returned to Headquarters. J M Blockley	
"	27/11/15		Sgt Smith, Pte Anderson T.C. and Murphy T proceeded on leave. Sgt Page and Pte Foster A.S.C. returned from leave. Lieut Lee R.A.M.C. returned from leave. J M Blockley	

WAR DIARY
or
INTELLIGENCE SUMMARY
(Erase heading not required.)

Instructions regarding War Diaries and Intelligence Summaries are contained in F.S. Regs., Part II. and the Staff Manual respectively. Title Pages will be prepared in manuscript.

Place	Date	Hour	Summary of Events and Information	Remarks and references to Appendices
Popuringhe	28/10/15		Sgt Major Neil RAMC returned from leave	
"	29/10/15		2 Petrol lamps and 3 stoves were purchased for the hospital. Lieut Herriot proceeded to take up duty as M.O. to the 9th Northumberland Fusiliers in place of Lieut H.W. Wilson.	J P Blockley
"	30/10/15		Lieut H.W. Wilson formerly of this unit was evacuated to the C.C.S. 1000 francs were drawn from the Field Cashier. Surgeon General Porter visited the hospital. Lieut Gorman proceeded to Branshock to relieve Lieut T.P. Herriot. Cpl Jones A.S.C. M.T. was evacuated to the base. Hostile aeroplane dropped two bombs in the town.	J P Blockley Lt RAMC

J P Blockley
Lt RAMC

57th F.A.
Vol: 4

14thDiv
F/1571/1

51st F.A.

Dec 1915

WAR DIARY
or
INTELLIGENCE SUMMARY

(Erase heading not required.)

Army Form C. 2118

Place	Date	Hour	Summary of Events and Information	Remarks and references to Appendices
POPERINGHE	1/10/15	10am	[struck through] 1 officer and 7 men arrived for duty as reinforcement	
		5pm	Capt Reader A.S.C. returned from leave	W.B. Barclay
-do-	2/10/15	—	Capt Wallace proceeded to YPRES for duty at A.D.S.	W.B. Barclay
-do-	3/10/15	8am	Lieut J.P. Beckley R.A.M.C. & Sgt Sayer R.A.M.C. proceeded on leave. Lt Lewis proceeded to BRANDHOEK for duty in A.D.S. Lt H.J. Cotter returned to POPERINGHE	W.B. Barclay
-do-	4/10/15	8am	Lt/Cpl Jones R.A.M.C. proceeded on leave.	
		9am	Lt H.J. Cotter assumed duty as M.O. 6 Sth N. Staff Regt	W.B. Barclay
-do-	5/10/15	5am	Pte Clease R.A.M.C. proceeded on leave	
		9pm	1 Siddeley-Deasy Motor Ambulance and its driver (ASCmT) reported here for duty.	W.B. Barclay
-do-	6/10/15		Major Poolland assumed temporary duty at RENINGHELST as D.A.D.M.S 17th Division. Capt W. Barclay assumed command of this unit.	W.B. Barclay

WAR DIARY
or
INTELLIGENCE SUMMARY
(Erase heading not required.)

Army Form C. 2118

Instructions regarding War Diaries and Intelligence Summaries are contained in F. S. Regs., Part II. and the Staff Manual respectively. Title Pages will be prepared in manuscript.

Place	Date	Hour	Summary of Events and Information	Remarks and references to Appendices
POPERINGHE	7/12/15		The men of Headquarters were paid	W.S. Barclay
do	8/12/15		The men at BRANDHOEK and YPRES were paid	W.S. Barclay
do	9/12/15	2pm	Sgt Wright (Conferring) transferred to 3rd DIVISION R.A.M.C. Capt C. Kingston R.A.M.C. was posted to this unit for temporary duty. 1 n.c.o. and 1 sergeant proceeded to YPRES to relieve staff A.D.S.	W.S. Barclay
do	10/12/15	9pm	Capt. G. Wallace returned to POPERINGHE with remainder of personell of A.D.S. YPRES, staff being relieved by D. Carsworth and 6 men	W.S. Barclay
do	11/12/15		Nothing to report.	W.S. Barclay
do	12/12/15		Pte Barnett Barnet examined (Eving).	W.S. Barclay
do	13/12/15	2am	Lt. J.P. Barkley returned from leave	W.S. Barclay
do	14/12/15	9am	3 drivers and 1 heavy draught horses provided to D.M.S. II Army for duty with Hoangs.	W.S. Barclay
do	15/12/15	9am	Pte Holford proceeded to take up Sanitary duty under the town Major, Poperinghe and was struck of the strength	W.S. Barclay

WAR DIARY or INTELLIGENCE SUMMARY

Army Form C. 2118

Place	Date	Hour	Summary of Events and Information	Remarks and references to Appendices
POPERINGHE	16/10/15	3/pm	Surgeon Gen. Porter inspected the hospital at POPERINGHE. Capt Q.V.R. Wallace proceeded to Asylum YPRES	
		2/pm	Lieut Coatsworth R.A.M.C. was Lieut Coatsworth transferred to No 12 C.C.S. HAZEBROUCK.	W.J.Bagely
to —	17/10/15	4/pm	1 NCO and 8 men proceeded to A.D.S. YPRES to relieve a similar no. of men.	W.J.Bagely
— do —	18/10/15	8am	A/Lt/Col Roble proceeded for duty to D.D.M.S. 1 Corps ABEELE and was struck off the strength	W.J.Bagely
— do —		6am	The town was shelled all day, to shells landed near the hospital.	W.J.Bagely
		7.30am	The presence of asphyxiating gas was felt at BRANDHOEK and gas helmets had to be worn for 2½ hours. The motor ambulance wagons were kept in action all day. The drivers and orderlies carried out their duties in an exemplary manner, and no difficulty was experienced in preventing any examination of cases. The wind became strain and BRANDHOEK were clear by 10.30pm	
		10.30pm		W.J.Bagely
		2/pm	14 Privates R.A.M.C. and 1 Driver A.S.C.(TT) were transferred to Base M.T. Depot ROUEN and struck off the strength	
		6/15	Lt Coatsworth returned from No 12 C.C.S.	

Army Form C. 2118

WAR DIARY
or
INTELLIGENCE SUMMARY
(Erase heading not required.)

Instructions regarding War Diaries and Intelligence Summaries are contained in F. S. Regs., Part II. and the Staff Manual respectively. Title Pages will be prepared in manuscript.

Place	Date	Hour	Summary of Events and Information	Remarks and references to Appendices
POPERINGHE	20/12/15	1 am	The A.D.M.S. 17th Division inspected the Hqs. of the unit.	Pte Praine Rene transferred to No 10 C.C.S.
		10.30 am	The D.A.D.M.S. V Corps visited Hqs. of the unit.	
		3 p.m.	S/Sgt Coard Reid reported to the unit for duty.	W.M. Barclay
-do-	21/12/15		Nothing to report.	
-do-	22/12/15		Capt J. S. Lewis transferred to 6/6th Dorsets for temporary duty. Lieut J. P. Blockley proceeded to BRANDHOEK to take command of Brewery Station.	W.M. Barclay
-do-	23/12/15	10 am	Lieut J. R. Mitchell Rainie reported for duty. Pte Hayes was evacuated to No 10 C.C.S.	W.M. Barclay
-do-	24/12/15		Nothing to report.	W.M. Barclay
-do-	25/12/15		Nothing to report.	W.M. Barclay
-do-	26/12/15		Major E. L. Agnew-Gland returned to Division Headquarters to his unit.	W.M. Barclay
-do-	27/12/15		Pte Armiga on holiday transferred for the unit to the 26th A.T. Coy Br. Cpl Potter A.S.C.(MT) transferred to MT Depot Rouen as unfit for duty with the unit.	W.M. Barclay

Army Form C. 2118

WAR DIARY
or
INTELLIGENCE SUMMARY
(Erase heading not required.)

Instructions regarding War Diaries and Intelligence Summaries are contained in F. S. Regs., Part II. and the Staff Manual respectively. Title Pages will be prepared in manuscript.

Place	Date	Hour	Summary of Events and Information	Remarks and references to Appendices
POPERINGHE	28/1/15		Nothing to report. W.M.Barela	
—do—	29/1/15		Lt. Cogsworth was transferred to 52nd Fd. Amb. for duty. W.M.Barela	
—do—	30/1/15	4 P.	Lt. Emo a.d. & NCO & men proceeded to Coy. in YPRES for duty at A.D.S. Capt. Rawson proceeded to BRANDHOEK for duty. Lt. N.E. Gordon proceeded on leave to London. W.M.Barela	
—do—	31/1/15	10 am	Capt. O. Wallace proceeded to 7 Bonders for duty. W.M.Barela	

14th Div
F/152/2.

31 F.A.

6
Jan 1916.

51st F.A.
Vol: 5

17

Army Form C. 2118

WAR DIARY
or
INTELLIGENCE SUMMARY
(Erase heading not required.)

Instructions regarding War Diaries and Intelligence Summaries are contained in F.S. Regs., Part II. and the Staff Manual respectively. Title Pages will be prepared in manuscript.

Place	Date	Hour	Summary of Events and Information	Remarks and references to Appendices
POPERINGHE	1/1/16	—	Nothing to report.	W/Barala
do	2/1/16	—	Nothing to report	W/Barala
do	3/1/16	9am	Lieut J.P. Mitchell with 30 men ad transport? as escorts set out for HOULLE. This was occupied two days, and the party was billeted at Meneers - Cappel for the night.	W/Barala
do	4/1/16	—	Nothing to report	W/Barala
do	5/1/16	2pm	A party of 2 Officers and 22 O.R. reported for 72⟨?⟩ 7a Cav⟨?⟩.	W/Barala
		11am	The O.D.S. at Coylin YPRES, was handed over to the 72⟨?⟩ 7a Amb. and the personnel of this unit withdrawn to POPERINGHE. The halfora⟨?⟩ g. returned to duty with the ⟨?⟩	W/Barala
		11am	The transfer of BRANDHOEK (less 20) withdrawn to POPERING⟨?⟩	W/Barala
do	6/1/16	3am	Transport, less 195 wagon, 1 ambes wagon, 1 water cart and 1 malcoe⟨?⟩ car entrained at POPERINGHE.	

Army Form C. 2118

WAR DIARY
or
INTELLIGENCE SUMMARY
(Erase heading not required.)

Instructions regarding War Diaries and Intelligence Summaries are contained in F.S. Regs., Part II. and the Staff Manual respectively. Title Pages will be prepared in manuscript.

Place	Date	Hour	Summary of Events and Information	Remarks and references to Appendices
POPERINGHE	6/1/16	9am	Journey of the Staff Personnel of 57 F.A. less 3 M.Os, 19 M and 56 O.R. entrained for ST OMER.	
		1pm	Arrived at ST OMER and detrained	
		4pm	The party arrived at HOULLE and were billeted	
HOULLE	7/1/16	10am	Established a hospital in buildings at HOULLE	
-do-	8/1/16	12.30pm	Remainder of Personnel reports at HOULLE. Bar transport and were billeted.	W.P. Bazeley
-do-	9/1/16	5pm	2/Lieut E Jones returned from leave. Lt J.C. Beale came with remainder of transport arrived at HOULLE. Inspected by A.D.M.S. 17th Div.	W.P. Bazeley
-do-	10/1/16		Hospital organised — scheme of collection organised	W.P. Bazeley
-do-	11/1/16		Nothing to report	W.P. Bazeley
-do-	12/1/16		Capt. Rowan transferred to 8 No. Staffs. Lt. A.J. Other rejoined this unit for duty	W.P. Bazeley

WAR DIARY
or
INTELLIGENCE SUMMARY

Army Form C. 2118

Place	Date	Hour	Summary of Events and Information	Remarks and references to Appendices
HOOGE	13/7/16	—	Nothing to report	W.Barela
do	14/7/16	—	do	W.Barela
do	15/7/16	—	do	W.Barela
do	16/7/16	—	do	W.Barela
do	17/7/16	—	Capt J.S. Lewis Ranie rejoined the unit for C. Jones	W.Barela
do	18/7/16	—	Nothing to report	W.Barela
do	19/7/16	—	do	W.Barela
do	20/7/16	2.30p	1k Ranie left the Coy from 3 7An of 1k division to return to G. West Ridings in cons. of 17th Division orders for trench competition.	W.Barela
do	21/7/16		Lt B.B. Gorst joined this unit for duty. Pt R. Smelded transferred to 57 mt/k Amb. 3 drivers A.S.C. (TT) joined the unit for duty.	W.Barela

WAR DIARY
or
INTELLIGENCE SUMMARY
(Erase heading not required.)

Army Form C. 2118

Place	Date	Hour	Summary of Events and Information	Remarks and references to Appendices
HOULLE	21/7/16	10—	Pte Byrne Rene evacuated sick.	W/Barada
do	22/7/16	—	Nothing to report.	
do	23/7/16	—	Nothing to report	W/Barada W/Barada
do	24/7/16	—	2nd O.C. 17th Divisional train inspected the horses, harness and vehicles of the unit.	W/Barada
do	25/7/16	—	Lieut J.R. Evans R.A.M.C. proceeded to 7th Brigade for duty.	W/Barada is on duty
do	26/7/16	—	The Rama team drew with 10th Kansas Fusiliers (Score 2-2).	W/Barada
do	27/7/16	—	Routine. Major J.E.G. Carstairs together with Capt A.E. report Sick.	W/Barada
do	28/7/16	2.30p 2.30p	Attached to A.D.M.S. 17th Division. The Rama team were defeated by 10th Lancs. Fusiliers (Score 6-0 to Lancs Fus. 2 goals Rama nil).	
do	29/7/16	1p	Capt W. Murdoch transferred to 7th Division for temporary duty.	W/Barada for
do	30/7/16	9.30p	A.Cpl Gouveia and Capt. W/Barada attended a lecture by Lt Col McDonald G.S.O.I. 9th Division at NORDAUSQUES on the work of the G.Staff in the G.Staff at LOOS.	W/Barada

Place	Date	Hour	Summary of Events and Information	Remarks and references to Appendices
ADCLE	30/1/16	10am	Capt. Lewis and Coper, 7th Gorran and Sgt attended a demonstration on Chemical Defence at OXELAERE. W. Barclay	
-do-	31/1/16	10am	Lt. Col. E. Gorran, R.A.M.C. proceeded to 79th Bge R.F.A. for tempory duty. W. Barclay	

S

Feb 1918

51st Field Amb.

51ṃ 7a.
vol: 6

WAR DIARY or INTELLIGENCE SUMMARY

Army Form C. 2118

(Erase heading not required.)

Place	Date	Hour	Summary of Events and Information	Remarks and references to Appendices
MOULLE	1 Feb/16		Captain 10th Barclay R.A.M.C. proceeded to OXYLEARE for a two days course of instruction on protective measures against gas attacks.	Capt. Barclay instruction in gas
do	2 Feb/16		Lieut. Col. E.L. Goodland R.A.M.C. attended D.M.S. II Army, also D.G.M.S. at H.Q. Ep. Stans	
do	3 Feb/16		Two M Drug horses Evacuated: one from Establishment + one attached (chaplain)	2 R.H. Evacuated
do	4 " "		Captain H.J. Cotter R.A.M.C. proceeded on leave.	Capt. Cotter on leave
			Captain 10th BARCLAY R.A.M.C. & 10 O.R. proceeded by car to RENINGHELST to take over hospital	Advanced party to Reninghelst
			Lieut G. JOUGHIN R.A.M.C. reports for temporary duty of this unit	Lieut G. Joughin arrives
do	5 Feb		Ptes. HAYNE + WINTERSCALE Evacuated sick Nothing to report.	2 ptes R.A.M.C. Evacuated sick
do	6 Feb. 16	6am	Transport & 2 sections under Capt. Blackday left HOULLE for RENINGHELST by road	W. Sparrow Captain R.A.M.C.
RENINGHELST		7am	Hospital at RENINGHELST taken over by advance party from 7th Fd. Amb.	W. Sparrow Capt.

WAR DIARY
or
INTELLIGENCE SUMMARY
(Erase heading not required.)

Army Form C. 2118

Place	Date	Hour	Summary of Events and Information	Remarks and references to Appendices
HOULLE RENINGHELST	27.2.16	5 p.m.	Capt Beasley's party arrived. No casualties.	
		6 p.m.	Lt Col Gostlard arrived	
		4 p.m.	Lt B.B. Gough proceeded to 6 & 8 Staffs for temporary duty	
HOULLE	28.2.16	8 am	Personnel and remainder of transport under Capt P. Rawson vice w/T. Barclay started by road for ST OMER and entrained for GOEDWAERSWELDE	
"	"	1 p.m.	The hospital at HOULLE was handed over to 142nd Fd. Ab. Pte Yates evacuated sick.	W.T. Barclay
RENINGHELST	"	7 p.m.	Capt. Lewis and party arrived aft.	
-do-	9.3.16	4.30 am	Lt Col E.L. Gostlard proceeded on special leave to England. In his absence Capt. W. Barclay assumed command.	W.T. Barclay
			Capt. P.H. Rawson assumed temporary duty with this unit	
			Capt. Q.V.B. Wallace returned from leave and proceeded to 7 Border and Lt P.B. Evans returned to this unit from 7 Border.	
-do-			Lt J.D. Evans assumed duty as O.C. Divisional Baths.	

Army Form C. 2118

WAR DIARY
or
INTELLIGENCE SUMMARY
(Erase heading not required.)

Instructions regarding War Diaries and Intelligence Summaries are contained in F.S. Regs., Part II. and the Staff Manual respectively. Title Pages will be prepared in manuscript.

Place	Date	Hour	Summary of Events and Information	Remarks and references to Appendices
RENINGHELST	9/1/16		The day was occupied in clearing up the hospital. The nervy sick & regimental units without an M.O. are seen and sick collected from the road camps. By arrangement with the S.M. Ambs. cases passing through the unit suitable for Divisional Rest Station and scabies cases are sent to this unit for disposal. Cleaning is done chiefly by horsed wagons. The roads are very bad, and it is impossible to have the heavy draught horses for wagon. The arrangement is this arrangement is the sloth passes to the vehicles, and the patients get very cold.	W.M. Sanders Capt W.M. Sanders
-do-	10/1/16		The A.D.M.S. 17th Division inspected the hospital, and billets of the unit.	W.M. Sanders
-do-	11/1/16		Nothing to report.	

WAR DIARY
or
INTELLIGENCE SUMMARY
(Erase heading not required.)

Army Form C. 2118

Place	Date	Hour	Summary of Events and Information	Remarks and references to Appendices
RENINGHELST	11/4/16	4 P.	One of our [?] road to Crony Aeroplanes passed over the village and dropped some bombs in the neighbourhood. 2 men of the 24th Division were killed.	
do	13/4/16		Nothing to report.	
do	14/4/16	2 pm	The men of the unit were paid.	W.T. Barclay
		7 pm	The O.C. received instructions to hold himself in readiness as a gas attack was in progress in front of BEDFORD HOUSE.	W.T. Barclay
		8.30 pm	Horses under Sgt. Doutton reported to O.C. 52nd Fd Amb for duty. All cars were despatched under the orders	
		11 pm 12 Mn	of O.C. 52 Fd Amb. Capt Begg a Car proceeded with 3 horsed amb. wagons to OUDERDOM. Capt Ravin and Lt Evans with 3 men of this unit and 1 man of 52 Fd Amb. set out in motor buses for BEDFORD HOUSE.	W.T. Barclay
do	15/4/16	12.30 am	61 wounded and 4 sickmen (all army cases) were brought from OUDERDOM by horse amb. wagons. These cases were dealt with.	
		7 am	3 large motor amb. wagons and one Ford with 9 men reported from 53rd F.A. 2 cars with 16 men proceeded to BEDFORD HOUSE.	
		6 am	The 5th M.A.C. cleared the wounded and sick (hand [?] from 52 Fd FA)	

WAR DIARY
or
INTELLIGENCE SUMMARY

(Erase heading not required.)

Army Form C. 2118

Place	Date	Hour	Summary of Events and Information	Remarks and references to Appendices
RENINGHELST	15/7/16	7 p.m.	Lt Cumberland and Lt Clements with 36 men reported for 53rd F.A.	
- do -		8 p.m.	36 men & 53rd F.A. proceeded to OUDERDOM to report to 52nd & 70th Amb. W/Barala	
- do -	16/7/16	2.30 p.m.	Capt. P.H. Ransom R.A.M.C. proceeded to BEDFORD HOUSE to relieve Lt. R.B. Gough, R.A.M.C. 2 So. Staffs, killed.	
		9 a.m.	Capt Walker, Lts Murray, Harper, and Coy R.A.M.C. reported	
		10.30 a.m.	Lts Cumberland and Clements with remainder of 53rd F.A. proceeded to BEDFORD HOUSE.	
		12.30 p.m.	Capt Walker and 21 men proceeded to OUDERDOM to 52nd F.A. Amb.	
		3 p.m.	Lt. Harper proceeded to OUDERDOM. During the day notification was received that Pte Hurst R. of the unit had been evacuated wounded	
	17/7/16	12.30 a.m.	Lt Evans R.A.M.C. returned for BEDFORD HOUSE. Comp Barelay	
- do -		1 p.m.	Lt. Stuart Rowe reported to this unit for temporary duty. Pte Laing of the unit evacuated sick.	

Army Form C. 2118

WAR DIARY
or
INTELLIGENCE SUMMARY
(Erase heading not required.)

Place	Date	Hour	Summary of Events and Information	Remarks and references to Appendices
RENINGHELST	17/9/16	4 p.m.	2/Lieut H Hayne reported on arrival from No 10 Stationary Hosp. W J Barclay	
-do-	18/9/16	9 a.m.	L.Cpl Gouillard returned from leave.	
		8 p.m.	3 O.R. arrived as reinforcements.	
		10 a.m.	Capt G Walker and Lt E.F. Key were attached to this unit	
		4 p.m.	Capt for temporary duty. moderate arrivals for duty from 7 Times. W J Barclay	
			Nothing to report. W J Barclay	
-do-	19/9/16	—	Nothing to report. W J Barclay	
-do-	20/9/16	11 a.m.	Capt H J Osler returned off leave.	
-do-	21/9/16	2 p.m.	A store of bricks was obtained from QUENTIN Siding, nr POPERINGHE. Work was commenced on the paths round the two piano W J Barclay	
-do-	22/9/16	—	Nothing to report W J Barclay	
-do-	23/9/16	—	Nothing to report W J Barclay	

Army Form C. 2118

WAR DIARY
or
INTELLIGENCE SUMMARY
(Erase heading not required.)

Instructions regarding War Diaries and Intelligence Summaries are contained in F. S. Regs., Part II and the Staff Manual respectively. Title Pages will be prepared in manuscript.

Place	Date	Hour	Summary of Events and Information	Remarks and references to Appendices
RENINGHELST	25/2/16	—	Nothing to report. WMBarclay	
–do–	26/2/16	—	Pte Honan R.A. transferred to No 2 C.C.S. Bailleul for obsn. Sgt Nuthall R.A.M.C. evacuated sick.	
		H.Q.	Capt. Colyer and Lt. Lee with 1 Sgt and 14 men proceeded to Ka Laiterie. DICKEBUSCH take over from 52nd F. Amb. 2 Motor Ambulance waggons proceeded with them. WMBarclay	
–do–	26/2/16	5a.	RENINGHELST was bombed by hostile air-craft. 1 man killed and 2 wounded in 51st M.G.C.	
		10a.m. noon	1 Regiment of bombs came through the roof of the hospital. 42 cases were transferred to No 12 C.C.S. HAZEBROUCK. 56	is C.C.S. HAZEBROUCK. (ADMS 11th Div F 444). WMBarclay
–do–	27/2/16	—	Nothing to report	WMBarclay
–do–	28/2/16	—	Nothing received of evacuation of Pte S. Darkes	WMBarclay

WAR DIARY or INTELLIGENCE SUMMARY

Place	Date	Hour	Summary of Events and Information	Remarks and references to Appendices
RENINGHELST	29/8/16	9:30a.m.	1 mule was shot by order of A.D.V.S. 17th Division. Post-mortem showed acute suppurative condition of the off hind fetlock. The mule was turned at 3 p.m. During the past three days the O.C. 7A.W.C. has been arranging to exchange the Damber Cos. of this unit & account the improbability of getting spare gear for this make of Cos., these Damber Cos. have not been repaired by Talbots.	

W.H. Bagalan

51 J. Anl.
Vol 6

S.I.
March 1916

WAR DIARY
or
INTELLIGENCE SUMMARY
(Erase heading not required.)

Army Form C. 2118

Place	Date	Hour	Summary of Events and Information	Remarks and references to Appendices
RENINGHELST	1/3/16	6 p.	Capt. Lewis, Capt. W. Murdoch with 1 sergeant and 20 men proceeded to BEDFORD HOUSE to report to Capt. 53rd Wischer. Proceeded 6 33rd F.A. for duty. W.W. Base Oxy. The O/C Lahore Dickiebrach regretted that 30 men were despatched rest up to Dickiebrach. These men were sent to and his more cars, making it in all, were sent to DICKIEBUSH for duty. Lt Col. Gouland proceeded to DICKEBUSCH.	
-do-	2/3/16 4 am			
		12.30 p.	46 cases were transferred to No 12 C.C.S. under orders from D.D.M.S. 5th Corps.	
			A number of German prisoners were brought through the village between the hours of noon and 5 p.m. Several of the wounded were redressed in the hospital of this unit.	
Caimusafa	1/3/16 3 p.		One officer and 25 OR from the R.A.M.C of the 3rd Division reported here for duty.	

WAR DIARY
or
INTELLIGENCE SUMMARY

(Erase heading not required.)

Army Form C. 2118

Place	Date	Hour	Summary of Events and Information	Remarks and references to Appendices
REINFORCEMENTS	7/9/16	9a	Lt. Col. Garland returned for Disbandment. W.J. Bagala	
-do-	8/9/16	9am	1 Officer and 50 O.R.'s of 3rd Division proceeded to Bedford House for duty with 52nd F.A. R.A.M.C.	
		1pm	L/Cp Pearce and Pte Harris and Smith H.H. proceeded to Havre. No 1 & 2 Base Depots on transfer to R. Anson. W.J. Bagala	
-do-	11/9/16	9a	Notification has been received that Cp'l G. Johnson Pte. Beckwith as flash tone had been evacuated (wounded at BEDFORD HOUSE).	
		10a	Capt. Lewis and Murdoch returned to duty with this unit with their detachment.	
	12/9/16	5pm	Cap'l J. Walker returned to duty with this unit. W.J. Bagala	

WAR DIARY or INTELLIGENCE SUMMARY

Army Form C. 2118

Place	Date	Hour	Summary of Events and Information	Remarks and references to Appendices
RENINGHELST	5/3/16	11am	LCpl Atkins was evacuated sick. W.J.Bagnall Capt	
			The hospital was increasingly crowded visit and who were only slightly ill had great difficulty in being experienced in getting the hospital anywhere. W.J.Bagnall Capt	
-do-	6/3/16	10am	130 sick were transferred from the 57 & 7a. Amb to 15 C.C.S.	
		4pm	75 cases were sent to D.R.S. and 50 to 15 C.S. The Hospital is still greatly overcrowded. W.J.Bagnall Capt	
		11pm	Capt J. Walker, Lewis and Murdoch proceeded with C section to accompany 52nd Brigade. W.J.Bagnall Capt T. & 2h Co	
-do-	7/3/16	12.15p	A & B sections less R.C.E. Gow[?]... marched for STEENVOORDE and 19 O.R.	
		4.30pm	Above reached party arrived and were billeted in STEENVOORDE. The men in a barn, horses in them. W.J.Bagnall Capt	
-do-	8/3/16		The C.O. and party headed out in RENINGHELST to re 5H Fd. Amb. and proceeded to STEEN VOORDE. W.J.Bagnall Capt	

Army Form C. 2118

WAR DIARY
or
INTELLIGENCE SUMMARY
(Erase heading not required.)

Place	Date	Hour	Summary of Events and Information	Remarks and references to Appendices
STEENVOORDE	9/3/16	7a-	Lt Evers R.A.M.C. proceeded to 7th Divn to duty vice Lt H.V. Wells, transferred to Base.	W.My Bagae Coy
-do-	10/3/16	1245 p.	A.T.B sections marched to OUTTERSTEENE and were billeted in village. The horses were evacuated.	W.My Bagae Coy
OUTTERSTEENE	11/3/16	1p.	S.M. Crosby transferred to 103rd A.T. Coy. Lt J Duke Rake appointed to supersede Pavitt under orders from A.P. this 17th Division.	W My Bagae Coy
-do-	12/3/16		Nothing to report.	W My Bagae Coy
-do-	13/3/16	7p.	A.T.B sections were paid.	W My Bagae Coy
-do-	14/3/16	2.30p.	Casualer at La Crèche was paid.	E My Bagae Coy
-do-	15/3/16		Nothing to note.	W My Bagae Coy

WAR DIARY
or
INTELLIGENCE SUMMARY

(Erase heading not required.)

Army Form C. 2118

Place	Date	Hour	Summary of Events and Information	Remarks and references to Appendices
OUTTERSTEENE	10/3/16	—	Nothing to note. W.J.Bagnall	
— do —	11/3/16	—	do. W.J.Bagnall	
OUTTERSTEENE	12/3/16 9.30am		Section complete with transport proceeded to ARMENTIERES. C. Section complete do.	
ARMENTIERES	13/3/16	11 noon	C Section arrived at ARMENTIERES.	
— do —		2 pm	B	
— do —		4 pm	Capt. Macdonald 1 N.C.O. and 11 men proceeded to A.D.S at HOUPLINES to take over from 64th Fd Amb.	
— do —		9 pm.	Orders received from A.D.M.S. 7th Division to change A.D.S. from HOUPLINES to BRIGQUERIE at CHAPPELLE d'ARMENTIERES. W.J.Bagnall	
— do —	14/3/16	10 am.	Capt Macdonald and detachment proceeded to HOUPLINES and relieved the party of 63rd Fd Amb. at BRICQUERIE.	
		12 noon	51st Fd. Amb. took over the hospital from the	

WAR DIARY
or
INTELLIGENCE SUMMARY
(Erase heading not required.)

Place	Date	Hour	Summary of Events and Information	Remarks and references to Appendices
ARMENTIERES	19/5/16		The hospital is situated in the CERCLE ST JOSEPH, RUE DENIS PAPIN. There is no large ward, but beds, we during hall for meals, offices, dispensary & officers' mess etc. The situation is a good one. The A.D.S. is 20 minutes walk from the hospital and to aid posts a further 10 minutes. The roads are good.	
do	20/5/16	2pm	New transport lines are in Port de Nieppe, under Lt. C.C. Gulland arrived at Armentières.	w/Sgde Car
do	21/5/16	6am	A section under Lt. C.C. Gulland arrived at Armentières. None received but I noticing horse had to be destroyed.	w/Sgde Car
do		2pm	2 NCOs and 13 men report to R.E. for duty in reasonable further notice. Lt Smith relieved Capt Murdoch at A.D.S.	w/Sgde Car

Army Form C. 2118

WAR DIARY
or
INTELLIGENCE SUMMARY
(Erase heading not required.)

Place	Date	Hour	Summary of Events and Information	Remarks and references to Appendices
ARMENTIERES	22/9/16	2 P.	Capt. W Thurgood proceeded to 17th Manchester Regt for duty vice Lt. G H Reid who is attached to them unit for temporary duty. W.H.Bare Capt	
do	23/9/16	2 P.	Sgt Major T Neil, of the unit evacuated sick to England ex France. W.H.Bare Capt	
do	24/9/16	Noon	Lt J.M.M Reid proceeded to England ex France. on this contract.	
		3 P.	Capt H.J. Copper proceeded to A.O.S. W.H.Bare Capt	
			Lt G Burke proceeded to H Bgde R.F.A vice Lt G Reid Lt M.L. Garman RAMC	
		3.30pm	Lt The C Wheeler evacuated sick	
			Pte S Shaw arrived duty with this unit W.H.Bare Capt	
do	25/9/16	5am	19 Reinforcements arrived.	
			Capt J.S. Lewis and Lt. R.L.Foy proceeded on leave. W.H.Bare Capt	
do	26/9/16	—	Nothing to note	

WAR DIARY
or
INTELLIGENCE SUMMARY

(Erase heading not required.)

Army Form C. 2118

Place	Date	Hour	Summary of Events and Information	Remarks and references to Appendices
ARMENTIERES	27/3/16	9/pm	The men of the went out at the Hqtrs were paid. P.R.E. goes forward A.D.S. to relieve Capt. M.J. O'Mar.	W.J. Barclay
do	28/3/16	10.30 am	The men at K.A.D.S. were paid	
		2.30 pm	The men of the A.S.C.(T.T.) were paid.	W.J. Barclay
do	29/3/16	—	Nothing to report.	
do	30/3/16	2/pm	Capt. J. Walker proceeds to A.D.S. in relief of to the guns.	W.J. Barclay
do	31/3/16	9 am	The presentation car driven by Pte Hoskins was withdrawn and Pte Hoskins proceeded to to the 14 M.A.C. with the car.	W.J. Barclay

14th Div.

No. 51 F. Amb.

5 April 1916.

COMMITTEE FOR THE
MEDICAL HISTORY OF THE WAR
Date 9 - JUN. 1916

SI J avab

Army Form C. 2118.

Vol 7

WAR DIARY
or
INTELLIGENCE SUMMARY.
(Erase heading not required.)

Instructions regarding War Diaries and Intelligence Summaries are contained in F. S. Regs., Part II. and the Staff Manual respectively. Title pages will be prepared in manuscript.

Place	Date 1916	Hour	Summary of Events and Information	Remarks and references to Appendices
In The Field	April 1st		Nothing to Note	Walker Capt RAMC
"	April 2nd		" " "	Walker Capt RAMC
"	April 3rd		" " "	Mallas Lieut RAMC

Army Form C. 2118.

WAR DIARY
or
INTELLIGENCE SUMMARY.
(Erase heading not required.)

Instructions regarding War Diaries and Intelligence Summaries are contained in F. S. Regs., Part II. and the Staff Manual respectively. Title pages will be prepared in manuscript.

Place	Date	Hour	Summary of Events and Information	Remarks and references to Appendices
	April 1916			
	4th		Capt Walker proceeded on leave and hand over temporary command of the Fld Amb to Capt J.S. Lewis.	Lewis
	5th		Capt H.S. Butter relieved by Lieut Ley at A.D.S. Lieut Lee proceeded on leave.	Lewis
	6th		Lieut Ley proceeded to 10th New York Regt. to relieve Capt Hunter. Lieut Ley relieved from A.D.S. by Lieut Gorman. Nothing to record.	Lewis
	7th			Lewis
	8th		Lieut Col Akers, Lieut Col Butler, & Capt Wilson Australian A.M.C. 1st Division (Australian) were attached to this Field Ambulance and A.D.S. Regimental Aid Posts for instructional purposes.	Lewis
	9th		Nothing to record.	Lewis

WAR DIARY
or
INTELLIGENCE SUMMARY.
(Erase heading not required.)

Army Form C. 2118.

Place	Date	Hour	Summary of Events and Information	Remarks and references to Appendices
	April 1916 9th		Capt H.S. Otter relieved Lieut McGorman at A.D.S.	
				Stevens
	10th		15 R.A.M.C. men under Staff/Sergt were attached to the 34th Sanitary Section for duty	
			Lieut Col Akers, Lieut Col Buller, and Capt Wilcox A.M.C., 1st Australian Division returned to their units	
				Stevens
	11th		Major Solley, Capt Johnson and Capt Fitzpatrick A.M.C. 1st Australian Div Sup Steps were attached to Dilky units for instructional purposes. Traded A.D.S. Regtl. Aid Posts &c	
			Lieut T.R. Davis reported to this unit for duty	
				Stevens
				Stevens
	12th		Nothing to record	

WAR DIARY or INTELLIGENCE SUMMARY.

(Erase heading not required.)

Army Form C. 2118.

Place	Date	Hour	Summary of Events and Information	Remarks and references to Appendices
	April			
	13th		Major Jolly; Capt Johnson and Capt Fitzpatrick A.M.C. 1st Australian Division returned to their Unit. Lieut R.C Bridgman R.A.M.C reported to this unit for duty. Cpl Purcelos A.M.C 1st Australian Division was attached Company for instructional purposes	J.K.Lewis
	14th		Lieut Col Gordon has returned to this Unit. Lieut R. Gorman relieved Capt H.S Little at A.D.S Lieut L.P. Ray left this unit to take up duty with W.O. 2 X Ray Unit in the Field.	J.K.Lewis W.M.Barley
	15th		Nothing to report.	
	16/4/16		Capt Purcelos, A.M.C. 1st Aust Div returned to his unit	W.M.Barley

WAR DIARY
or
INTELLIGENCE SUMMARY.
(Erase heading not required.)

Army Form C. 2118.

Instructions regarding War Diaries and Intelligence Summaries are contained in F. S. Regs., Part II. and the Staff Manual respectively. Title pages will be prepared in manuscript.

Place	Date	Hour	Summary of Events and Information	Remarks and references to Appendices
ARMENTIERES	24/4/16	5.30 pm	Pay Parade. The men at headquarters were paid. W. Barclay	
-do-	25/4/16		The remainder of the men of the unit were paid. W. Barclay	
-do-	26/4/16		Leave reopened after being stopped since 16.4.16. A/Cpl Instead assumed duty as A.D.M.S. Orderly during the absence on leave of Cpl O'R.A. Julian A.M.S. Cpl H. L. Orton relieved Capt Walker at A.D.S.	JHeron
-do-	27/4/16		Capt Walker took temporary command of Unit. Capt W.E. Barclay proceeded on leave. Inspection of Gas Helmets of Unit took place	JHeron
-do-	28/4/16		Nothing to record.	JHeron

WAR DIARY
or
INTELLIGENCE SUMMARY.
(Erase heading not required.)

Army Form C. 2118.

Place	Date	Hour	Summary of Events and Information	Remarks and references to Appendices
ARMENTIERES	17/4/16	—	Capt. J.S. Lewis proceeded to A.D.S. to relieve Lt. Jorman	W.R.Barclay
- do -	18/4/16	—	Nothing to record.	W.R.Barclay
- do -	19/4/16	—	- do -	W.R.Barclay
- do -	20/4/16	—	Lt. Col. Davis proceeded to A.D.S. to relieve Capt. J.S. Lewis	W.R.Barclay
- do -	21/4/16	—	Nothing to record	W.R.Barclay
- do -	22/4/16	—	Sergt. Maj. T. Neil returned to duty with the unit from No. 6 Stationary Hospital. Lt. Kirkell rejoined the unit.	W.R.Barclay
- do -	23/4/16	—	Capt. F. Walker proceeded to A.D.S. in relief of Lt. Col. Davis	W.R.Barclay

Army Form C. 2118.

WAR DIARY
or
INTELLIGENCE SUMMARY.
(Erase heading not required.)

Place	Date	Hour	Summary of Events and Information	Remarks and references to Appendices
to -	April 29th		Lieut Bridgeman relieved Capt H.J. Ottley at J.J.S.	[signature]
- do	30th		Nothing to record.	[signature]

5 May 1916.

No. 51 F. Amb.

14th D⟨iv⟩

COMMITTEE FOR THE
MEDICAL HISTORY OF THE WAR
Date 26 JUN 1916

Vol. 8

Army Form C. 2118.

WAR DIARY of 51st FIELD AMBULANCE 17th DIVISION. B.E.F. MAY 1916

INTELLIGENCE SUMMARY
(Erase heading not required.)

Instructions regarding War Diaries and Intelligence Summaries are contained in F.S. Regs., Part II. and the Staff Manual respectively. Title pages will be prepared in manuscript.

Place	Date 1916	Hour	Summary of Events and Information	Remarks and references to Appendices
In the field	1st May		37388 Pte Rowntree, and 1420 Pte Smith, S, of this unit left on 8 days leave.	Mueller
" "	2nd "		1256, Cpl. Houlston A.S.C, att. this unit, granted 8 days leave. Under instructions R.D.M.S. 17th Division, Lieut. Bridgman remains on duty for 3 more days at our A.D.S. keeping in touch & R.M.O. 10th Notts Derby for instructional purposes.	JW JW
" "	3rd May		Nothing to note.	JW
" "	4th May		Capt. J.P. BLOCKLEY RAMC. (T.C.) transferred to 12. C.C.S. 7 reinforcements (O.R.S.) join	JW
" "	5th "		Nothing to note: Lt Gorman RAMC. of this unit transferred sick to 12. C.C.S.	JW
" "	6th "		Colonel GEDDES. A.M.S. DDMS. II Corps, inspected unit.	JW
" "	7th "		Capt. Barclay rejoins from leave.	JW
" "	8th "		Nothing to note. Capt. J.S. Lewis, RAMC relieves Lt Bridgman at A.D.S.	JW
" "	9th "		Major Martin, New Zealand A.M.C, also Lts ROCHE, THOMAS, & CORKHILL R.A.M.C. attached for 3 days duty (instructional) Sergt Ahern A.S.C joins unit for duty	JW
" "	10th "		Capt. J.P. BLOCKLEY, & Lt GORMAN of this unit return for duty on discharge from 12. C.C.S.	JW
ARMENTIERES	11		Sgt Ahern A.S.C. returned to dispersal train. Lt White ASC joined this unit for duty. Major J.S. Lewis and detachment returned to HQ on relief by NZ Fd Amb. detachment from N.Z. Fd Amb.	W.R. Barclay

WAR DIARY
or
INTELLIGENCE SUMMARY.

Army Form C. 2118.

Place	Date	Hour	Summary of Events and Information	Remarks and references to Appendices
ARMENTIERES	12/5/16	9am	Capt. J.S. Levis and 10 N/Rank proceeded to Estaires as advance billeting party	
		11.30	Crossum under Capt. J. Walker, with 16 Carls Dawn proceeded en route for Estaires	W. Bazalay
-do-	13/5/16	1.30am	No 3 N.Z. Ft Amb arrived in Armentieres. The men of the unit were met, given hot food and conducted to their billets.	
-do-		2pm	The dressing station was taken over by No 3 N.Z. Ft Amb. B. Section under Capt.	
-do-	14/5/16	10.45am	Lt. M.C. Poingma R.A.M.C. sick	
-do-		8pm	Capt. Ha. Smith R.a.m.c. proceeded to 1st Cans Fns, in relief of Capt. Ha. Smith R.a.m.c. sick	W.T. Bazalay
-do-	14/5/16	11.50am	B Section under Capt. H.J. Coker proceeded with 2 barris. 51st Bgde en route for Estaires	W. Bazalay
-do-	15/5/16	1.15am	Headquarters of unit with A Section left en route for Estaires with 51st Bgde Group.	W. Bazalay

WAR DIARY
or
INTELLIGENCE SUMMARY.

Army Form C. 2118.

Place	Date	Hour	Summary of Events and Information	Remarks and references to Appendices
Balance	13/5/16	5 a.m.	Headquarters established in Hospice.	
		2 p.	- do - marched for MORBECQUES.	LCpl Harkin awarded 2nd Class Certificate. Contact regarged. Signed Brazier. W.P.Baralar
		8 p.	- do - arrived in MORBECQUES and joined Brazier.	
MORBECQUES	16/5/16	9.30 a.m	A&B sections marched for WARDRECQUES with 51st Bgde Group.	W.P.Baralar
- do -		3 p.	- do - arrived	
WARDRECQUES			- do -	W.P.Baralar
- do -	17/5/16	9.30 a.m.	- do - marched with 51st A. Bgde Group.	
		10.30 a.m.	Notification received from Captain J Walker Kay he had taken over on 15/5/16 duties previously carried on by 2nd and 3rd 3rd Divs. in HELLEBROUCK, and had been ordered by the actn. Staff Captain of 51st Bgde to remove to HOULLE.	
HOULLE		3 p.	A&B sections arrived in HOULLE and found that billets for Officers NCOs and men had not been found. After a great deal of trouble billets were found for personnel and accomadation for horses in HOULLE. A hospital was opened in the	

WAR DIARY
or
INTELLIGENCE SUMMARY.

Army Form C. 2118.

Place	Date	Hour	Summary of Events and Information	Remarks and references to Appendices
HOULLE	17/5/16	8p	Makings parade stamped by this unit not settled in Billets. W.S. Barclay	
	18/5/16	9am	During the whole move men with field ambulance attacked by the motor ambulance wagons. This was found to work very well and the care to the sick in the billets of this unit and have been examined and treated. Minor cases were remained to their units. Other cases were disposed of in accordance with A.D.M.S. 17th Div. letter 74/C/16.	
		9am	Capt. Allen proceeded to inspect and 17th Div. Cyclist Cr.	
		10am	Capt. J. Walker assumed duty in the A.D.M.S. office in the absence of Lt. Col. Gouland a leave. W.S. Barclay	
-do-	19/5/16	9am	Lt. Col. Daw assumed his duty at 9 a/c 10 Peinoth. W.S. Barclay	

Army Form C. 2118.

WAR DIARY
or
INTELLIGENCE SUMMARY.
(Erase heading not required.)

Instructions regarding War Diaries and Intelligence Summaries are contained in F.S. Regs., Part II and the Staff Manual respectively. Title pages will be prepared in manuscript.

Place	Date	Hour	Summary of Events and Information	Remarks and references to Appendices
HOULLE	20/3/16	10am	In accordance with instructions for DA QMG 17 Div 1 Sgt and 1 driver ASC (HT) 1056, 1 HD horse and 1 mule were sent to Base HT Depot.	W.F.Bayala
-do-	21/3/16		Nothing to report.	W.F.Bayala
-do-	22/3/16		All the men of the unit were paid.	W.F.Bayala
-do-	23/3/16		Nothing to report.	W.F.Bayala
-do-	24/3/16		One motor cycle returned to 17 D.S.C. ad and anoth[er]	Lt W.F.Bayala
-do-	25/3/16		Nothing to report.	W.F.Bayala
-do-	26/3/16		Nothing to report.	W.F.Bayala
-do-	27/3/16	8am	The inoculation of the men of the 51st Inf. Bgd with mixed antityphoid vaccine was carried out today.	Lt W.F.Bayala

T2134. Wt. W705—776. 500000. 4/15. Sir J.C. & S.

Army Form C. 2118.

WAR DIARY
or
INTELLIGENCE SUMMARY.
(Erase heading not required.)

Place	Date	Hour	Summary of Events and Information	Remarks and references to Appendices
HOULLE	26/3/16		Dr Harris A.S.C.(T.T.) of this unit evacuated sick to U.S. Base Coy	
-do-	27/3/16	9am	Lt Earle-Page returned to duty with this unit.	
		1pm	Pte Taylor R. transferred to A.Vet Corps.	U.S.Base Coy
-do-	29/3/16		Nothing to note	U.S.Base Coy
-do-	3/4/16	10am	Lt M.C. Bridgeman R.A.M.C returned to duty with this unit. R.A.M.C Routine Order No 53 by Col O.R.A. Green, C.M.G. A.D.M.S 17th Div. No 84. Lt Col E.R. Gowland, R.A.M.C 51st Fd Amb, will be in England, having been granted sick leave of absence from 20.5.16 - 19.6.16 ceases to command the 51st Fd Amb. from 20th inst. in accordance with D.G.M.S. letter 2297/21 of 5.4.16 para A(9) Capt W. Barclay, R.A.M.C. (S.R.) 51st Fd Amb. pending	

WAR DIARY
or
INTELLIGENCE SUMMARY.

(Erase heading not required.)

Army Form C. 2118.

Instructions regarding War Diaries and Intelligence Summaries are contained in F. S. Regs., Part II. and the Staff Manual respectively. Title pages will be prepared in manuscript.

Place	Date	Hour	Summary of Events and Information	Remarks and references to Appendices
			Confirmation is temporarily appointed to command K. 51st Bde. Cmd. as from 16 20th inst.	

W.P. Barclay

No. 51 - F.A.

June 1916.

51

Army Form C. 2118.

WAR DIARY
of 51st FIELD AMBULANCE.
INTELLIGENCE SUMMARY. 17th DIVISION.
(Erase heading not required.)

Vol 9

Page 1.

Instructions regarding War Diaries and Intelligence Summaries are contained in F.S. Regs., Part II. and the Staff Manual respectively. Title pages will be prepared in manuscript.

Place	Date	Hour	Summary of Events and Information	Remarks and references to Appendices
HOULLE	1/6/16	8.30	The unit paraded for a route march with 51st Bgd. Gp. and marched past E.S.S. an O Lavasach motor was carried. Sufficient personnel were left at Houlle to work the Hospital. Old cooks also were left behind. On 9.25 am the unit passed the starting point. Map 27(B) K 29 a 1.3 and returned to billets at noon. There was no transport minded very well and there was no trouble of any description. I visited the 7th Jehad Lancers horse field up. W. Barclay	
-do-	2/6/16	9p-	Sports were held in a field near HOULLE. An invitation to be present was extended to the Officers of N°10 Stationary Hospital and also the nurses and sisters. W. Barclay	
-do-	3/6/16	5:45pm	A.Y.C. section paraded for to take part in a divisional	

WAR DIARY OF INTELLIGENCE SUMMARY

Army Form C. 2118.

Page 2

Place	Date	Hour	Summary of Events and Information	Remarks and references to Appendices
HOULLE.	June		Raining day. The B.S.T. Regt. attacked our K. INGLINGHEM ridge. C section established Regimental station in an invisible point behind the INGLINGHEM Mill Ridge and established communication with the regimental medical officer. A section represented a main dressing station in NORDAUSQUES. Major G.E. FERGUSON, R.A.M.C. arrived at HOULLE and took over command of the unit.	
	Mon			A.D.M.S. 17th Div. 20.11.17.I.7.
HOULLE	3rd	—	Journed at War Headquarters of 51st Field Ambulance at 11 a.m. today to take over command of the Unit vice Lieut-Col (Temp) E.L. GOWLAND R.A.M.C. who is on the sick list in England.	
"	4th	—	Inspected Section kitchens with Quarter Master & Sgt Major. Voluntary Church parade at 11 G.M. Visited A.D.M.S. 17th Division to report arrival etc	
"	5th	—	At 10 a.m. inspected R.A.M.C. personnel in Drill order; also smoke helmets & identity discs. Ditto A.S.C. (H.T.) at 11 a.m. and R.A.M.C. (H.T.) at 2 p.m. Inspected all weapons and motor ambulances. Inspected office records & books. Re-allotted officers to Sections	

Army Form C. 2118.

WAR DIARY
or
INTELLIGENCE SUMMARY.
(Erase heading not required.)

Page 3

Instructions regarding War Diaries and Intelligence Summaries are contained in F.S. Regs., Part II. and the Staff Manual respectively. Title pages will be prepared in manuscript.

Place	Date	Hour	Summary of Events and Information	Remarks and references to Appendices
HOULLE	June. 6th	—	Inspected Medical & Surgical equipment in charge of sections. Also greater-coats & stores. Pay day for unit. Rain.	
"	7th	—	Lieut. BRIDGEMAN. R.A.M.C. posted to 4th BORDERS temporary duty. Lectures on "First Aid" to Bearer - Sub-division by O.C. Sections. Inspected Dressing Station, Dispensary, Packstore etc. at 3p.m. Inspected arms pistols & holsters. Capt. V. M. Rich. R.A.M.C. reported his arrival for duty at 4-30p.m. Dvr. Anderson A.S.C. ex attached to Divisional Supply Colum.	Dvr. Anderson A.S.C. ex attached to Divisional Supply Colum.
"	8th	—	Route March 10 a.m. to 12-30 p.m. Marching order. Nos 1,2,3 & 4. Dvr CULLEN A.S.C. to Supply Colum. Three privates R.A.M.C. arrived for duty from Base. Visited O.D.M.S.	No
"	9th	—	Returned all maps on charge to unit except HAZEBROUCK (5a); LENS; AMIENS. Visited A.D.M.S. at 5pm. Received orders by wire to detail two reliable N.C.Os. as Advanced Billetly Party in conjunction with forthcoming move: detailed Sgts. PAGE & JONES R.A.M.C.	
"	10th	—	Cpl. GORHAN T.A.M.C. detailed for temporary duty with 7th East Yorks. Unit employed packing waggons etc. Capt. Rich R.A.M.C. attended at Mr. J. Pearson of 10th Sherwoods for instruction. Visited A.D.M.S.	
"	11th	→	No.17084 Cpl. WILD. R.A.M.C. evacuated to Base. Issued detailed orders re move to AMIENS.	
"	12th	→	Reveille 4 a.m. Paraded 7 a.m. Unit proceeded to AUDRICQ STATION by March - 2½ mile arriving	

Army Form C. 2118.

WAR DIARY
or
INTELLIGENCE SUMMARY.
(Erase heading not required.)

Instructions regarding War Diaries and Intelligence Summaries are contained in F. S. Regs., Part II. and the Staff Manual respectively. Title pages will be prepared in manuscript.

Page...

Place	Date	Hour	Summary of Events and Information	Remarks and references to Appendices
In the Train	June 12th	—	at station at 10-30am. Entraining began at once & was completed by 11-15am. Train worked very well & there was no hitch in the proceedings. Hot meal served at 12 noon & train left about 1-30pm. Capt BARCLAY R.A.M.C. went on ahead of the unit to report to R.T.O. all motor ambulances & cycles went by road to Amiens under Capt COTTER R.A.M.C. accompanied by the Interpreter & sundry cooks. Capt BLOCKLEY R.A.M.C. returned from leave & rejoined unit at AUDRIER Station. The train passed through ABBEVILLE about 6-30pm & those were fed & watered & men supplied with tea; left at 7-30pm and arrived at LONGEAU (4 mls S.E. of	
LONGEAU	"	11-15p.	AMIENS) at 11-15pm. Detraining took place at once, two motor ambulances & one Kam & reported that on their extra equipment. Capt COTTER with motor ambulances diet Kam & reported that on their arrival he found that no billets had been allotted to the unit & only after great difficulty had he been able to get a field & 12 billets for all ranks. Jumped on	
ALLONVILLE.	"	12.9.	ahead with him to see about matters & found that No.23 Field Ambulance had their use 22 tents in their Divisional Rest Station & also the use of their Mess & cookhouse. The main body & transport arrived about 3 a.m. having had to march 6 miles from the station; all ranks had all day & was forming on arrival & prem as every one dog & got up by traffic but nobody fell out. The men were given a hot meal on arrival in Camp & turned to bed about 4-30 a.m.	

Army Form C. 2118.

WAR DIARY
or
INTELLIGENCE SUMMARY.
(Erase heading not required.)

Page 5

Instructions regarding War Diaries and Intelligence Summaries are contained in F. S. Regs., Part II. and the Staff Manual respectively. Title pages will be prepared in manuscript.

Place	Date	Hour	Summary of Events and Information	Remarks and references to Appendices
ALLONVILLE	June 13.	—	Paraded as fatigues parties detailed for various duties. The unit is encamped on a sloping grass field at ALLONVILLE, about 5 miles from AMIENS, the rest of the 17th Division being billeted in various villages round about. Heavy rain all day. Lieut EARLE-DAVIS R.A.M.C struck off the Strength on departure to England.	
"	14"	→	Route-March in morning. Visited A.D.M.S. Drew extra tents & completed camp.	
"	15"	→	Re-employed Building bivouacs etc. Still very wet. Visited A.D.M.S. — Conference re forthcoming operations. Received instructions to indent for a very large amount of extra drugs & to increase to 1000 blankets, 200 stretchers, etc. Worked out indents in afternoon. Inspection of goggles & smoke helmets.	
"	16"	→	Route march (8 miles). Conference at A.D.M.S office. Capt H.V. RICH R.A.M.C left at 5pm for duty with	
"	17" 18"	→ →	9 York & Lancs at BOIS DU TAILLES. Lectures to Bearer sections on "First Aid". Nothing special to note. Visited Advanced Depot of Medical Stores at CORBIE. Two H.D. Lamps seized with severe colic on emerging and recovered after treatment by A.D.V.S. (? Castor oil then).	
"	19"	→	Self with Capt. BARCLAY. R.A.M.C went up to BRAY to reconnoitre A.Dr Stations & R.A. Posts on right sector of Corps area (7th Division). Saw Minden Post etc.	
"	20"	→	Visited left Sector of line (21st Division) with Capt. BARCLAY R.A.M.C. (MEAULTE: QUEENS REDOUBT etc). Capt LYONS R.A.M.C arrived for duty & posted to "C" Section. S/Sgt JOHNSTONE R.A.M.C and to drawn train for duty vice S/Cpl ANDERSON. R.A.M.C	

T2134. Wt. W708—776. 500000. 4/15. Sir J.C. & S.

Army Form C. 2118.

WAR DIARY
INTELLIGENCE SUMMARY.
(Erase heading not required.)

Page 6.

Instructions regarding War Diaries and Intelligence Summaries are contained in F.S. Regs., Part II. and the Staff Manual respectively. Title pages will be prepared in manuscript.

Place	Date	Hour	Summary of Events and Information	Remarks and references to Appendices
ALLONVILLE	June 21st	→	Capts. COTTER, BLOCKLEY, LEVIS, & WALKER R.A.M.C. reconnoitered the new trench line & R.A. Roads.	
"	22nd	→	" LYONS R.A.M.C. with O.i/c of 51st Brigade went up to the trenches (MEAULTE). Unit went on 10 mile route march under Capt WALKER R.A.M.C. Capt RICH R.A.C. rejoined for duty. One N.C.O (Cpl Wellington) & 5 privates R.A.M.C. joined for duty.	
"	23rd	→	Capt LYONS & M.O. of Brigade went to MERICOURT to reconnoitre Capt GORMAN R.A.M.C. rejoined for duty. Returned to Bearer Section as "First Aid". In evening received information that the 63rd Field Ambulance (21st Division) had orders to move at 6.30am next morning — in accordance with previous orders from A.D.M.S. Capt LEVIS R.A.M.C. & first sub-division of "C" section went to the Chateau & took over the Rest Station & equipment.	
"	24 "	→	"C" tent sub-division completed "taking over" & are now running the Rest Station (4 officers + 30 [others]). Disinfection of blankets begun. Sent up a lorry load of straw to MORLANCOURT. Inspected wagon equipment & detailed new wagon orderlies.	
"	25 "	↑	Visited A.D.M.S. detailed 2 men for duty as messengers with units of 51st Brigade; also Corporal WHITTAKER R.A.M.C. to 17th Divisional Headquarters. After church parade "Military Medal" ribbon to L/Cpl JOHNSTONE R.A.M.C. on full parade. In afternoon took over the 7th Divisional Rest Station from 22nd Field Ambulance in accordance with A.D.M.S. orders. The H.Q. horse evacuated by advice of A.D.V.S. Drew out new mule.	

WAR DIARY
INTELLIGENCE SUMMARY
(Erase heading not required.)

Army Form C. 2118.

Page 1.

Place	Date	Hour	Summary of Events and Information	Remarks and references to Appendices
ALLONVILLE	JUNE 26	→	"C" tent sub-division under Capt LEWIS. R.A.M.C. assisted by Capt LYONS R.A.M.C. are now running the two Rest Stations & will remain behind when unit moves up. At 8.30 a.m. I inspected all patients left sick & wounded & fit for duty & 13 for evacuation. Handed over kit of patients from tents to Chateau. Handed in blankets & surplus kits of officers & men to divisional dump in Allonville. Struck all spare tents.	
"	27	→	Struck all equipped tents & sundries in preparation of a move tomorrow. Personnel moved into vacant tents in Rest Station. Sent up more places to Halencourt. Two Officers (Lieuts THOMAS and BUSH, R.A.S.C.) carried for duty with 52nd & 53rd Field Ambulance. Four drivers A.S.C. H.T. Subenred to 2 days F.P. No I for refusing to obey an order given by a superior officer. At 9 pm received orders from A.D.M.S. for unit to move tomorrow at 3 pm.	
"	28"	→	Very wet day. At 2-10 pm received a wire cancelling the move ordered for 3 p.m. Continued packing up tents etc but moved officers tents into the tents recently taken over from 28th Field Ambulance version the Chateau, latrines etc as this place is not being used. Visited A.D.M.S. at 4 p.m. Sent up four car loads of equipment to MORLANCOURT. At 7 p.m. received news from A.D.M.S. to hand over the Rest Station to a Field Ambulance at 3rd Corps on arrival. Sent two officers to 52nd & 53rd Ambulances as.	
"	29"	→	Handed over Rest Station to 69th Field Ambulance (23rd Division). Struck marquees in Rest Camp	

Army Form C. 2118.

WAR DIARY
OF
INTELLIGENCE SUMMARY.
(Erase heading not required.)

Page 8

Place	Date	Hour	Summary of Events and Information	Remarks and references to Appendices
ALLONVILLE	June 29th	→	At 10-30pm received orders from A.D.M.S. to move to MORLANCOURT tomorrow at 5pm meeting the 51st Brigade at HEILLY.	
"	30th	10am	Sent Capt WALKER R.A.M.C. to HEILLY for orders from 57th Brigade & to MORLANCOURT for billets etc.	
"	"	5pm	An advance party of 17 cooks, servants & fatigue men started in motor ambulances for MORLANCOURT to prepare billets: this party was under Capts BARCLAY & WALKER R.A.M.C.	
"	"	7pm	Main body with horsed transport marched via QUERRIEUX to HEILLY arriving at the latter place at 11pm where we joined on behind the 51st Brigade arriving at MORLANCOURT about 4pm	
MORLANCOURT	July 1st 12am - 12pm		Found billets all ready & detailed for sections. Men had marched very well up to HEILLY but latter part of march very slow as the Brigade was in front: No one fell out. Tea issued to all ranks on arrival, blankets chosen, & men then sent to bed. Horse transport marched well though wagons very heavily loaded.	

1/7/16

Meynon
Major R.A.M.C.
Commanding 51st Field Ambulance

Vol 10

17

Confidential

War Diary
of
51st Field Ambulance

from 1.7.16 to 31.7.16.

July 1916.

COMMITTEE FOR THE
MEDICAL HISTORY OF THE WAR
Date 31 AUG. 916

Army Form C. 2118.

WAR DIARY
of 51st Field Ambulance
17th Division

INTELLIGENCE SUMMARY.
(Erase heading not required.)

July 1916

Page 1.

Instructions regarding War Diaries and Intelligence Summaries are contained in F.S. Regs., Part II. and the Staff Manual respectively. Title pages will be prepared in manuscript.

Place	Date	Hour	Summary of Events and Information	Remarks and references to Appendices
MORLANCOURT	July 1st		Very heavy bombardment of FRICOURT: MAMETZ etc during the night. At 7am. an attack was carried out by 7th & 21st Divisions + 1 brigade of 17th Division. Unit billeted at MORLANCOURT + under orders to move at short notice. Packed A.D.M.S. at TREUX.	
"	2nd	1-30am	Received orders from A.D.M.S. to send 6 Talbot cars to help 21st Division; these were sent out at once & proceed to LA BOISELLE & returned at 5 p.m. Visited A.D.M.S. at 10 am. On return found that orders had been received to send out the BEARER DIVISION with 3 officers to report to A.D.M.S. 21st Division in MEAULTE.	
		11-15am	Bearers paraded & moved off under CAPTS BARCLAY: WALKER: & GORMAN R.A.M.C. Strength 110 N.C.Os men. They took 50 stretchers with them + additional surgical haversacks for the wheeled stretchers. Capt Rich R.A.M.C. joined 17th Divisional Headquarters and returned as they had to accommodation for the No:- 80205 Pte Horry R.A.M.C. joined for duty. Remainder of unit stayed at Morlancourt for the day. Visited Meaulte at 4 – but found that the Bearer half gone out to collect wounded from FRICOURT.	
"	3rd	–	At 7.30am Visited MEAULTE but found that the Bearer were still out. The A.D.M.S. visited our camp at 4pm + directed me to proceed to MEAULTE + to take over the collection of wounded from front area, the R.D. Stations at QUEENS REDOUBT: the SUBWAY: + at MEAULTE village; also the Divisional Collecting Station at the FILE FACTORY outside MEAULTE from the 65th Field Ambulance (21st Division). Saloner went to Meaulte + interviewed the O.C. 65th Field Ambulance & returned to Morlancourt.	
		9pm	The three unit sub-divisions moved to MEAULTE at 8pm + the "taking over" was completed by midnight.	

T2134. Wt. W708–776. 500000. 4/15. Sir J. C. & S.

Army Form C. 2118.

WAR DIARY
or
INTELLIGENCE SUMMARY.
(Erase heading not required.)

Page 2.

Place	Date	Hour	Summary of Events and Information	Remarks and references to Appendices
	July.			
MEAULTE	3rd	11pm	The Unit were thus distributed as follows :- QUEENS REDOUBT :- Capts. WALKER & RICH. R.A.M.C. with "B" Section Suf. division (units) & 6 bearers of "A" section. SUBWAY :- Capts. LEVIS & LYONS. R.A.M.C. with "C" section Suf. division (units) & 4 bearers of "A" section. FILE FACTORY :- Headquarters: Capt. COTTER R.A.M.C. Lieut. LEE. R.A.M.C.; "A" Section tent subdivision & 6 men of bearer suf. division. The small collecting post at corner of Meaulte village was staffed by one Nursing N.C.O. & one man. Horse transport after unloading returned to MORLANCOURT for the night. The File factory was in a very dirty condition & personnel of 65th Field Ambulance remained there for the night by Capt. Cotter R.A.M.C. went on with the cleaning of cases. Inspected the QUEENS REDOUBT & the SUBWAY during the night & superintended the taking over of those places. The bearer division continued to work under Capts. BARCLAY & GORMAN. R.A.M.C. & made their Headquarters at the QUEENS REDOUBT. The motor ambulances of 21st Division worked with all the large cases of the 17th Division clearing the night and were withdrawn about 4 a.m. A.D.M.S. inspected Factory about 11.30 pm. About 50 cases admitted during the night but were all cleared to MARICOURT & VECQUEMONT.	
"	4th	5am	Visited QUEENS Redoubt & "SUBWAY" all bearers in & asleep: front reported clear of wounded.	
		10am	65th Field Ambulance moved out. men then started to clean up the File Factory & other places & to settle down properly. With cheer "A" sleepy bivouac to MEAULTE for 24 hours rest. Very heavy rain during the afternoon & the grounds at File factory were converted into a swamp.	

WAR DIARY
INTELLIGENCE SUMMARY.
(Erase heading not required.)

Army Form C. 2118.

Page 3.

Place	Date	Hour	Summary of Events and Information	Remarks and references to Appendices
MEAULTE	July 4th	8p.	In the evening visited Subway & "Queens Redoubt" again & found everything going on satisfactorily, the bearers had been out in evening & had cleared all the R.A. Posts. A collecting post had been started about TRICOURT Village & this was now manned by 53rd Field Ambulance. On return found A.D.M.S. at File Factory, he told me that an attack was to take place at dawn on 5th & that he had ordered up all bearers from 52nd & 53rd Field Ambulances. Steady flow of cases through A.C.Stn all day but these were cleared easily by cars, lorries etc. Capt BLOCKLEY, R.A.M.C. took a convoy of 4 horsed ambulances with 48 cases to HEILLY at 11p.m. Horse transport moved to MEAULTE.	
"	5th	—	Under instructions from A.D.M.S. landed over Subway to 53rd Field ambulance & withdrew my personnel to Headquarters at 11a.m. Cases coming in steadily all night. O.D.M.S. visited File Factory at 3p. & arranged for Worship Unit to come into our Courtyard. At 5pm. received an urgent message from O.C. 53rd F.A. to clear up all available cars to Subway & 3 horsed ambulances to TRICORT. These returned at 11/p having cleared all the cases. All horsed ambulances of Division placed under my supervision. During the day 189 wounded, 10 Germans, & 1 Frenchman passed through D.C.Stn. "B" Section brought back to billets to rest: "A" & "C" Section on duty at Queens Redoubt. Owing to heavy rain & line moving on practically no cases are coming through the Queens Redoubt - the Tricourt - Becourt road being the only practicable method of bringing the cases down.	

Army Form C. 2118.

WAR DIARY
INTELLIGENCE SUMMARY.
(Erase heading not required.)

Page 1.

Place	Date	Hour	Summary of Events and Information	Remarks and references to Appendices
MEAULTE.	July 6th	8 a.m.	Urgent message from "Subway" for all cars & 3 horsed wagons. "B" Section relieved "A" Section at Queens Redoubt (10am). Visited Picard in afternoon with Lt. Col. 53rd Field Ambulance with a view to finding another chez-used capable of being used as an A.D. Stn. in neighbourhood of PATCH ALLEY & SUNKEN ROAD. The only one suitable is being used as an R.A. Post by four battalions. Visited Queens Redoubt on way back & found very few cases coming in. On return to Headquarters met A.D.M.S. & he told me that an attack was timed to take place at 2 a.m. & another at 8 a.m. the objectives being the Quadrangle Support trench "ACID DROP COPSE" & "PEARL ALLEY". He required "A" Section subdivision to reinforce Bearers at Queens Redoubt & with Bearers of 52nd & 51st F. Ambs. to road from the front to "Subway" under Major Bryden R.A.M.C. whilst Major Key, R.A.M.C. remained at Divisional Collectg. Station (FIRE FACTORY). Capt COTTER R.A.M.C. with 6 horsed ambulance wagons & "A" Section Bearers went to Subway at 11 p.m.	
"	7th		Steady stream of wounded passed through D.C. Stn. all night & at 3 a.m. they began to come in fast. Two motor buses reported for duty at 10.30 & these with horsed wagons, G.S. wagons, & empty motor lorries from the road kept us clear. In 24 hours 690 patients passed through D.C. Stn. Stretcher cases sent to 64th Field Ambulance at MERICOURT. Sitting cases to 36th C.C.S. at HEILLY or 34th C.C. Stn at VECQUEMONT. Reports received at intervals from O/c Bearer Division showed	

WAR DIARY
or
INTELLIGENCE SUMMARY.
(Erase heading not required.)

Army Form C. 2118.

Page 5.

Place	Date	Hour	Summary of Events and Information	Remarks and references to Appendices
MEULTE	July 7th		That the Bearers had a very hard task all night & day to clear. The fact that managed to do so & there was no congestion in an A.D. Stn. at any time. Heavy rain came on at 4pm & continued until down on the 8th inst. This made the Bearers work much harder. Owing to casualties amongst Regimental Stretcher bearers the R.A.M.C. personnel had to work in front of the R.A. Posts & during the night the men were caught in the QUADRANGLE trench at a time when the Germans made a heavy counter attack & shore our troops out of the QUADRANGLE SUPPORT trench & back to the Quadrangle. At this place certain casualties occurred & No. 78040 Pte ATTWELL W. R.A.M.C. was killed by a shell and the following wounded No. 66308 Pte J.T. BARRETT (right hand) No. 110278 Pte HOWARTH H. (thigh) No. 81635 Pte TATE H. R.A.M.C. (Chest). Several others received slight wounds & were buried whilst several N.C.Os & men had to be sent back to hosptls suffering from "Exhaustion & shock". Numerous reports of N.C.O.s & men were reported to me for meritorious work at this time amongst them being:—	
	8th		Fell started at 3am & continued till early in evening. Capt. Barclay & Walker R.A.M.C. returned from Green Richards on being relieved by Capts Lewis & Sansom R.A.M.C. Rain on & off all day & roads & patients covered with mud. Evacuated No. 73061 Pte TODD R.A.M.C. (shell-shock)	
	9th		Steady stream of patients sent in during the night. Lead very quiet all day till noon. Cleared 2 motor buses & those motor lorries attached to us emergency clay to carpenter. Visited Queens Redoubt & Fricourt: men very dirty but resting.	

WAR DIARY
INTELLIGENCE SUMMARY

Army Form C. 2118.

Page 6

Place	Date	Hour	Summary of Events and Information	Remarks and references to Appendices
MEAULTE	July 10th	—	Steady flow of wounded during the night & morning; motor lorries & lorries attached returned at 1/pm to their headquarters. Evacuations continued to VECQUEMONT & MARICOURT by our ambulances & commenced lorries Vende A.D.M.S. at VILLE at 4pm & received notice to move out from all our stations on relief by 21st Division. O.C. 61st Field Ambulance (21st Divn) visited FILE FACTORY in morning & scheme to cover ran et. At 7.30 p visited QUEENS REDOUBT & on finding that our bearer division had been ordered to "rest" for the night - sent them back to billets in MEAULTE. Returned to FILE FACTORY & sent up Section wagons (3 H. bring down famished officers at Headquarters by 2am (11th inst). In return to Headquarters issued orders for unit to move by train to AILLY-SUR-SOMME by train at 7am on 11th inst; transport to follow by road (2 days march)	
"	11th	4 a.m	Reveille. Arrived at HEAULTE JUNCTION at 7am to entrain; received orders to wait, and other units, till ammunition train arrived & unloaded. Advance party under Capt. BARCLAY & WALKER R.A.M.C. with cooks etc. left at 11am by road for FOURDRINOY. Horse transport under Capt BLOCKLEY. R.A.M.C. left at 2pm with all Spare Officers, horses, grooms etc. They had orders to bivouac for the night at QUERRIEU. The main body eventually entrained at 2pm & arrived at SALEUX after many "stops" on part of "entraining Officer". On arrival at this station we were told to get out of train & march to SAISSEVAL (10 miles). did so & arrived in new billets about 11pm with help of our motor ambulances. It appears that	

WAR DIARY
INTELLIGENCE SUMMARY

Army Form C. 2118.

Part 7

Place	Date	Hour	Summary of Events and Information	Remarks and references to Appendices
SAISSEVAL	July 11th	11p	The Divisional Billetting area had been altered during the day & that an advance party had received new orders. The men had been working hard for 10 days or so & arrival quite "done up" but the hay journey enabled them to get some rest & they did the last mile march in good order. Several other units were landed in the same manner & it was an example of "Staff work".	
"	"	11.30p	Received orders from A.D.M.S. to detail two sections to take over the Corps Rest Station at ALLONVILLE as soon as possible on 12th inst. Issued orders accordingly	
"	12th	10a	Dispatched Capts. BARCLAY & WALKER R.A.M.C. with various N.C.Os & nursing orderlies & motor ambulances to take over Rest Station at ALLONVILLE. The previous night had arrived to Transport officer to stop "B" & "C" Section transport with all officers horses etc at ALLONVILLE & also sent there a load of forage. This message could not be delivered & after a good deal of trouble I managed to find them on the outskirts of AMIENS. Capt. COTTER R.A.M.C. with "A" Section transport arrived at SAISSEVAL about 4p. Selected billets for personnel, patients etc & left they in running order. Cars returned at 11p & later returned to ALLONVILLE with more men.	
SAISSEVAL	13th	1p	Sent off ammunition of "B" & "C" sections and Headquarters Staff to ALLONVILLE by motors. Also sent off one S.S. wagon & one limbered wagon with the days stores forage for "B" & "C" sections as supplies for full unit are arriving at this place. Settled all mess debts & left Capt. COTTER R.A.M.C. in charge with promise to send out another officer next morning	
		2p	Headquarters with some patients left by car for ALLONVILLE & arrived at 2.45p	

WAR DIARY or INTELLIGENCE SUMMARY.

Army Form C. 2118.

Page 2

Place	Date	Hour	Summary of Events and Information	Remarks and references to Appendices
ALLONVILLE	July 12th	4p	Found 'B' & 'C' Section had settled down well at Rest Station & had taken over Officers & 242 other ranks as patients. Owing to frequent changes in past three weeks this place is in a very dirty state & there is no clean linen for beds.	
		11p	At midnight received orders by wire from A.D.M.S. to detail two "Talbot" ambulances for duty with 25th M.A. Convoy; to join at LES ALENÇONS at 2 a.m. on 13th inst	
	13th	7.30a	Two Talbots cars left for duty with 25th M.A.C. ('A' Section) at LES ALENÇONS. At Les ALENÇONS. At 4pm received a message from Capt. COTTER R.A.M.C. ('A' Section) at SAISSEVAL to the effect that he had received orders from A.D.M.S. to move with 51st Brigade at once to BUSSUS, & that he wanted transport at once sent off. One "Talbot" & one Ford car to help him, also the F.S. wagon & linen wagon & hand ambulance wagon by road to by & catch them at SAISSEVAL. Inspected Rest Station & opened Possible Field Ambulance.	
		4p	down.	
		4p	received orders to prepare to hand over Rest Station to a relay Field Ambulance.	
ALLONVILLE	15th	12.30	An Officer & party of men from 39th Casualty Clearing Station arrived to take over Rest Station.	
		4p	Received orders to move the FAMECHON as soon as "handing over" complete; also to send a representation to D.D.M.S. XV Corps at HEILLY to hand over list of stores material & equipment left behind at HEAULTE. Lieut. LEE R.A.M.C. performed this last duty at & at 4pm our motors having returned from 25th M.A. Convoy at SAISSEVAL — the unit moved by road to new fields at FAMECHON. (25 miles.) Advance party sent on ahead.	

WAR DIARY or INTELLIGENCE SUMMARY

Army Form C. 2118.

Place	Date	Hour	Summary of Events and Information	Remarks and references to Appendices
FAMECHON	July 15th	11 p	Arrived at FAMECHON after long march via POULAINVILLE – ST. VAAST – FLEXICOURT etc. Transport arrived two hours later. Everybody ready & a very comfortable village.	
"	16th	—	Capt. C.M. BERNAYS, T.R.A.M.C. reported his arrival for duty; he has been with "A" Section since the 11th inst. One new "Douglas" motor cycle received in place of one broken on 13th inst.	
"	17th	—	Visited A.D.M.S. at PONT REMY. Inspected billets, arms, feet etc. Nothing to report.	
"	18th	—	Very wet night; finished move into hut for men & patients; generally settled down in billets. Capt. BERNAYS, R.A.M.C. left for duty with No. 6. C.Cl.Sh at CORBIE.	
"	19th	—	Capt. GORHAM, R.A.M.C. attached to see "morning sick" of General Supply Column. Pay day. Visited A.D.A.S. Heard that Division may move within 48 hours. Instructed wagons & inspected equipment etc. Issued new clothing & underclo. for stores.	
"	20th	—	Hour of Division postponed. Capt. J.T. KIRKLAND R.A.M.C. joined for duty from 5. C.Cl.Sh.	
"	21st	—	Received warning orders from 51st Brigade to move on 22nd or 23rd inst. From Maj. R.G.L.C. joined for duty. At 10pm received orders for all horsed transport of our Coma eta to move off on 22nd inst. "Starting point" at SUR CAMPS at 7am.	M.61250 Pte Bernard S(?)1934 Pte Bayliss F 51597 Pte Barton J. 67492 Pte Batty H
"	22nd	2-30 a	Reveille 2-30am. All horsed wagons loaded up with sick & equipment, forage etc & moved off at 4-30am. under Capts BARCLAY & BLOCKLEY R.A.M.C. They will billet for the night at CARDONNETTE. A large number of sick sent to Field Ambulance during the day from 51st Brigade units; many of these should have been sent in Several days ago as quite unfit for duty for 7–14 days	

Army Form C. 2118.

WAR DIARY
INTELLIGENCE SUMMARY
(Erase heading not required.)

Page 10

Instructions regarding War Diaries and Intelligence Summaries are contained in F.S. Regs., Part II. and the Staff Manual respectively. Title pages will be prepared in manuscript.

Place	Date	Hour	Summary of Events and Information	Remarks and references to Appendices
	July			
TAMECHON.	22nd	6pm	Capt J.T. KIRKLAND R.A.M.C. detached for temporary duty with 7th Bn.Durs. vice Capt. LYONS R.A.M.C. (sick)	
"	23rd	9am	Received orders for "a fatiguing party" to meet Staff Captain 57th Brigade at HANGAST Station at 11 P.M.; detailed Capt. COTTER R.A.M.C. & 2 N.C.Os. At 9.30am received orders to entrain at HANGAST at 8pm. Advance party under Capt WALKER R.A.M.C. left with all TALBOT cars at 3pm. Unit paraded at 5.45pm & marched via FLEXICOURT to HANGAST. On arrival found that the usual delay had occurred; men eventually entrained at 1 A.M. on 24th instl	
near BUIRE (about 1/2 N.E. of D.1 a. 8.2.)	24th	4am	Train arrived at MERICOURT-L'ABBE at 4am & unit detrained & marched about 4½ miles to a Camping ground near BUIRE (just off AMIENS-ALBERT road) Shed. Advance party had finished tents & then set down to sleep about 6.30am. Transport bivouaced in a field about 1/2 mile away; they arrived about 4pm on 23rd inst having marched from CARBONNETTE. Visited A.D.M.S at midday — no news but may arrive at any time.	
"	25th		Inspection of gas helmets, followed by physical drill. Completed camp & arranged Dressing Station for patients	
"	26th		Usual camp duties; physical drill. Inspection of motor ambulance by Inspection Staff — all correct. Visited ADMS	
"	27th		Detailed 50 N.C.Os men under Capt. GORMAN R.A.M.C. for fatigue work at "Y" Corps Dressing Station. Funeral parade of Division at 6pm for presentation of "MILITARY MEDAL" ribbon by G.O.C. 17th Division. Two N.C.Os from the unit received this decoration for conspicuous gallantry & devotion to duty during the recent operations round FRICOURT, viz:— No. 30932 Sgt. DOULTON. R.A.M.C. No. 36763 L/Cpl. A. ABEL. R.G.M.C.	

WAR DIARY

INTELLIGENCE SUMMARY.
(Erase heading not required.)

Army Form C. 2118.

Part II

Place	Date	Hour	Summary of Events and Information	Remarks and references to Appendices
SHEET 62dNE D. 18. C.9.2. Nr BUIRE	July. 28th	—	Visited A.D.S. but there is no news of Division moving though we have been under orders to move at 1½ hours notice for past two days. Capt LEVIS R.A.M.C. i/c fatigue party of 50 N.C.O.s then on duty at "Y" Corps Dressing Station all day. Moved G.S. wagons to main camp.	
"	29th	→	Detailed Capts. LEVIS & RICH R.A.M.C. with "C" Tent Sub-division completed for duty at "Y" Corps Dressing Station. Inspected Horse, transport & wagons on parade. Visited A.D.M.S.	
"	30th	→	Relieved 50 N.C.O.s men for fatigue work at "Y" Corps Dressing Station. Very hot weather but men are very fit & well. Our three A.S.C.(M.T.) evacuated the Base.	
"	31st	→	Visited A.D.M.S. in morning. received warning orders that we would probably take over from 34th Field Ambulance all Stations tomorrow. In afternoon visited Advanced Dressing Station etc in vicinity of MAMETZ & LONGUEVAL with O.C.s 52nd & 53rd Field Ambulances. 11.9 pm visited A.D.M.S & received orders to take over the Divisional Collecting Station from 10th Field Ambulance (3rd Division) as soon as possible on 1st August. issued orders accordingly.	

Jnapr
Major R.A.M.C.
Commanding, 57th Field Ambulance

3/7/11

51. J. Amb.
Vol II

Confidential

War Diary
of
51st Field Ambulance

From Aug 1st 1916 to Aug 31st 1916.

(Vol III)

Army Form C. 2118.

WAR DIARY
or
INTELLIGENCE SUMMARY.
(Erase heading not required.)

51st Field Ambulance
17th Division
Page I

MEDICAL

Place	Date	Hour	Summary of Events and Information	Remarks and references to Appendices
BECORDEL - BECOURT P.7.d.9.9.	August 1st	→	M.O.s. left by motor for Divisional Collecting Station in order to take over: the Quartermaster, Sgt Rogers, Wagonmasters & Engineers accompanied me. By arrangement with O.C. 114th Field Ambulance I took over the A.D. Post from 12 noon. At 1.30 pm the tent sub-division of 'A' section under Capts Walker & Cotter R.A.M.C. had arrived & are now responsible for patients from 3 pm. Horsed lorries Capt BARHAM R.C.C. moved out of camp at 1 pm & arrived at 3.30 pm; transport arrived at 4 pm. No. 114 Field Ambulance marched out and at 4.30 pm the Divisional Collecting Station consists of a wood & canvas hut & two small marquees erected on a triangular piece of ground where the FRICOURT - ALBERT and FRICOURT - MEAULTE roads join; it is surrounded by artillery waggon lines &c. & horse lines through the grounds to water - traffic - this & the traffic on the MEAULTE roads makes it a very dusty spot. Water is drawn from tank-lorries in BECORDEL village during the day & is scarce. There are 10 motor Chars-a-bancs attached for evacuation of "sitting-cases" to 34th & 45th C.C. Stations at VECQUEMONT. The A.D. St. is on MAMETZ - MONTAUBAN Road with an Advanced Collecting Post in the CATERPILLAR RAVINE: both places are staffed by 52nd Field Ambulance. Two Ford Cars & three Horsed Ambulance Wagons work between Advanced Collecting Post & A.D. St.	
"	2nd	→	Very quiet night during day cleaned up camp moved cook-house & generally settled down. Capts WALKER & COTTER R.A.M.C. on day and field duty alternately, nothing special to note	

Army Form C. 2118.

WAR DIARY
INTELLIGENCE SUMMARY.
(Erase heading not required.)

Page 2

Instructions regarding War Diaries and Intelligence Summaries are contained in F. S. Regs., Part II. and the Staff Manual respectively. Title pages will be prepared in manuscript.

Place	Date	Hour	Summary of Events and Information	Remarks and references to Appendices
Becordel – Becourt	August 3rd	→	Very heavy bombardment all night but very few patients passed through D.A. Stn. during the day. D.A.D.M.S. visited the camp in morning. At 6pm. received report from Lt. 52nd Field Ambulance to send up 15 stretcher squads to be in reserve at A.D. Stn. as 52nd Brigade were to make an attack at 11 p.m. 4th inst, also to send up extra motor Amb. at 10 p.m. Detailed 60 men from "B" & "C" Bearer Sub-divisions under Capts. BARCLAY & GORHAM, R.A.M.C. & sent them up the line at 8pm.	
"	4th	→	Very heavy bombardment again during the night from both sides, very few cases sent in up to 8 a.m. but between 8 a.m. & 9 a.m. about 100 battle cases passed through. Remainder of day very quiet. Request of OC 52nd Field Ambulance sent up 3 Horsed Ambulances at 3 p.m. to work between Caterpillar Ravine & Advanced Collect. Post near MONTAUBAN. Also sent up all available stretcher carriers (5). Capt. BARCLAY, R.A.M.C. & men of Bearer sub division returned from A.D. Stn. about 8pm. & reported to me that orders had been received from A.D.M.S. to open another Advanced Dressing Station in BERNAFAY WOOD (S.28 d 8.8.) in a dug-out at present occupied by 6th Field Ambulance. He inspected this place & & arrangement with OC 6th Field Ambulance detailed Capt. GORMAN R.A.M.C. & 7 stretcher squads to be attached for duty. Rations, dressings etc sent up later in evening. Two Rouge Cars & one Ford car from 53rd Field Amb attached to us for duty.	
"	5th	→	Orders received here to report to D.M.S. 4th Army ad GUERRIEUX at 9.30 am. Ford Car & returned about 1pm. very little doing during the night or daytime shall of heavy shell fire. D.D.D.S. XVth Corps visited camp & ordered 5 motor busses to return to	

T2134. Wt. W708-776. 500000. 4/15. Sir J. C. & B.

Army Form C. 2118.

WAR DIARY
or
INTELLIGENCE SUMMARY.
(Erase heading not required.)

Part 3

Place	Date	Hour	Summary of Events and Information	Remarks and references to Appendices
BECORDEL - BECOURT	August 5th	—	There are Headquarters as there is so little doing. Capt. BARCLAY R.A.M.C. awarded the "Military Cross". Sent up rations, forage, water etc. to the A.D.Sn. in BERNAFAY WOOD	
"	6th	—	Very quiet night & morning though there was a good deal of promiscuous shelling of neighbouring wagon lines & transport during the night. Up to 12 noon 13 Officers + 432 other ranks have passed through the D.Cl.Sn. Capt. BARCLAY & WALKER R.A.M.C. went to A.D.St. at BERNAFAY WOOD in the morning & found everything going on well. Two horse Ambulance wagons returned at 7pm. One wagon remains at A.D.Sn. for the present. Lud. hoses & drivers have returned. One N.D. horse slightly wounded.	
"	7th	—	Nothing special to note during the night (36 cases through from 9th to 6am.) Capt BARCLAY R.A.M.C. with 30 N.C.O.s & men went up to A.D.Sn. in Bernafay Wood at 2.5pm. Capt. GORMAN R.A.M.C. returned about 6pm with his 'bearer Squads'. Major E.L. COWLAND R.A.M.C. arrived about 6.30pm.	
"	8th	—	Little special to note. At 1.30pm received orders to hand over Command of the Unit to Surgeon E.L. Gouilland R.A.M.C. this was completed by 4pm.	

M[...]
OC, R.A.M.C.

Army Form C. 2118.

WAR DIARY
or
INTELLIGENCE SUMMARY.
(Erase heading not required.)

Instructions regarding War Diaries and Intelligence Summaries are contained in F.S. Regs., Part II. and the Staff Manual respectively. Title pages will be prepared in manuscript.

Place	Date	Hour	Summary of Events and Information	Remarks and references to Appendices
BECORDEL - BECOURT	August 8th	4 p.m.	Lieut Col (T/Lt Col) E. L. GOWLAND R.A.M.C. assumed Command of 51st Field Ambulance	E.G.
		7 p.m.	Capt T. WALKER R.A.M.C. proceeded to the Main Corps Dressing Station at DERNANCOURT in relief of Capt J. S. LEWIS R.A.M.C. who rejoined Headquarters of this unit	
			Number of wounded sitting cases admitted and dealt with from 6 A.M. 8th Augt to 6 A.M. 9th inst. 4 Officers 188 O.R.	E. Gowland RAMC Lieut Col R.A.M.C.
"	9th		O.C. visited the Dressing Station on MAMETZ - MONTAUBAN road, also ADS Collecting Post at N.E. corner of the Bois de BERNAFAY.	
			D.D.M.S XVth Corps inspected arrangements accompanied by a Russian Medical Officer	
			NCOs + men at Headquarters were paid	
			Sitting Cases 4 Officers, 135 O.R., Evacuated between 6 A.M. 9th & 6 A.M. 10th inst	E.G.

WAR DIARY
or
INTELLIGENCE SUMMARY.
(Erase heading not required.)

Army Form C. 2118.

Place	Date	Hour	Summary of Events and Information	Remarks and references to Appendices
BECORDEL - BECOURT	August 10th		D.D.M.S. XV Corps called re Relief of A.S.C. Division 18 Aux Bn & Captain BARCLAY who has since returned to H.Q. for the Advanced Collecting Post at BERNAFAY WOOD on being ordered by Capt. M.E. GORMAN with C sect. trans. O.C. 43rd Div. Aux. inspected arrangements he will take over from this unit Sitting Cases 6am 10th to 6pm 11th inst. Official OR37	
	11th		Nothing to report.	E.g.
	12th	A.M.	Packing up equipment etc. Advance party 43rd Div Aux. arrived 11:30 a.m. to take over, handed over completed at 4 P.M. Unit moved to DERNANCOURT. O.C. reported to A.D.M.S. at BELLEVUE FARM S. of ALBERT.	E.g. E.g.
DERNANCOURT	13th		Transport moved off by road to new area	E.g.
	14th		M.T. Drivers & Motor Cyclists with their vehicles leave the unit & report to N°17 Supply Column	E.g.

WAR DIARY
or
INTELLIGENCE SUMMARY.
(Erase heading not required.)

Army Form C. 2118.

Instructions regarding War Diaries and Intelligence Summaries are contained in F.S. Regs., Part II. and the Staff Manual respectively. Title pages will be prepared in manuscript.

Place	Date	Hour	Summary of Events and Information	Remarks and references to Appendices
DERNANCOURT	Aug 15		Unit leo transport march to MERICOURT & entrain. Entrain at CANDAS march via GÉZAINCOURT to BRETEL; in billets	E.G.
BRETEL	16		Unit moves by road via HEM to NEUVILLETTE billets. M.T. transport & cars minus motor cycles join too BOULEMAISON	E.G.
NEUVILLETTE	17		O.C. & Capt⁰ Barclay Walker. Tom & Gorman motor to GAUDIEMPRÉ to inspect medical arrangements in rear part of the line	E.G.
"	18		Advanced parties to GAUDIEMPRÉ. O.C. takes over from the 2/1 London Fd Amb⁰ O.C. takes on duties of Town Major GAUDIEMPRÉ Main Body 51st Field Ambulance arrived at GAUDIEMPRÉ	E.G. E.G.
GAUDIEMPRÉ	19		2/2 London Fd Amb⁰ handed over at 4 p.m.	E.G.
"	20		Capt. J. WALKER & Capt. GORMAN to B Sec⁰ trailers to Adv⁰ Dressing Station FONQUEVILLERS Capt. T. S. LEWIS & Capt. GOTTER with C section trailers to Adv⁰ Dressing Station BIENVILLERS	E.G.

WAR DIARY
or
INTELLIGENCE SUMMARY.

Army Form C. 2118.

Place	Date	Hour	Summary of Events and Information	Remarks and references to Appendices
GAUDIEMPRÉ	1916 August 20th		Advance Collecting Post established at HANNESCAMP, one N.C.O. and 3 trained chiefly for maintaining communication with A.D.S. at BIENVILLERS. E.g.	
	21st		Pte N.D left behind at NEUVILLETTE in medical charge of 17 Div. Troops remaining. Reported at Headquarters. E.g.	
	22nd		Paid men at Headquarters. E.g.	
	23rd		3 reinforcements A.S.C. Horse Transport arrived	
	24th		5 reinforcements R.A.M.C. arrived including Sergt. CAISLEY E.g. Took over huts at GAUDIEMPRÉ FONQUEVILLERS and Capt. McNEILL, Walker & Leeson busy BIENVILLERS	
	25th		Placed in charge respectively E.g. Capt. T.P. BUCKLEY R.A.M.C. reported for duty. E.g.	
	26th		Nothing to report.	
	27th P.M.		O.C. inspected Advd. Dressing Station FONQUEVILLERS. E.g.	
	28th P.M.		O.C. " " " BIENVILLERS, other further work to be done relating accommodation for sick & wounded. E.g.	

WAR DIARY
or
INTELLIGENCE SUMMARY.

Army Form C. 2118.

Place	Date	Hour	Summary of Events and Information	Remarks and references to Appendices
GAUDIEMPRE	1916 August 29th		Conference of O.C's Field Ambulances at Office of A.D.M.S. re medical arrangements.	
	30th		Lieut. BARBER R.A.M.C. Gas Expert arrives at 11.30 p.m. No previous intimation of operations had been received by this unit from 46th Division. E.S.	
	31st		9 O.R. Gassed (Drift) were admitted from Special Bn. R.E. about 5.15 A.M. all slight, as all apparently caused by a faulty valve joint in gas cylinder the most serious of these cases was of a sergeant who was obliged to remain in the tube of his antigas apparatus to give orders and it was who continued to work though slightly gassed, the administration of oxygen was tried in these two cases with good results. Capt. D. McNEILL R.A.M.C. of this unit k to 2/1 S. Staffs. during temporary absence on leave of Capt. Rawson R.A.M.C. E.S.	

140/1734.
1st Div.

Confidential

War Diary
of
51st Field Ambulance

From Sept 1st 1916   to Sept 30th 1916

(Volume 3)

Sept. 1916
51

COMMITTEE FOR THE
MEDICAL HISTORY OF THE WAR
Date 30 OCT. 1916

detached

Gassed Cases treated
during Sept 1916
    Filed Medicine "9"

Army Form C. 2118.

MEDICAL

WAR DIARY
INTELLIGENCE SUMMARY.
(Erase heading not required.)

Place	Date	Hour	Summary of Events and Information	Remarks and references to Appendices
GAUDIEMPRÉ	1916 Sept 1st		Capt. V.M. RICH R.A.M.C. proceeded on leave from 1st to 6th Sept. Capt. H.J. COTTER to 95th Heavy Artillery Group as M.O. in the absence of Capt. RICH	
	Sept 2nd		Six gassed cases admitted (two of them most seriously) caused by the bursting of one of our own gas cylinders by hostile French mortar fire. Conference at A.D.M.S. Office 11 a.m.	
	Sept 3rd		Very heavy bombardment heard from the South. Lieut. General Sir A. d'O. Snow G.O.C. VIIth Corps visited the unit. Major General ROBERTSON C.M.G. G.O.C. 17 Div[n] " " " Arranged for Brig[d] Collecting Station (for walking wounded) at Y.M.C.A. Hut SOUASTRE.	
	Sept 4th		Lieut. CRAIG R.A.M.C. & 12 O.R. sent to 19. C.C.S. DOULLENS to assist in view of a large number of casualties being received.	
	Sept 5th		Paid men at Headquarters. O.C. visited & inspected BIENVILLERS & HAUNESCAMP.	

Army Form C. 2118.

WAR DIARY
INTELLIGENCE SUMMARY.
(Erase heading not required.)

Place	Date	Hour	Summary of Events and Information	Remarks and references to Appendices
GAUDIEMPRÉ	1916 Sept 5th	P.M 8.30	Our Gas Discharged on our Front. First four cases arrived at 11 p.m. Gassed These had intimated walked down communication trench, & were much exhausted.	Our GAS Discharge
	Sept 6th	1 A.M.	12 more cases arrived by 1 a.m. one an officer of 16 Lancs Fus. who went over the parapet with his party 35 minutes after the discharge of our Gas. They arrived with Gas helmets as they could not see the wire and the crump holes, and were gassed when close to the German parapet.	7/-APPENDIX NoI full report on Gassed cases. Cases treated in the Unit from Aug 30th to Sept 10th
		4 A.M.	By 4 A.M. 31 cases had been admitted, one of which had died in the Car returning SOUASTRE & GAUDIEMPRE	
		12.30 pm	One more Gassed Case was admitted. Due to escape of Gas from Inlets on Decoincating [?] SOUASTRE & GAUDIEMPRE	
		4 P.M.	Post mortem examination of Case which died from Gas poisoning shewn:- Early Post Mortem rigidity - Early Post mortem staining - browning of lips, tongue, & inflammation of technical [?] membranes of trachea & larger bronchi, oedema of lung. The heart stopped in systole & was empty	

T2134. Wt. W708—776. 500000. 4,15. Sir J. C. & S.

WAR DIARY
or
INTELLIGENCE SUMMARY.
(Erase heading not required.)

Army Form C. 2118.

Place	Date	Hour	Summary of Events and Information	Remarks and references to Appendices
GAUSTEN PRÉ	1916 Sept 6th	A.M.	D.D.M.S. VIII Corps called & in Effect to arrangements for the telegraph of gassed cases. A.D.M.S. 17th Div in attendance. The Scott Carthie "Yoke Pattern" stretcher sling was given extensive trial and favourably reported upon for work outside the trenches. E. Eastland Lieut Col RAMC	
	Sept 7th	A.M.	Conference at A.D.M.S. Office. A second case died in the Unit from own gas drift at the P.M. 4 hours after death when the Corps transport station was found. As in the former case, very obvious signs of inflamed trachea, but in this case the head was tilted as to 15th Vertebra, with a much rising like clot, & had no tripe blisters in Bycole. In this case I had endeavoured to perform Venesection, & Venesection	

WAR DIARY

INTELLIGENCE SUMMARY.
(Erase heading not required.)

Army Form C. 2118.

Place	Date	Hour	Summary of Events and Information	Remarks and references to Appendices
GHYVELDE	1916 Sept 7th		Revised the modern Battle Kit. The Blood Clothes so quickly that a satisfactory venesection could just be performed. In active Service Cases venesection was wanted to interveneously good quality v. Appendix No 1.	
		9h	Issued to Officers from the South. E.g.	
		10h	Conference at A.D.M.S. Office 11 a.m. 2/Lt + 2Pte Audrie went to St AMAND of the Main Body. Dr 51 + 260 Audrie went to 19th Field Ambulance handing over main dressing Station to 19th Field Ambulance Battery. Conference at A.D.M.S. Office re army arrangements to new station	
St AMAND	11th		The Advanced Dressing Stations at FONQUEVILLERS and BIENVILLERS are divided Dr to 101st Field Ambulance Detachment and 19 Field Ambulance Detachment respectively. E.S.	
St AMAND	12th		Cleaning up new quarters Inspection of gas helmets, iron rations and Steel Helmets. 2x Box Ration, instead being issue the grocery ration iron rations	

T134. Wt. W708-776. 500000. 4/15. Sir J. C. & S.

Army Form C. 2118.

WAR DIARY
of
INTELLIGENCE SUMMARY.
(Erase heading not required.)

Instructions regarding War Diaries and Intelligence Summaries are contained in F. S. Regs., Part II. and the Staff Manual respectively. Title pages will be prepared in manuscript.

Place	Date	Hour	Summary of Events and Information	Remarks and references to Appendices
ST. ANAND	19th Sept 12		was found to have deteriorated, the biscuits were broken & mouldy; it is thought that the presence of the Oxo cubes in the grocery ration, combined with the fact that the tin containing same is not air-tight, contributes to this deterioration. Oxo cubes are hygroscopic, the sugar becomes damp, the tea mouldy & very quickly goes the tun. Even when it had not been previously opened, contained a mouldy impregnated debris. It is suggested either that the Oxo cubes shall be excluded from the ration or that the tins containing same shall be hermetically sealed.	

WAR DIARY
or
INTELLIGENCE SUMMARY.

(Erase heading not required.)

Army Form C. 2118.

Place	Date	Hour	Summary of Events and Information	Remarks and references to Appendices
ST AMAND	1916 SEPT 13		Nothing to report. EG	
	14th	11 am	Conference at Office of A.D.M.S. VII Corps attes + inspected Headquarters D.D.M.S. Capt H.J. Carter RAMC returned to the unit a/c Sany Duty, as M.O. of 19. Heavy Artillery Group EG	
	15th		Conference 3 pm at Office D.A.D.M.S. at sixteen Corps taking over Main Dressing Station at HEBUTERNE. EG	
	16th		O.C. + several Officers visited Dressing Station at MHP Sheet 57D D 26 central. EG 10.000	
	17th		Capt D. McNEILL RAMC returned to their unit from Temporary Duty with 8th BN. Sth Stafford. Regt. EGellard	

Army Form C. 2118.

WAR DIARY
or
INTELLIGENCE SUMMARY.
(Erase heading not required.)

Place	Date	Hour	Summary of Events and Information	Remarks and references to Appendices
ST AMAND	1916 Sept 18		Nothing to report. EG	
	19		Orders at short notice Capt J WALKER RAMC proceeded to 78th Field Amb'y Brigade for temporary duty. EG	
	20		Lieut & Q.M. H.B. Lee RAMC proceeded on leave till Oct 1st Lieut CRAIG returned from temp'y duty at 19 C.C.S. DOULLENS Lieut E.V. BEAUMONT RAMC reported for duty from No 14 Ambulance Train. EG	
	21st		Col D. McNEILL RAMC left this unit for duty with 14 Amb'e Train. EG	
	22nd		Capt M.E. GORMAN RAMC on leave. Capt J.S. LEWIS " proceeded to 17th Div'l Train to temp'y duty as M.O. EG	

WAR DIARY
or
INTELLIGENCE SUMMARY

Army Form C. 2118.

(Erase heading not required.)

Instructions regarding War Diaries and Intelligence Summaries are contained in F. S. Regs., Part II. and the Staff Manual respectively. Title Pages will be prepared in manuscript.

Place	Date	Hour	Summary of Events and Information	Remarks and references to Appendices
ST AMAND	1916 Sept 2nd	8.30 A.M.	The Unit marched from ST AMAND to billets in MONDICOURT. E.G.	
MONDICOURT	2nd 3rd	7.45 A.M.	Unit marched to BARLY via MEZEROLLES and DOULLENS. Accompanied by certain details from Infantry and 52nd Fd Amb. who has been on duty at Baths & Laundry at PAS. E.G.	
BARLY	"	12.50 P.M.	Arrived new billets at BARLY. Heavy draught filling 250 ? colic on ptomaine stomach. E.G.	
BARLY	24th		Unit II marched in rear of 51st Inf'y Brigade to billets at AUXI LE CHATEAU, South of AUXI. LE CHATEAU, 2 kilometers.	
AUXI.LE CHATEAU			MONDEVIS FARM about " " " " Capt. J. P. Blockley R.A.M.C sent to 81st Brigade R.F.A for temporary duty. Capt. H. J. COTTER " " 10th Sherwood Foresters " E.G.	

WAR DIARY or INTELLIGENCE SUMMARY

Army Form C. 2118

Place	Date	Hour	Summary of Events and Information	Remarks and references to Appendices
AUXI-LE-CHATEAU	1916 Sept 25th	6 pm	Settling in new billets, erecting tents for patients, & O.C. to St RIQUIER to consult with A.D.M.S. re arrangements. E.G.	
"	26th		Lieuts. Craig & Beaumont R.A.M.C. sent to 7th Lincs. I.M.O. for instruction in the duties of a Regimental Medical Officer. E.G.	
"	27th		New R.D. horse has been sent for to replace casualty, but none were available. E.G.	
"	28th		To A.D.M.S. at 11 a.m. for conference. E.G.	
"	29th		Lieut. J.M. CRAIG R.A.M.C. to 17th D.A.C. for temporary duty during the absence on leave of Capt. G. Toughin R.A.M.C. E.G.	
"	30th		The A.D.M.S. visited the unit. The Machine Gunnery & Trench Mortar Batteries were visited the last day of the month. This unit- E.G.	

140/1811 17

Confidential

War Diary of

51st Field Ambulance 11th Div

From October 1st 1916 to October 31st 1916

(Volume 3)

COMMITTEE FOR THE
MEDICAL HISTORY OF THE WAR
Date -9 DEC. 1916

Army Form C. 2118.

WAR DIARY
or
INTELLIGENCE SUMMARY.
(Erase heading not required.)

"MEDICAL"

Place	Date 1916 Oct	Hour	Summary of Events and Information	Remarks and references to Appendices
AUXI LE CHATEAU	1st		Lieut & QrMr H.R.B.LEE R.A.M.C. returned from leave	
"	2nd	11 AM	D.Ch.A.D.M.S. 3rd Army also to 57th Bde Headquarters. EG. Unit moves to billets at BARLY. Capt. W. BARCLAY R.A.M.C. with advanced party for billeting. EG.	
BARLY	3rd	9 AM	Move by march route from BARLY to HALLOY, a very wet day.	
HALLOY	4th		HALLOY wet weather frost. EG. O.C. reports at Office of 48th Divn under whose administration this unit devolves until arrival of 17th Divn. EG.	
"	5th		O.C. to St RIQUIER to report to A.D.M.S. 17th Divn. Capt. C. HUNTER R.A.M.C. reports for temporary duty with this unit. The Interpreter Monsieur M. L. DE BELLEFONDS returnes from leave EG.	
"	6th		Capt. J WALKER R.A.M.C. reported for duty with the unit after temporary duty with 78th Field Artillery Brigade. EG.	

WAR DIARY
or
INTELLIGENCE SUMMARY.
(Erase heading not required.)

Army Form C. 2118.

Place	Date 1916	Hour	Summary of Events and Information	Remarks and references to Appendices
HALLOY	OCT. 7th		O.C. and Lieut + Q.M. + R.LEE R.A.M.C. visited D 26 Central, HEBUTERNE and SAILLY au BOIS Capt. J. S. LEWIS R.A.M.C. and 6 O.R proceeded by car to D. 26 Central. Map ref: 57 D. 1/40 000 EG	
HALLOY	8th	8 a.m.	Capt WALKER, HUNTER and 26 O.R. proceeded to ADV. Dressing Station at HEBUTERNE (K 9 d 22 Map 57D 1/40000) for whole of party. From 1/2 S Motors Hq Amb 48 F.D. One Staff Sergeant and 4 O.R to Collecting Post at SAILLY au BOIS (J.16 b 9-). relief of party from same Hq Amb. 9 a.m. (Lorry arrived to camp at D.26 central stores SQUASTRE and COUIN, arrived at 11 a.m. took over "Establishing" at 12 noon Capt. M. E. GORMAN R.A.M.C. returned for leave. Lieut SARGEANT A.S.C. and 23 O.R. A.S.C. M.T. from No 4y Supply Column reported to this unit for duty as Hq Ambce Workshop Unit. EG	

WAR DIARY
or
INTELLIGENCE SUMMARY.
(Erase heading not required.)

Army Form C. 2118.

Place	Date	Hour	Summary of Events and Information	Remarks and references to Appendices
Map Ref. 57D N.E. & N.W. 1: 40,000 D 26 Central 9.5	19/10		O.C. to office of A.D.M.S. at P.A.S. re Medical Arrangements 3 lorry loads of I.P. large dressings issued. D.A.D.M.S. Corps called re arrangts. to Corps Dressing Stations. Capt. A.L. ROBERTSON R.A.M.C. O.C. Laundry at P.A.S. stays the night at D 26 Central. E.G.	
"		10:45	Brigdier General TRUEN D.M.S. Third Army Called with Col. SWAN the D.D.M.S. XVth Corps re arrangements at D 26 Central. Capt. A. MASSEY R.A.M.C. reports for duty with this unit from No 12 Stationary Hospital. Capt. J.P. BLOATLEY R.A.M.C. returned to duty with his unit from 81st Bde. R.F.A. O.C. called on No 20 & No 43 C.C.S. re arrangements in case of having to deal with a large number of casualties. E.G.	

Army Form C. 2118.

WAR DIARY
or
~~INTELLIGENCE SUMMARY.~~
(Erase heading not required.)

Place	Date	Hour	Summary of Events and Information	Remarks and references to Appendices
D. 26 Cabot nr. COUIN	1916 Oct 11th		Work as usual E.G.	
	12th	12N	A.D.M.S. visited station Col. Grey F.R.C.S. lectures to Officers on treatment of wounds R.A.M.S. work as usual	
	13th		E.G.	
	14th		Capt. Gorman R.A.M.C. to HEBUTERNE A.D.S. lecture by Col. Grey A.M.S. offrs on treatment of wounds work as usual E.G.	
	15th		Capt. J.S. Lewis on leave for 14 days E.G.	
	16th		Capt. WALKER returns to Headquarters from A.D.S. HEBUTERNE Lieut. E.J. BEAUMONT to HEBUTERNE for duty Surgeon General Macpherson called. E.G.	
	17th		work as usual E.G.	
	18th		" " " E.G.	
	19th		Capt. A. MASSEY to 7th Bde. Stn. in relief of Capt. Lyons on leave.	

WAR DIARY or INTELLIGENCE SUMMARY

Army Form C. 2118.

Place	Date	Hour	Summary of Events and Information	Remarks and references to Appendices
D. de. ait. 19th Cov/N	1916 Oct 19th		Unit proceeded by March route in very bus weather to LUCHUEL about 10 miles — having now to 3rd South Midland Field Ambu 48th Div	
LUCHUEL	20th		Capts BARCLAY & WALKER on leave for 10 days had an parade	
	21st			
	22nd		Unit moved to VILLE	
VILLE	23rd		Capt GORMAN & Lieuts CRAIG & BEAUMONT proceeded with the whole of personnel of tent subdivision and equipment to CORPS REST STATION (XIV Corps) near SAILLY LAURETTE a party of 12 O.R. left for Corps Main Dressing Station at CARNOY.	
	24th		Lieut R.S. GASKELL proceeded to New Ambulance reported in Duty	
	25th		Captain E. GORMAN returned to duty with 51st Fd Ambce, and Lieut R.S. GASKELL was sent to XIV Corps Main Dressing Station in his stead	

Army Form C. 2118.

WAR DIARY
or
INTELLIGENCE SUMMARY
(Erase heading not required.)

Instructions regarding War Diaries and Intelligence Summaries are contained in F. S. Regs., Part II and the Staff Manual respectively. Title Pages will be prepared in manuscript.

Place	Date	Hour	Summary of Events and Information	Remarks and references to Appendices
VILLE	1916 Oct 26		Work on road EG	
			W. Aubce.	
	27th		Into A.D.M.S. & O.C. 52nd in Car to MONTAUBAN. Inspected A.D.M.S. Dressing Station of 8th Divn. Thence walked thro' GINCHY along FLERS road to ADS Relay Posts. A.D.M.S. 8th Divn + O.C. 52nd then walked across country to inspect Post at LESBŒUFS. 52nd Fd Amb: Dress Divn by Sunken route to CITADEL Camp near FRICOURT.	
	28th		Lecture by O.C. on Trench Fill Sanitation to 77th Coy R.E. Walkover meant EG	
	29th		Capt M.E. GORHAM. R.A.M.C. + 16 O.R. to LESBŒUFS to take over advanced Post from 8th Divn EG	
	30th		Bearer Divn 52nd Fd Amb: marched to Camp at BERNAFAY, very bad early Day EG	
	31st		Work in Camp, + reliefs to Advanced Post, arrangements for hutters &c.	
			E Garstland Lieut Col RAMC	

140/282   Vol 14

Confidential

War Diary

of

51st Field Ambulance R.A.M.C.

From November 1st 1916 to November 30th 1916

Volume 3.

COMMITTEE FOR THE
MEDICAL HISTORY OF THE WAR
Date -3 JAN. 1917

Army Form C. 2118.

MEDICAL

WAR DIARY
or
INTELLIGENCE SUMMARY.
(Erase heading not required.)

Place	Date	Hour	Summary of Events and Information	Remarks and references to Appendices
BERNAFAY	1916 Nov 1st		Capt. J. S. LEWIS R.A.M.C. returned from leave. Corporal WHITTIKER R.A.M.C. lately wounded whilst attached to 51st Infy Bde Headquarters.	
	2nd		Very hot day. Much artillery activity in the neighbourhood Col. O.R.A. Julian promoted D.D.M.S. Cavalry Corps. Col. H. BARRON the new A.D.M.S. visited works as usual E.S.	
	3rd		Relay post of bearers at LESBOEUFS relieved. D.E. visited post and R.A.P. near GUILLEMONT, much shelling own area. Visited. Capt. A. Massey R.A.M.C. from temp'y duty with 76 Bde ars reported sick & was evacuated. Capt. H. N. COTTER R.A.M.C. reported for duty from No 21 C.C.S. where he has been detained sick.	
	4th		Capt. M. E. GORMAN R.A.M.C. returned from this Unit and posted to 12th Labour Bn. The Black Watch, on this lose the services of	

WAR DIARY
or
INTELLIGENCE SUMMARY
(Erase heading not required.)

Army Form C.

Places	Date	Hour	Summary of Events and Information	Remarks and references to Appendices
BEAUFRAY	1916 Nov. 4th cont.		of one of the best brave officers it is possible to have, who has been with the unit since its arrival in this country & who knows every man in the unit, and thus is to go as 2/I.C. in charge a labour Bn.	
	5th		Pte. J. BROWN of this unit killed by shell fire on duty. Capt. J. WALKER & 17 O.R. proceed at day break to relieve Capt. LEWIS & his party at ad. Relay Post LESBOEUFS. News received of Capt. J.S. Lewis gallantry on Nov 4th in attempting wounded under heavy shell fire. Capt. N.J. COTTER orders to report to O.C. 7th B.N. Lincoln Reg for duty. E.g.	
	6th		A.D.M.S. visited the unit work as usual E.g	
	7th to 8th		Capt W. BARCLAY orders Capt J. WALKER at sunken Road LESBOEUFS. Hostile aeroplane dropped 3 bombs in camp of this unit. killed 2 horses & wounded 10 other horses & mules 9 p.m. E.g	

WAR DIARY
INTELLIGENCE SUMMARY

Army Form C. 2118.

Place	Date	Hour	Summary of Events and Information	Remarks and references to Appendices
BERNAFAY	1916 Nov 9th 10th		Work as usual. EJ. Met the A.D.M.S. 8 to 10.15. OC Met the A.D.M.S. 17 to DSW on behalf of A.D.M.S. visited relay posts from GINCHY to LESBOEUFS &c. Work as usual. EJ.	
"	11th		Met M.O. of a Fd Amb[?] Guards Divn at 10 AM & explained to him routes & methods of evacuation in area under care of this unit. EJ	
"	12th		Relieved at relay post LESBOEUFS EJ by Fld Ambce [?] Guards Divn at 12.30 p.m. EJ.	12.6/13
"	13th		Camp shelled during night. O.C. with transport left camp at 10 a.m. for SANDPITS Camp nr MEAULTE owing 3 p.m. our excessively bad roads. Dismounted party marched to CITADEL camp nr FRICOURT EJ	
"	14th		Dismounted party ordered to move to SANDPITS Camp in order to start with remainder of Group on 15th inst for EGGEMIE[?] STAT[?] EJ	

WAR DIARY
or
INTELLIGENCE SUMMARY.

Army Form C. 2118.

Place	Date	Hour	Summary of Events and Information	Remarks and references to Appendices
HQ	15/6		Dismounted party entrenched at EDGEHILL and detached at HENGEST. Shell near fort for HENGEST to a farm between the village and SOUES. This party held the earthwork to a flank of the 9th Dist. (No 6). The remainder formed the reserve of the Corps and then joined the remainder of the unit at EDGE HILL. The rear part of this party stayed at BEAUMONT RAGE joined with remainder by transport at DAOURS at 1:30 Cumbria 9.30. Remainder of the party was spent in organizing the flashy area as a hospital at the request of each for 5th Inf Bde Group. ARMS ot Dist moved to hospital.	
		6 PM	Transport arrived	
HENGEST	16/6		W. Saturday	
	17/6		Further organization of area	Sunday

WAR DIARY
or
INTELLIGENCE SUMMARY.

Army Form C. 2118.

Place	Date	Hour	Summary of Events and Information	Remarks and references to Appendices
HENGFET	18/4/16		Lt Col Garland proceeded on leave to U.K. a Canteen for the use of the personnel of the unit was established. W. Barclay	
-do-	19/4/16		A/QMS G. Du?Snake F.W.City proceeded to Thos. Tno. for temporary duty. W. Barclay	
-do-	20/4/16		Reports of unit proceeded with weekly & Hungarian sets. W. Barclay	
-do-	21/4/16		G.S.O. 1st Division visited the unit. W. Barclay	
-do-	22/4/16		Nothing to report. W. Barclay	
-do-	23/4/16		Capt. T. Walker proceeded to Paris on short leave. W. Barclay	
			Lt E.V. Beaumont proceeded to 7th Border Regt	

WAR DIARY
or
INTELLIGENCE SUMMARY.
(Erase heading not required.)

Army Form C. 2118.

Place	Date	Hour	Summary of Events and Information	Remarks and references to Appendices
HENGEST ?	24/1/16		For tefrom duty vice Capt Lyons.	W.J.Barclay
- do -	24/1/16		Nothing to report	W.J.Barclay
- do -	25/1/16	6p.	Capt. J. Walker returned from leave.	W.J.Barclay
- do -	26/1/16		Nothing to report.	W.J.Barclay
- do -	27/1/16	3p.	Visited by D.A.D.M.S. 17th Div. who inspected the area occupied by unit. Lt Bennett attended to duty with Thornwick.	W.J.Barclay
- do -	28/1/16		Nothing to report	W.J.Barclay
- do -	29/1/16		- do -	W.J.Barclay
- do -	30/1/16		- do -	W.J.Barclay

40/903 Vol 15

Confidential

War Diary of

51st Field Ambulance

From December 1st 1916 To December 31st 1916

Volume 3.

COMMITTEE FOR THE
MEDICAL HISTORY OF THE WAR
Date 31 JAN. 1917

Army Form C. 2118.

MEDICAL

WAR DIARY
or
INTELLIGENCE SUMMARY.
(Erase heading not required.)

Place	Date	Hour	Summary of Events and Information	Remarks and references to Appendices
HENGEST	1/2/16		Nothing to report	W.J. Barclay
do	2/2/16	10.30a	A.D.M.S. 17th Div. inspected the area occupied by unit and inspected various sanitary improvements	W.J. Barclay
do	3/2/16		Nothing to report	W.J. Barclay
do	4/2/16		— do —	W.J. Barclay
do	5/2/16	10a	Capt. J. Walker R.A.M.C. proceeded to 7th E. YORKS in relief of Capt. GREIG on leave to Paris	
		2p	Revd. F. McGUINNESS C.F. proceeded to 149th Inf. Bde.	
		4p	Lt. Col. E.R. Gourland R.A.M.C. returned from leave in United Kingdom	W.J. Barclay
do	6/2/16		Lt Col E Gourland sick in billet	W.J. Barclay

WAR DIARY
or
INTELLIGENCE SUMMARY

Army Form C. 2118.

Place	Date	Hour	Summary of Events and Information	Remarks and references to Appendices
HENGEST	7/12/16		Lt Col Goullard sick in billet.	
-do-	8/12/16		Lt-Col Goullard admitted to No 1 N.Z. Stationary Hospital Amiens	W/Barala
-do-	9/12/16		Nothing to report.	W/Barala
-do-	10/12/16		Capt. J. Walker RAMC returned to duty with this unit.	W/Barala
			Lt Craig — do — — to — — do —	
-do-	11/12/16		Capt. J. Walker proceeded to Corbie on advance billeting party.	W/Barala
			Lt Craig proceeded for temporary duty to artillery and Divisional Schools at DOULLENS.	
-do-	12/12/16	7300	Horse transport proceeded by road to Corbie enroute	W/Barala
			Capt. J.S. Stevens RAMC	

WAR DIARY
or
INTELLIGENCE SUMMARY.
(Erase heading not required.)

Army Form C. 2118.

Place	Date	Hour	Summary of Events and Information	Remarks and references to Appendices
		9.15a.m.	Advanced party proceeded from HENGEST to Corbie by train arriving at 12.30 p.m and were billeted in Chateau. The transport arrived at 5.30 p.m without incident. Capt. R. Wicker R.A.M.C. transferred to No 4 Fd. Amb.	W/Barala Cpy W/Barala Cpy
CORBIE	13/7/16		7 reinforcements arrived	W/Barala Cpy
do	14/7/16	1.30 p	Lt. A. Gaston R.A.M.C. transferred from D.D.M.S. XIV Corps. Under orders from D.D.M.S. XIV Corps 1 No. 50 bearers, 1 NCO, A.S.C.(M.T.) 4 drivers 6 mules and 4 wagon G.S.t proceeded to No 25 M.A.C. in advance.	W/Barala Cpy
do	15/7/16 — 16/7/16		Nothing to report. 4 Class with drivers and orderlies and groom proceeded to XIV Corps Rest Stams	W/Barala Cpy XIV Corps DIVE CORPS

Army Form C. 2118.

WAR DIARY
or
INTELLIGENCE SUMMARY.
(Erase heading not required.)

Place	Date	Hour	Summary of Events and Information	Remarks and references to Appendices
		10am	Capt W. Barclay and Capt J. Walker visited 61st Fd Amb 75th Div to inspect arrangements for evacuation of sick and wounded for Forward area. W.Base Coy	
CORBIE	17/12/16	11am	Lt A. GASTON proceeded to 6th So. Staff for temporary duty. 2 O.R. proceeded to XIV Corps Officers rest station TREUX for temporary duty. W.Base Coy	
		5pm		
do	18/12/16	9.30p	OC 17th Fd.l Svn inspected hospr's Rw hunt and gave a very favourable report. Capt C.A. KEEGAN joined this unit for duty. W.Base Coy	
do	19/12/16		Nothing to report. W.Base Coy	
do	20/12/16		A chief of staff office was formed a MEAULTE — to be arranged for a move to Forward area. W.Base Coy	

WAR DIARY
or
INTELLIGENCE SUMMARY.

Army Form C. 2118.

Place	Date	Hour	Summary of Events and Information	Remarks and references to Appendices
CORBIE	20th Sept		Lt Col E Gowland reported sick not on discharge for hospital. W. Bearer Co	
do	21/9		Nothing to report. W. Bearer Co	
do	22/9		Nothing to report. W. Bearer Co	
do	23/9	9am	Capt Pairs and 8 OR proceeded to take over A.D.S. at GINCHY from 61st Fd Amb. no Bin.	W. Bearer Co
			Capt J Walker proceeded to MEAULTE as Orderly Officer. Capt Kaye and 4 OR with proceeded to march to MEAULTE arriving there at 1 pm.	W. Bearer Co
MEAULTE	23/9	9am	Capt Walker proceeded to BEARER CAMP TRÔNES	

Army Form C. 2118.

WAR DIARY
or
INTELLIGENCE SUMMARY.
(Erase heading not required.)

Instructions regarding War Diaries and Intelligence Summaries are contained in F. S. Regs., Part II. and the Staff Manual respectively. Title pages will be prepared in manuscript.

Place	Date	Hour	Summary of Events and Information	Remarks and references to Appendices
Apt 2.5 (Albert) Confce Huaotro	25/10/16	9.30	NCOO with guides to ascertain details of collection of wounded from front line Bearer and details of tent subdivisions marched to new area.	
		1 pm	Arrived at A.D.M.S (Headquarters) with details of new position. Bearer subdivisions marked to Rear	W.T.Bars Coy
	26/10/16	9 am	Day spent in organisation Capt REGAN reported to D.H.Q as two for duty vice Capt. Skeag evacuated sick.	W.T.Bars Coy
- do -		8 am	Bearers of this unit relieved bearers of 67th F.A. at the relay aid regimental aid posts.	W.T.Bars Coy
- do -	27/10/16		Nothing to report	W.T.Barclay
- do -	28/10/16	7.30 am	Under orders from A.D.M.S 17 Div. 2 horse amb wagons proceeded to GARNY M.D.S. for duty	W.T.Barclay
		9 am	Bearers relieved by those of 573 Fd Amb.	W.T.Barclay

T2134. Wt. W708—776. 500000. 4/15. Str J. C. & S.

WAR DIARY
or
INTELLIGENCE SUMMARY.
(Erase heading not required.)

Army Form C. 2118.

Place	Date	Hour	Summary of Events and Information	Remarks and references to Appendices
A.D.S. 5th ARMY MONTAUBAN Rd.	29/12/16 30/12/16		Nothing to report. One hundred duck boards were obtained for board camp and a water tank and pump for A.O.S. GINCHY. The stabling material obtained for headquarters.	W.J. Barclay W.J. Barclay
do	31/12/16		The A.D.S. at GINCHY and the neighborhood was heavily shelled during the day	W.J. Barclay W.J. Barclay

17

140/19+3 Vol 16

1st Sea
Confidential

War Diary
of
51st Field Ambulance

from 1-1-17 to 31-1-17

(Volume +)

Nov 1917
S

COMMITTEE FOR THE
MEDICAL HISTORY OF THE WAR
Date 13 MAR. 1917

Army Form C. 2118.

MEDICAL

WAR DIARY
or
INTELLIGENCE SUMMARY.
(Erase heading not required.)

Place	Date	Hour	Summary of Events and Information	Remarks and references to Appendices
CARNOY MONTAUBAN RD A.25.5 —do—	1/7 2/7	9am 9am	Lt Col Gowland took over temporary command of Capt M.D.S. Nothing of special interest. W.P.Barclay Under instructions from A.D.M.S. 7 Div. Capt Barclay and Walker proceeded to the R.A.P. of the left Battalion of the Guards Division to arrange if possible for its retirement to Bearer post at T9 & when taken over to a battalion of 17th Div. The R.A.P. is not approachable by daylight except in urgency and the ground is extremely bad. A duck-walk leads B to R.A.P. from Maid Wood (T23.c) so it was arranged with the 20 F Amb that 9 squads be kept at a F Bay post on T1.a.4.9 to clear the R.A.P. at night. This arrangement was approved by A.D.M.S (A6.29). The R.A.P. was taken over the same night and this arrangement put into operation. W.P.Barclay	
3/7		6a	Lt Craig returned to duty with this unit.	W.P.Barclay

Army Form C. 2118.

WAR DIARY
or
INTELLIGENCE SUMMARY.
(Erase heading not required.)

Instructions regarding War Diaries and Intelligence Summaries are contained in F. S. Regs., Part II. and the Staff Manual respectively. Title pages will be prepared in manuscript.

Place	Date	Hour	Summary of Events and Information	Remarks and references to Appendices
-do-	4/7		Nothing to report.	
-do-	5/7		Nothing to report	WinBar=0a
-do-	6/7		-do-	WinBar=0a
-do-	7/7		Work had been going on during the previous ten days in the erection of NISSEN HUTS at headquarters. These huts are now occupied.	WinBar=0a
-do-	8/7		Nothing to report	WinBar=0a
-do-	9/7		Nothing to report	WinBar=0a
-do-	10/7		Nothing to report	WinBar=0a
-do-	11/7		Nothing to report	WinBar=0a
-do-	12/7		Nothing to report	WinBar=0a
-do-	13/7		S.M. Double R ans applied for duty	WinBar=0a
-do-	14/7		Nothing to report	WinBar=0a
-do-	15/7		Lt Freeman proceeded to England to Cadet school. Lt J.M. Craig proceeded to school of instruction at ALBERT for short course.	WinBar=0a

Army Form C. 2118.

WAR DIARY
or
INTELLIGENCE SUMMARY.
(Erase heading not required.)

Instructions regarding War Diaries and Intelligence Summaries are contained in F. S. Regs., Part II. and the Staff Manual respectively. Title pages will be prepared in manuscript.

Place	Date	Hour	Summary of Events and Information	Remarks and references to Appendices
do —	16/7	8am	Capt M⁼ James Rae M.O. for duty in exchange for Lt Col. Ban Black watch. Advance party back to MEAULTE, to take over billets.	
do —	17/7/16	11a	The personnel at the A.D.S. GINCHY were relieved by 69/70 and as per order to MEAULTE. The Rear division proceeded to MEAULTE.	
MEAULTE		11p	Headquarters moved to MEAULTE & Para Co that arrived in MEAULTE. The billets (No 1 Works Road) very unsatisfactory at present. Bed ret, beds etc. Necessary extensive repair to be made out and forwarded to 4/5 Div Para Co	
do —	18/7/16	—	Morning spent in cleaning up billets and	
		2/c	Mens Pay Parade.	

WAR DIARY
or
INTELLIGENCE SUMMARY.
(Erase heading not required.)

Army Form C. 2118.

Place	Date	Hour	Summary of Events and Information	Remarks and references to Appendices
MEAULTE	18/9/16		A.D.M.S. 17th Div: inspected the Unit and gave directions as to the unit and gave directions as to various improvements	in Barracks
- do -	19 to 20/16		Improvements carried out. Nothing to report	in Barracks
- do -	21/16		Capt F.M. Craig R.A.M.C. proceeded to England	on Leave
- do -		8p	Capt Barclay and Lieut Lewis attended a meeting of 4th Army Medical Society at No 1/1 to 11/1 C.C.S. A paper on Shell Shock was read by Capt Porter Neurologist to 4th Army. The paper was of little value to officers of Field Ambulances or regiments, on no indication was given as to treatment or R.A.P.'s or dressing stations very little also was said about the aetiology of the condition. Nothing to report	by Capt Barclay
- do -	22/16			

Place	Date	Hour	Summary of Events and Information	Remarks and references to Appendices
MEAULTE	24/9/16	9 am	Capt. W.E. GORMAN proceeded on leave to PARIS. Orders received from A.D.M.S. 17 Div. that bearer division move on 25th inst to bearer camp at GUILLEMONT. Sent advance guard on same date to C.O. Bearer Station at CARNOY.	
— do —	25/9/16	10.0	Capt Barclay visited 61st Fd Amb to arrange move of Bearer division.	
		10.30	QM. Stf at details sent to Carnoy as advance party.	
		10/p	Ambulance to A.D.M.S. orders waiting at 2½ to proceed direct via arrival to go to M.D.S. Camp [?]	
do	25/9/17	10.30	Unit moved to CARNOY arriving 12.15 pm. N.C.O. and 36 men proceeded as working party to REGICOURT arriving 3.30 pm. They are employed making a reserve (bearer) post and R.A.P.	
	1/a		CORPS M.D.S. taken over by 51st Fd. Amb. W. Riding Cy. Capt W.E. Gorman returned from PARIS.	

Army Form C. 2118.

WAR DIARY
or
INTELLIGENCE SUMMARY.
(Erase heading not required.)

Place	Date	Hour	Summary of Events and Information	Remarks and references to Appendices
— do —	21/7		Capt J. Walker Rowe proceeded to 7th E. Yorks for temporary duty. Capt G.S. Lewis Rowe proceeded to 9th Bn. D.L.I. for temporary duty.	W. Bazar Coy
CARNOY	24/7		Further inspection of the duties etc in the Cotton Dressing Station were carried out. Nothing to report	W. Bazar Coy
— do —	25/7		— do —	W. Bazar Coy
— do —	26/7		— do —	W. Bazar Coy
— do —	27/7		— do —	W. Bazar Coy
— do —	30/7		Lt. R.R. Gourlad visited site of new dressing station at M.A.B. Court to some Bearers of the ex. Nothing to report.	W. Bazar Coy
— do —	31/7			W. Bazar Coy

1/4th Divn.

Confidential 140/1919 Vol 7

War Diary
of
51st Field Ambulance

From Febry 1st 1917   To Febry 28th 1917

Volume (IV)

COMMITTEE FOR THE
MEDICAL HISTORY OF THE WAR
Date 4 — APR. 1917

Feb. 1917
5

Army Form C. 2118.

MEDICAL

WAR DIARY
or
INTELLIGENCE SUMMARY.
(Erase heading not required.)

Place	Date	Hour	Summary of Events and Information	Remarks and references to Appendices
CARNOY	1/2/17		Nothing to report	
- do -	2/2/17		- do -	
- do -	3/2/17	10 am	Working party at FREGICOURT relieved by 53rd Fd Amb, and withdrawn to Bearer Camp at S.30 c.8.5.	W⁴ Baraclay W⁴ Baraclay W⁴ Baraclay
- do -	4/2/17		Nothing to report	
- do -	5/2/17		Capt. R. Mitchell 53rd Fd Amb. temporarily attached to this for duty at Convalescent Camp at Bonfray Farm	W⁴ Baraclay
		11 pm	Bombs were dropped by hostile aircraft in the neighbourhood	W⁴ Baraclay
- do -	6/2/17		Nothing to report	W⁴ Baraclay
- do -	7/2/17	10.30	Hostile shelling of Plateau Station; one shell fell near the horse lines of this unit, and severely wounded Lt Creery, A.S.C. attached	W⁴ Baraclay
- do -	8/2/17		Nothing to report	W⁴ Baraclay
- do -	9/2/17	4.0	Orders received to send stretcher squads to A.D.S, Combles. These men were supplied from Bearer Camp and	

Army Form C. 2118.

WAR DIARY
or
INTELLIGENCE SUMMARY.
(Erase heading not required.)

Instructions regarding War Diaries and Intelligence Summaries are contained in F.S. Regs., Part II. and the Staff Manual respectively. Title pages will be prepared in manuscript.

Place	Date	Hour	Summary of Events and Information	Remarks and references to Appendices
CARNOY	18/5/17		Regiment at reserve. Beaver Post Corbies	W. Barclay
-do-	2/6/17	10 am	Battalion to Capt J Walker. Capt returned this unit.	W. Barclay
			Beaver div under Capt Barclay and James relieve	
			Beaver div. 9 32nd 7th Amb in line.	
			Capt J.E Lewis he returned to his unit.	W Barclay
-do-	12/6/17		Nothing to note	W Barclay
-do-	13/6/17		Beaver div received wire at 9.30 pm to send	
			11 stretcher squads with bearers all attached	
			to 12th Manchesters. These squads reported at	
			Headquarters 12th Manch. and proceeded to	
			front line where the casualties were. Ptes Saunders	
			and Rotherwood showed great bravery and ingenuity	
			in rescuing wounded from holes at Hill 60.	
			The cases were all removed before daylight.	W Barclay
-do-	15/6/17		Nothing to note	W Barclay

Army Form C. 2118.

3

WAR DIARY
or
INTELLIGENCE SUMMARY.
(Erase heading not required.)

Instructions regarding War Diaries and Intelligence Summaries are contained in F. S. Regs., Part II. and the Staff Manual respectively. Title pages will be prepared in manuscript.

Place	Date	Hour	Summary of Events and Information	Remarks and references to Appendices
CARNOY	15/5/17	—	Capt. W.S.T. Craig returned from leave.	W.T.Base Coy
-do-	16/5/17	—	Capt. W.T. Scorgie evacuated to hospital	W.T.Base Coy
-do-	17/5/17	—	Bearer div. relieved that of 53rd Fd. Amb. in line and returned to camp	W.T.Base Coy
MEAULTE	19/5/17	9pm	Unit moved to MÉAULTE and took over camp near Dressing Station to 87th Fd. Amb.	W.T.Base Coy
BONNAY	21/5/17	9.30am	Unit moved to BONNAY taking over billets from 59th Fd. Amb.	W.T.Base Coy
-do-	24/5/17	9am	Billets cleaned etc.	W.T.Base Coy
-do-	25/5/17	10am	Inspector of all ranks; men looked very fit; clothing renewed etc.	W.T.Base Coy
-do-	28/5/17	9a-	Lt.Col. E.R. Garland proceeded on leave to England	W.T.Base Coy
-do-	29/5/17	—	Capt. G.D. Shirley returned from hospital Lt. E.N. Beaumont returned to duty with this unit.	W.T.Base Coy

WAR DIARY.

4.

Place	Date	Hour	Summary of events and information	
BONNAY	24/2/17	9.30 a.m.	Capt. J. W. Craig proceeded to 6/6 Dorsets for duty vice Capt. G. R. Grant.	Wm Barclay
-do-	25/2/17	—	Nothing to note	Wm Barclay
-do-	26/2/17	3p.	Capt. D. Dougal Ranic delivered a lecture "Gas" to the Officers of the 51st Inf. Bde.	Wm Barclay
-do-		4p.	Nt. E. V. Beaumont evacuated sick to No 1 N.Z. Stat. Hosp. Amiens.	Wm Barclay
-do-	27/2/17	3p.	The D.A.D.M.S 17th Div. inspected the billets of the unit and commented unfavourably on the sanitary condition.	Wm Barclay
-do-	28/2/17	3p.	The small box respirators recently issued were tested at the gas school - HEILLY.	Wm Barclay

140/2042

Confidential

War Diary of

51st Field Ambulance

17th Div.

From March 1st 1917

To March 31st 1917

(Volume IV)

Y8/18

Mar 1917
S

COMMITTEE FOR THE
MEDICAL HISTORY OF THE WAR
Date 11 MAY 1917

Army Form C. 2118.

WAR DIARY
or
INTELLIGENCE SUMMARY
(Erase heading not required.)

MEDICAL

Place	Date	Hour	Summary of Events and Information	Remarks and references to Appendices
BONNAY	1/3/17	12 noon	The personnel & the unit marches to the Baths at HEILLY. The clothing issued was in an unsatisfactory condition and in very bad repair.	
		10 am	Athletic party paraded & proceeded to HERRISART	W. Bare Cay
do	2/3/17	7.30 am	Unit marched on route for HERRISART, arriving	W. Bare Cay
		12.15 pm	Billets first rate ad aa	
HERRISART	3/3/17		Nothing to report	W. Bare Cay
do	4/3/17	8.45 a	Sgt Stinson under Capt J. Walker and J. Steward proceeded for duty to T Corps Rest Station for duty in relief of 56 Fd Amb	W. Bare Cay
		10 am	Arrangements made to collect "sick" from RUBEMPRE ad PUCHVILLERS daily by horse ambulance wagon	W. Bare Cay
do	5/3/17	6 pm	Capt A. RANDLE RAMC joined this unit for duty	W. Bare Cay
do	6/3/17		H Col E E Gould returned from leave	W. Bare Cay
do	7/3/17	5 pm	Capt J S Black Cay proceeded to I Corps rest Station for duty	W. Bare Cay

T2134. Wt. W708—776. 500000. 4/15. Sir J. C. & S.

Army Form C. 2118.

2.

WAR DIARY
or
INTELLIGENCE SUMMARY.
(Erase heading not required.)

Instructions regarding War Diaries and Intelligence Summaries are contained in F. S. Regs., Part II. and the Staff Manual respectively. Title pages will be prepared in manuscript.

Place	Date	Hour	Summary of Events and Information	Remarks and references to Appendices
HERRISART	6/5/17	—	Nothing to report	
do	8/5/17	11 a.m.	A.D.M.S. Inspected the personnel of the W.Bar.Coy Unit and the billets etc	W.Bar.Coy
do	9/5/17		4 reinforcements arrived	W.Bar.Coy
do	11/5/17		Nothing to note	W.Bar.Coy
do	12/5/17		Capt. J. F. Burke proceeded on leave to U.K.	W.Bar.Coy
BRETEL	13/5/17	9.30 a.m.	Unit proceeded by road to BRETEL arriving 4.30 p.m. The last mile of R. road was in very bad condition and considerable difficulty was experienced in getting the wagons in. Billets were in good condition.	W.Bar.Coy
BERNATRE	14/5/17	9.15 a.m.	Unit proceeded by road to BERNATRE arriving 6.4 p.m. The roads were in fair condition. The men ad horses marched well and arrived good condition. Billets good	W.Bar.Coy
HAUTEVILLE	15/5/17	10.10 a.m.	Unit proceeded by road to HAUTEVILLE arriving 3.30 p.m. This area has not been occupied as a Fd.Amb. billet	W.Bar.Coy

Army Form C. 2118.

WAR DIARY
or
INTELLIGENCE SUMMARY.
(Erase heading not required.)

Place	Date	Hour	Summary of Events and Information	Remarks and references to Appendices
HAUTEVILLE	14/3/17		Reveillé	
			Day spent in cleaning up	W.P. Barclay
- do -	17/3/17		A.D.M.S. 17th Div. inspected area	W.P. Barclay
			& also hospital & read a Nissen hut in transport field	W.P. Barclay
- do -	18/3/17		Capt. A. Randle proceeded for temporary duty to the Divisional Rest Station (Whit N° 52) 7th A.C.	W.P. Barclay
- do -	19/3/17		Nothing to report	W.P. Barclay
	22/3/17		Lieut. [illegible] Capt. J. Walker proceeded to 7th Yorks for duty	W.P. Barclay
- do -	24/3/17		Lt. Col. Beamont proceeded to 8.G. Staff for temporary duty.	W.P. Barclay
BOTTLES	25/3/17	8.30am	Orders received from 51st Inf. Bde re move to [illegible] to Grand Bileaming. party proceeded at 9 am	W.P. Barclay
		11.30am	Unit moved off road to BOTTLES. Good billets.	W.P. Barclay
BREVILLERS	27/3/17	9am	Unit marched to BREVILLERS, arriving 11 am.	W.P. Barclay

WAR DIARY
or
INTELLIGENCE SUMMARY.
(Erase heading not required.)

Army Form C. 2118.

Place	Date	Hour	Summary of Events and Information	Remarks and references to Appendices
ARQUEVES	24/7/17	—	Billets left in a very unsatisfactory condition by previous occupiers. 31st Inf Bde on LE SOUICH. Hospital opened	Lt W. J. Barclay
- do -	25/7/17		Capt A. Randle returned to duty with H.Q. and 9 miner huts taken over from 31st Inf Bde and Divisional Rest Camp opened	Lt W. Barclay Lt W. J. Barclay
- do -	26/7/17		Nothing to report	Lt W. Barclay
- do -	27/7/17		Capt J. J. Back Coy returned off leave	Lt W. Barclay
- do -	28/7/17		Nothing to note	Lt W. J. Barclay
- do -	29/7/17 9a	Extra Rations returned to ordnance. Capt A. Randle proceeded to 7th YORKS for temporary duty	Lt W. J. Barclay
- do -	30/7/17 11a	Lecture delivered by Capt. ALEXANDER R.A.M.C. "On Iron in water. Testing"	Lt W. Barclay
- do -	31/7/17	Capt Vandendique departed for duty	Lt W. J. Barclay

No. 51 Fields Ante.

COPY.

B.E.F.

SUMMARY OF MEDICAL WAR DIARIES of

51st Field Ambulance,

17th Division,

18th Corps, till 1.5.17.
17th Corps, from 1.5.17.

3rd Army.

WESTERN FRONT, APRIL - MAY 1917.

O.C.   Lt.Colonel E. L. Gowlland.

Summarised under the following headings:-

PHASE "B" - BATTLE OF ARRAS. "APRIL - MAY 1917."

1st Period, April 1917. Attack on Vimy Ridge.
2nd Period, May 1917. Capture of Siegfried Line.

B.E.F.

1.

51st F.A., 17th Division,   WESTERN FRONT,
O.C. Lt.Col. E. L. Gowlland.   APRIL 1917.
18th Corps, 3rd Army.

Phase "B" - Battle of Arras. "April - May 1917."
1st Period, April 1917. Attack on Vimy Ridge.

April	H.Q. at Brevillers.
5th	Evacuation 100 cases transferred to C.R.S. at Gaudiempré - remainder to 6th Stn. Hospital Frevent.
5th-6th	Moves To Monts-en-Ternois.
7th	To Civenchy-Le-Noble.
8th	To Habarcq.
10th	To Arras.
12th-13th	Med. Arr. Ecole Normale, Arras, taken over fitted up as A.D.S.
14th	Casualties About 300 Sk. and 48 W. dealt with.
	Moves det. 2 Br. S.D's sent to "Brown Line" to assist 29th Divn. brs. Returned to H.Q. 15th.
15th	Casualties R.A.M.C. 0 & 2 W.
16th	Operations R.A.M.C. & Civilians. 2 Str. squads proceeded to Monchy and brought back 2 civilians left in the village Pte. McKeown P. showed great pluck and persistence in this operation.
22nd	Moves det. "C" section Br. S.D. to 88th F.A. to clear right Battln. of divisional front - Returned to H.Q. 26th. O & 9 to Decauville unloading point (Rivage) Returned to H.Q. 25th.
23rd	"B" section Br. S.D. to Blangy to assist 52nd F.A. Returned to H.Q. 25th.
	Evacuation During day evacuation of W. by Decauville Rly. from Feuchy worked excellently - no congestion at any point.
26th	Moves det. & Transport 1 & 12 with 2 cars to 51st Inf. Bde. Group to deal with evacuation of Sk. and W.

B.E.F.

51st F.A., 17th Division,   WESTERN FRONT,
O.C. Lt.Col. E. L. Gowlland.   APRIL 1917.
18th Corps, 3rd Army.

Phase "B", continued.
1st Period, continued.

April. H.Q. at Arras.
27th   Moves det. 1 & 2 Br. S.D's to Warlus for duty at 6th
        C.R.S. Returned 2nd May.

B.E.F.

1.

51st F.A., 17th Division, WESTERN FRONT,
O.C. Lt.Col. E. L. Gowlland. APRIL 1917.
18th Corps, 3rd Army.

Phase "B" - Battle of Arras. "April - May 1917."
1st Period, April 1917. Attack on Vimy Ridge.

April	H.Q. at Brevillers.
5th	Evacuation 100 cases transferred to C.R.S. at Gaudiempre - remainder to 6th Stn. Hospital Frevent.
5th-6th	Moves To Monts-en-Ternois.
7th	To Civenchy-Le-Noble.
8th	To Habarcq.
10th	To Arras.
12th-13th	Med. Arr. Ecole Normale, Arras, taken over fitted up as A.D.S.
14th	Casualties About 300 Sk. and 48 W. dealt with. Moves det. 2 Br. S.D's sent to "Brown Line" to assist 29th Divn. brs. Returned to H.Q. 15th.
15th	Casualties R.A.M.C. 0 & 2 W.
16th	Operations R.A.M.C. & Civilians. 2 Str. squads proceeded to Monchy and brought back 2 civilians left in the village Pte. McKeown P. showed great pluck and persistence in this operation.
22nd	Moves det. "C" section Br. S.D. to 88th F.A. to clear right Battln. of divisional front - Returned to H.Q. 26th, 0 & 9 to Decauville unloading point (Rivage) Returned to H.Q. 25th.
23rd	"B" section Br. S.D. to Blangy to assist 52nd F.A. Returned to H.Q. 25th. Evacuation During day evacuation of W. by Decauville Rly. from Feuchy worked excellently - no congestion at any point.
26th	Moves det. & Transport 1 & 12 with 2 cars to 51st Inf. Bde. Group to deal with evacuation of Sk. and W.

B.E.F.

<u>51st F.A., 17th Division,</u>　　　　　　WESTERN FRONT,

<u>O.C. Lt.Col. E. L. Gowlland.</u>　　　　APRIL 1917.

<u>18th Corps, 3rd Army.</u>

<u>Phase "B", continued.</u>

<u>1st Period, continued.</u>

April.　　H.Q. at Arras.

27th　　<u>Moves det. 1 & 2 Br. S.D's to Warlus</u> for duty at 6th C.R.S.　Returned 2nd May.

Army Form C. 2118.

MEDICAL

WAR DIARY
or
INTELLIGENCE SUMMARY.
(Erase heading not required.)

Instructions regarding War Diaries and Intelligence Summaries are contained in F. S. Regs., Part II. and the Staff Manual respectively. Title pages will be prepared in manuscript.

Place	Date	Hour	Summary of Events and Information	Remarks and references to Appendices
BREVILLERS	1/4/17		Nothing to report	
-do-	2/4/17		Nothing to report	
-do-	3/4/17	2.15p	A/Cpl E.L. Garland attended a conference at A.D.M.S. 7th Div.	W.Bases Co W.Bases Co
-do-	4/4/17	8.30am	Major O.C. travelled to Capt. W. Bean Co. proceeded to ARRAS with a view to making arrangements for a possible move	W.Bases Co
		4p.m.	Through the day. Information received from A.D.M.S. 17th Div. that all cases of 53rd F.A. were being transferred to 78th F.A. & the unit St Ev. Beaumont proceeded to LuBase Co	
MONTS TERNOIS	5/4/17	7am 10am	Unit cleared 2 officers and 12 other ranks personnel left for MONTS-TERNOIS with 51st Bde. Group. 100 cases were transferred to Corps Rest Station at GAUDIEMPRÉ; remainder to No 6 Sta. Hospt. Unit arrived 3 pm. Good billets.	W.Bases Co W.Bases Co
-do-	6/4/17	9p	Remainder of unit joined up.	W.Bases Co

Army Form C. 2118.

WAR DIARY
or
INTELLIGENCE SUMMARY.
(Erase heading not required.)

Instructions regarding War Diaries and Intelligence Summaries are contained in F. S. Regs., Part II. and the Staff Manual respectively. Title pages will be prepared in manuscript.

Place	Date	Hour	Summary of Events and Information	Remarks and references to Appendices
GIVENCHY-LE-NOBLE	7/7/17	9a.	Capt. Lewis Blackler and Gunner Plant with 3 G.D. Sergeants proceeded to ARRAS to reconnoitre the material arrangements in the horse lines.	
		12noon	Unit left Mont-au-Denis for GIVENCHY-LE-NOBLE arriving 3/8. W.T. Barrow Capt	
HABARCQ	8/7/17	6.30a	A section Lewis Bower outfits proceeded to Casualty Clearing Station ARRAS	
			(as H.Q. Aud) for duty.	
			Unit left GIVENCHY-LE-NOBLE for HABARCQ arriving 11a. Unit was divided into Echelons A.B.&C.	
			A echelon — Cooker tent orderlies B.O. bear orderlies with all officers. 4 limbered wagons 2 water carts	
		11a.	B echelon — 3-horse and wagons 1 maltese cart	
			C echelon — A&B 1st Battalion with remainder of transport.	
		10p.	Lt. T Vado&signs proceeded to Walker W. Coll. Post, to Reservoir ARRAS for duty.	W.T Barrow Capt

Army Form C. 2118.

WAR DIARY
or
INTELLIGENCE SUMMARY.
(Erase heading not required.)

Place	Date	Hour	Summary of Events and Information	Remarks and references to Appendices
ARRAS HABARCQ Road	9/4/17	9 pm	Wire rec'd from 57th Dgl. Bde to move 4.45 pm	
		9.30	No horses suspected to carry to establish relay posts in ARRAS in case of casualties while wires never through the town.	
		4.45 pm	A soldier started for starting point 400 yards E. of HABARCQ	
		10 pm	A echelon held up to K. west of ARRAS owing to convoys.	
		11 pm		
ARRAS	10/4/17	2 am	Relay posts in town withdrawn and personnel billeted. March of echelon continued.	
		10 am	Unit billeted in crypts of Cathedral in ARRAS.	
		Noon	Party composed of C. Walker ordered to proceed to case drawing	
— do —	11/4/17	1 a m	Station for duty.	
		9 am	Capt. H. Beale proceeded to Caves for duty. W.Y. Beale	
		11 am	H Reserve Brigade. do do under Capt. J. Lewis and Capt. W. F. Gomer.	
		11 pm	All personnel of this unit on duty at CAVES returned to	

WAR DIARY
or
INTELLIGENCE SUMMARY.
(Erase heading not required.)

Army Form C. 2118.

Place	Date	Hour	Summary of Events and Information	Remarks and references to Appendices
ARRAS	12/4/17	10am	Headquarters HQ. Cavan having been known all 9 wash of a stiffness.	
			Orders received to equip and take over ECOLE NORMALE as GARDENS as A.D.S in conjunction with 47 Fd Amb.	
	13/4/17		Day spent in cleaning out the building	W.S/Rand Co
			Day spent in cleaning and equipping the building.	W.S/Rand Co
			Red Cross and Grace Medical Stores received	
			From VI Corps Dump at HABARCQ	
do	14/4/17	9am	Hospital opened for reception of sick and wounded.	
			About 300 sick and 156 wounded dealt with in 12 hours.	
			Arrangement made with OC 47 Fd Amb to see sick and wounded	
			on alternate days in conjunction with him.	
		4pm	Under orders from ADMS 17 Div. 2 Bearer subsections under	
			Capt Lewis & Gorman were sent to "BROWN LINE".	
		8.30pm	Notification received that he had reached N's central (SCARPE) and	
			was awaiting instruction	

Army Form C. 2118.

WAR DIARY
or
INTELLIGENCE SUMMARY.
(Erase heading not required.)

Place	Date	Hour	Summary of Events and Information	Remarks and references to Appendices
ARRAS	15/5	1pm	Instructions received that these orderlies were to stand by to accompany 29th Div. Seners.	W.J.Bard Capt
		3pm	D.D.M.S. Vth Corps inspected billets	
		3.30pm	Instructions rec'd for A.D.M.S. 17th Div. recalling the two bearer subsections despatched yesterday.	
		4pm	Bearer subsection returned. Ptes Armitage and Mercy slightly wounded by shell	
		5pm	Lt J. Vandersaign returned to duty with the unit.	W.J.Bard Co
	16/5/17	11am	Capt. P. Moore R.A.M.C. reported for temporary duty. The D.D.M.S. 1st Army visited the dressing station.	W.J.Bard Co
			Capt. A. Randle R.A.M.C. & another 30 lads were sent to MONCHY to bring the civilian cases from the village to ARRAS. Pte P. McKEOWN shewed great pluck and persisted in his efforts.	
	17/5/17	11am	Capt A. Randle R.A.M.C. returned to duty with the unit. W.J.Bard Cap	
	17/5/17	6.30pm	Instructions received to send Capt P. Moore to Beaurains in relief	

Army Form C. 2118.

WAR DIARY
or
INTELLIGENCE SUMMARY.
(Erase heading not required.)

Instructions regarding War Diaries and Intelligence Summaries are contained in F. S. Regs., Part II. and the Staff Manual respectively. Title pages will be prepared in manuscript.

Place	Date	Hour	Summary of Events and Information	Remarks and references to Appendices
ARRAS	19/7		of Capt Fahy who was to be attached to the unit temporarily	
-do-	20/7	7pm	Lt Gill, RAMC reported for temporary duty with the unit	W/m Bar Co
-do-	21/7		whm report. attended a conference of O.C. Field Ambs at A.D.M.S. office	W/m Bar Co 19 Bar Co
-do-	24/7		Lt McGill transferred to 53rd Fd Amb.	W/m Bar Co
	20/7		High Gradig Examination Capt J.S. Capt W.E Gorm, RAMC reported on special leave to Canada	W/m Bar Co
-do-	22/7, 23/7		C section beries orderlies under Cpl J.T. Tait reported to O.C. 55th Fd Amb for duty to clear night bom[?] of wounded from	
-do-		3pm	Med. adjumm detailed for duty at DECAUVILLE Unloader POINT (RIVAGE).	W/m Bar Co
-do-	23/7	6.30	Bearer bearer orderlies (Capt H. Pleydell) proceded to BLANGY to 57th Fd Amb. Lt M.B Taylor RAMC reported for duty	

Army Form C. 2118.

WAR DIARY
or
INTELLIGENCE SUMMARY.
(Erase heading not required.)

Place	Date	Hour	Summary of Events and Information	Remarks and references to Appendices
ARRAS	24/5	—	During the day the evacuation of wounded by the Divisional railway from FEUCHY was excellent. There was no shelling at any point. W/Barn Ca	
—	25/5/17	—	Arrangements as before. W/Barn Ca	
		8.30a	B section bearer subdivision returned to Headquarters.	
—	26/5/17	9a	Party at RIVAGE relieved by 36 Ft. Amb. W/Barn Ca under orders from D.D.M.S. VI Corps. 51st Ft Amb remain in VI Corps.	
		10a	Offrs (Capt A Ra.d Q) an /2 OR. with 2 cars proceeded to 51st T.S grp to deal with evacuation of sick at. wounded at the Brigade grps.	
		10am	C section Bearer subdivision returned to Headquarters.	
		aft	A/SJ Fisk Royal distinguished himself by his conduct bravery under shell fire. from 23/4/17 to this date.	
— do —	27/5/17	10am	B section subdivision under Lt. Ev Roberts proceeded to EV Corps Rest Stn. W/Barn Ca	
			WARLUS for duty at VI Corps Rest Stn.	

WAR DIARY
or
INTELLIGENCE SUMMARY.

(Erase heading not required.)

Army Form C. 2118.

Place	Date	Hour	Summary of Events and Information	Remarks and references to Appendices
ARRAS	28/4/17	—	Nothing to report	W. Barclay
do	29/4/17 10a	1/1 & 2/1 Field Amb^s detailed for the unit for duty with 52nd Inf. Brigade	W. Barclay
do	30/4/17 6p.	Order received for D.D.M.S. VI Corps to be in readiness to move at short notice to XVIII Corps.	W. Barclay

COMMITTEE FOR THE
MEDICAL HISTORY OF THE WAR
Date   10 JUL. 1917

No. 51. F.A.

May 1917

Carbons.

B.E.F.

SUMMARY OF MEDICAL WAR DIARIES of

51st Field Ambulance,

17th Division,

18th Corps, till 1.5.17.
17th Corps, from 1.5.17.

3rd Army.

WESTERN FRONT, APRIL - MAY 1917.

O.C. Lt.Colonel E. L. Gowlland.

Summarised under the following headings:-

PHASE "B" - BATTLE OF ARRAS. ,"APRIL & MAY 1917."

1st Period, April 1917. Attack on Vimy Ridge.
2nd Period, May 1917. Capture of Siegfried Line.

B.E.F. 1.

51st F.A., 17th Division,   WESTERN FRONT,
O.C. Lt.Col. E. L. Gowlland.   MAY 1917.
17th Corps, 3rd Army.

Phase "B" - Battle of Arras. "April - May 1917."

2nd Period, May 1917. Capture of Siegfried Line.

May	
	H.Q. at Arras.
1st	Transfer To 17th Corps.
	Moves det. 1 & "B" section T.S.D. to 17th C.R.S.
3rd	Moves To St. Nicholas, relieved by 89th F.A.
	Operations Enemy & Casualties. Camp at St. Nicholas shelled. 2 Wounded.
10th	Moves Unit (less transport) to Hervin Farm H.13.b.9.3. (Sheet 51b) relieved 1st S.A. F.A.
	Med. Arr. & Evacuation. Collection of W. taken over from 28th F.A. and 1st S.A. F.A. Advanced Br. P. established at H.11.a.Central (junction of "Brown Line" and Sunken Rd.) O & 8 stationed at Decauville Railhead L'Abbayette to stop all 17th Divn. cases and load them on train. From Adv. Br. P. cases taken by wheeled stretcher carriers to Fampoux - Athies Rd. at H.16.d.3.5. - thence to car loading post at H.16.c.5.2. - thence by car to A.D.S. at Hervin Farm.
11th	Assistance 1 & 16 to 17th T.M.B. arrived for duty. Re-joined unit 20th.
	1 & 2 Br. S.D's 53rd F.A. reported for duty. Re-joined unit 27th.
11th-12th	Operations Enemy & Med. Arr. Owing to heavy shelling, rear Relay P. moved to H.16.c.9.1.
	1 Train despatched from L'Abbayette.
12th	Moves det. 6 squads of 53rd F.A. to A. Br. P. to reinforce.
	Med. Arr. & Evacuation. A.D.S. removed to H.13.b.5.7. Loading party at L'Abbayette removed. Cases brought from whole divnl. front to A.D.S. and evacuated/

B.E.F.

51st F.A., 17th Division,   WESTERN FRONT,

O.C. Lt.Col. E. L. Gowlland.   May 1917.

17th Corps, 3rd Army.

Phase "B" - Battle of Arras. "April 1917.- May "

2nd Period, continued.

May   H.Q. at St. Nicholas.

12th   Evacuation (contd.)   evacuated by rail to Arras.
(contd.)   Evacuation very satisfactory.

16th   Operations Enemy & Med. Arr.   Owing to heavy shelling A.D.S. removed to former situation H.13.b.9.4. where it is protected by Railway Embankment.

2 operating tents practically destroyed and some instruments damaged by shell fire - no casualties.

30th-31st   Moves   To Mondicourt.

10th-30th   Summary   During fighting 12th, 13th and 14th when all available brs. were required at A.D.S., H.11.a.Central, all duties carried out satisfactorily at the post by 7 squads with 2 officers, 2 N.C.O's and 2 nursing orderlies.

Personnel of rear br. post 0 & 7 - Relieved each 72 hours by reserve squads from A.D.S. at Hervin Farm, with exception of officers.

Casualties R.A.M.C. & Casualties R.A.M.C. Gas

     0 & 1 Killed.

     0 & 6 W.

     0 & 2 gassed.

Casualties A.S.C attd.

     0 & 1 Killed.

B.E.F. 1.

51st F.A., 17th Division,   WESTERN FRONT,

O.C. Lt.Col. E. L. Gowlland.   MAY 1917.

17th Corps, 3rd Army.

Phase "B" - Battle of Arras. "April - May 1917."

2nd Period, May 1917. Capture of Siegfried Line.

May	H.Q. at Arras.
1st	Transfer To 17th Corps.
	Moves det. 1 & "B" section T.S.D. to 17th C.R.S.
3rd	Moves To St. Nicholas, relieved by 89th F.A.
	Operations Enemy & Casualties. Camp at St. Nicholas shelled. 2 Wounded.
10th	Moves Unit (less transport) to Hervin Farm H.13.b.9.3. (Sheet 51b) relieved 1st S.A. F.A.
	Med. Arr. & Evacuation. Collection of W. taken over from 28th F.A. and 1st S.A. F.A. Advanced Br. P. established at H.11.a.Central (junction of "Brown Line"and Sunken Rd.) O & S stationed at Decauville Railhead L'Abbayette to stop all 17th Divn. cases and load them on train. From Adv. Br. P. cases taken by wheeled stretcher carriers to Fampoux - Athies Rd. at H.16.d.3.5. - thence to car loading post at H.16.c.5.2. - thence by car to A.D.S. at Hervin Farm.
11th	Assistance 1 & 16 to 17th T.M.B. arrived for duty. Re-joined unit 20th.
	1 & 2 Br. S.D's 53rd F.A. reported for duty. Re-joined unit 27th.
11th-12th	Operations Enemy & Med. Arr. Owing to heavy shelling, rear Relay P. moved to H.16.c.9.1.
	1 Train despatched from L'Abbayette.
12th	Moves det. 6 squads of 53rd F.A. to A. Br. P. to reinforce.
	Med. Arr. & Evacuation. A.D.S. removed to H.13.b.5.7. Loading party at L'Abbayette removed. Cases brought from whole divnl. front to A.D.S. and evacuated/

B.E.F.

51st F.A., 17th Division,   WESTERN FRONT,
O.C. Lt.Col. E. L. Gowlland.   May 1917.
17th Corps, 3rd Army.

Phase "B" - Battle of Arras.   "April 1917.- May "
2nd Period, continued.

May
12th (contd.) — H.Q. at St. Nicholas.
Evacuation (contd.) evacuated by rail to Arras. Evacuation very satisfactory.

16th — Operations Enemy & Med. Arr.   Owing to heavy shelling A.D.S. removed to former situation H.13.b.9.4. where it is protected by Railway Embankment.
2 operating tents practically destroyed and some instruments damaged by shell fire - no casualties.

30th-31st — Moves To Mondicourt.

10th-30th — Summary   During fighting 12th, 13th and 14th when all available brs. were required at A.D.S., H.11.a.Central, all duties carried out satisfactorily at the post by 7 squads with 2 officers, 2 N.C.O's and 2 nursing orderlies.
Personnel of rear br. post 0 & 7 - Relieved each 72 hours by reserve squads from A.D.S. at Hervin Farm, with exception of officers.

Casualties R.A.M.C. & Casualties R.A.M.C. Gas
  O & 1 Killed.
  O & 6 W.
  O & 2 gassed.

Casualties A.S.C attd.
  O & 1 Killed.

Army Form C. 2118.

"MEDICAL"

WAR DIARY
INTELLIGENCE SUMMARY.
(Erase heading not required.)

Instructions regarding War Diaries and Intelligence Summaries are contained in F. S. Regs., Part II. and the Staff Manual respectively. Title pages will be prepared in manuscript.

Place	Date	Hour	Summary of Events and Information	Remarks and references to Appendices
ARRAS	1/5/17	2:0 p	Verbal orders received fm A.D.M.S. 17 Div. to move that afternoon to XVII Corps Rest Stn., BERLETTE. 17 Regiment revealed fm Watkins as act with B tent subsec. W.B.Barclay	
	2/5/17		Lt MO Taylor detailed for duty to 33 Fd A.A. (A.D.M.S. Regt). Bearer subsection returned fm 6 Corps Rest Stn. Watkins, Lt 57 of Fd Amb. experienced motor of evacuation of wounded in XVIII Corps.	W.B.Barclay W.B.Barclay
St NICHOLAS	3/5/17	10 a.m.	Unit moved to St Nicholas on relief by 89 Fd Amb. Some men in billets in village.	
	4/5/17	9 am	At Vandadingne proceeds to XVII C Rest Stn for duty	W.B.Barclay
		11 p	Camp at St Nicholas attacked 2 casualties	W.B.Barclay
		7.15 p	Considerable discomfort from Canada by the explosion of a large ammunition dump on the Rivage, ARRAS.	W.B.Barclay
- do -	5/5/17		Nothing to report	W.B.Barclay
- do -	6/5/17		- do -	W.B.Barclay
- do -	7/5/17		- do -	W.B.Barclay

WAR DIARY
INTELLIGENCE SUMMARY.
(Erase heading not required.)

Army Form C. 2118.

Place	Date	Hour	Summary of Events and Information	Remarks and references to Appendices
ST NICHOLAS	8/5/17	Noon	OC 51st FA. with A.D.M.S. 7th Div. interpreted mode of evacuation of wounded in 9th Div. Nothing to report.	W.Pl.Bear.Coy W.R.Bear.Coy
-do-	9/5/17			
MERVIN FARM	10/5/17	10 am	Unit (less transport and PM Store moved to HERVIN FARM, (H.15.89.3 Map 51B.N.W.), relieving 1st Tank Africa F.A. (H.15.89.3 Map 51B.N.W.), relieving 1st Tank Africa F.A. Collection of wounded taken over from 26th F.A. and 1st Sth African F.A. An advanced bearer post established at H.11.a.central, at the junction of "Brown line" and wheeled ambce road. From here bearers are taken by wheeled stretcher carrier across country to the YPRES~ATHIES road at H.16.d.3.5, Hence along to road to car loading post at H.16.c.5.2.) Hence by car to A.D.S. at HERVIN FARM.	
		2pm	ACO and men stationed at Doorsils in charge of W.Bear.Co PARADISE will return to Coy 17th Divn away and transfer kits to Coy.	

Army Form C. 2118.

WAR DIARY
or
INTELLIGENCE SUMMARY.
(Erase heading not required.)

Instructions regarding War Diaries and Intelligence Summaries are contained in F. S. Regs., Part II. and the Staff Manual respectively. Title pages will be prepared in manuscript.

Place	Date	Hour	Summary of Events and Information	Remarks and references to Appendices
HERVIN FARM	11/17	10 a.	1 Officer and 16 OR 17th Tn B reported for duty.	
		2 p.m.	Capt A Robertson with 2 Bearer Relays 53rd T.A. reported.	
		10 a.	Lt Gill 23 T.A. reported.	
		7 p.m.	1 NCO and 7 men stationed at Desqueille notified in L'ABBAYETTE with instructions to stop all 17th R.B. cases and take to rear.	
-do-	12/5/17	9:30a.	Officers received from OC Reserve that near relay post moved to HR69. Long to heavy shelling during night.	
		8 p.m.	6 Squads of 53rd T.A. departed for L'ABBAYETTE 6 Squads of 53rd T.A. departed to advanced bearer post to reinforce.	W.R. Bendry
		6 p.m.	A.D.S removed to H18 b.5.7 and using party in L'ABBAYETTE removed. Cases are brought to this A.D.S for the walking wounded first and evacuated by rail to A.D.S who in ARRAS.	W.R. Bendry
-do-	13/7/17		Evacuation of wounded working very satisfactorily.	W.R. Bendry
-do-	14/7/17		Nothing to report.	W.R. Bendry

WAR DIARY
INTELLIGENCE SUMMARY

Army Form C. 2118.

Place	Date	Hour	Summary of Events and Information	Remarks and references to Appendices
MERVIN FARM	15/5/17	—	Nothing to report	Wilj Bare Cy
- do -	16/5/17	5.30pm	Enemy by heavy shelling A.D.S. was removed from M18 c.5.7 back to front where M18 b.9.4 where at no protection by railway embankment. Fortunately there were no shelter cases awaiting removal when the shells commenced, and the only damage sustained was two Company tents practically destroyed, one instrument damaged and another destroyed. The two nurses at M18 d.7.7 and in bunkers for the A.D.S. by	Wilj Bare Cy Wilj Bare Cy Wilj Bare Cy
- do -	17/5/17	—	Nothing to report	Wilj Bare Cy
- do -	18/5/17	—	Nothing to report	Wilj Bare Cy
- do -	19/5/17	—	- do -	Wilj Bare Cy
- do -	20/5/17	9a.m	1 Officer and 17 O.R. 1/7 T.M.B. regened kernit.	Wilj Bare Cy
- do -	21/5/17	5pm	1 N.C.O. and 12 O.R. for 32nd Inf Bde reported for duty	Wilj Bare Cy
- do -	22/5/17	—	Nothing to report	Wilj Bare Cy

Army Form C. 2118.

WAR DIARY
or
INTELLIGENCE SUMMARY.
(Erase heading not required.)

Instructions regarding War Diaries and Intelligence Summaries are contained in F. S. Regs., Part II. and the Staff Manual respectively. Title pages will be prepared in manuscript.

Place	Date	Hour	Summary of Events and Information	Remarks and references to Appendices
HERVIN FARM	23/5/17		Nothing to report	
- do -	24/5/17		do	
- do -	25/5/17		do	
- do -	26/5/17		do	
- do -	27/5/17	4pm	The attached personnel of 52nd Inf Bde returned to A.D.M.S. 17th Div.	W.Bare Co.
			under orders of A.D.M.S. 17th Div.	W.Bare Co.
		9pm	2 Officers and 36 O.R. 53rd Fd Amb reported for duty.	W.Bare Co.
			Lt. QM M.S. GEE and 2 O.R. proceeded to Coare to U.K.	W.Bare Co.
- do -	28/5/17		Lt. I. Vandaigu proceeded to U.K. with a draft	W.Bare Co.
			proceeding to Canada or Coare.	W.Bare Co.
			Nothing to report.	W.Bare Co.
- do -	29/5/17	10am	Bearer party proceeded to MONDICOURT.	W.Bare Co.
	30/5/17	9pm	Stretcher bearer party proceeded to ST NICHOLAS to arrange	
			billets for one night for unit.	
		8am	All but essential personnel despatched to ST NICHOLAS.	
		11am	Personnel at HERVIN FARM relieved by 102nd Fd. Amb., W.Barclay
	31/5/17	10am	Personnel at advanced dressing posts also were relieved
			by 102 Fd Amb.

WAR DIARY
or
INTELLIGENCE SUMMARY.
(Erase heading not required.)

Army Form C. 2118.

Place	Date	Hour	Summary of Events and Information	Remarks and references to Appendices
MONDICOURT	3/5/17	5am	Entire unit billeted in ST NICHOLAS. Transport moved en route for MONDICOURT.	
		6am	Personnel formed up and entrained for MONDICOURT arriving at entraining station at ARRAS station and arriving at 8pm.	
		9am		
		8pm	Billeted in CHATEAU. Horse lines in field near railway.	
			Reinforcements of 1 hour from 10 $\frac{5}{7}$ to 30 $\frac{7}{7}$. During the fighting after the 12th & 13th & 14th May when all available bearers were required at the A.D.S. at this centre it was found that the duties were carried out satisfactorily by Trumpeters at this post, with 2 N.C.O's and 2 men, others was 1 NCO and 6 men. This personnel (with the exception of the Officers) were relieved each 72 hours by reserve bearers from A.D.S. at HERVIN FARM.	

WAR DIARY or INTELLIGENCE SUMMARY

Army Form C. 2118.

Capt. J.S. Lewis remained at the advanced Report. Post during the whole tour with the exception of the night 15-16/5/17

Casualties. 1 the R.A.M.C. killed by shell fire between advanced and rear bearer posts.
1 pte A.S.C. M.T. killed at MERVIN FARM by a shell.
2 ptes R.A.M.C. gassed severely by shell gas near rear bearer post.
2 ptes R.A.M.C. severely wounded in forward area to do shelling wounded at Mervin Farm.

Relief. Some inconvenience was caused by the lateness of the relief. Owing to a breakdown the O.C. 102nd Fd Amb was unable to inform O.C. 57th Fd Amb of an alternative made in the arrangements for relief, much needless friction and unpleasantry was thus caused.

W. N. Rose Capt

MEDICAL 17

Lovrantini

War Diary wo/a696
of

51st Field Ambulance

From June 1st 1914
To June 30th 1914

(Volume IV)

COMMITTEE FOR THE
MEDICAL HISTORY OF THE WAR
Date -4 MAR.1918

WAR DIARY
or
INTELLIGENCE SUMMARY.
(Erase heading not required.)

Army Form C. 2118.

MEDICAL

Place	Date	Hour	Summary of Events and Information	Remarks and references to Appendices
MONDICOURT	1/6/17		Day spent in cleaning up the area occupied by the unit. Scheme for Rolokomehed established.	
-do-	2/6/17	9a.	The inoculation with T.A.B. vaccine of the 51st Inf. Bde. Group was carried out during the day. Officers & men detailed for this purpose all worked excellently, and there was no question at any time. Number inoculated 2008. The number of objectors was small, but no amount of persuasion appears to have any effect once the man's mind is made up. W. Baverley Lt. R.A.M.C.	
-do-	3/7	6	Nothing to report.	
		5p.	Capt J.S. Karis proceeded on leave 6/7 to U.K. Capt E.J. Beaumont proceeded for temporary duty to 7th Lines.	
-do-	3/7		Capt A. Radke proceeded on leave. Capt J.P. Beakley assuming temporary duty with 57 So. Staff.	

Army Form C. 2118.

WAR DIARY
or
INTELLIGENCE SUMMARY.
(Erase heading not required.)

Place	Date	Hour	Summary of Events and Information	Remarks and references to Appendices
MONDICOURT	4/6/17		Nothing to report	W.J. Barclay
- do -	5/6/17		- do -	W.J. Barclay
- do -	6/6/17		- do -	W.J. Barclay
- do -	7/6/17		All ranks given every opportunity to attend the Sports held Wednesday	W.J. Barclay
do	8/6/17	2 P.M.	Sports were carried through by the unit. The Tea of the 10th Hampshires was I afternoon. Lt. H.J. See returned from leave	W.J. Barclay
do	9/6/17		Capt. Barclay proceeded on leave to U.K. A dinner and concert were provided to the unit from Ambulance Cadres Funds. 6.O.R. proceeded on leave to U.K. It. Qr. M. H.F.C and 6 R. joined for duty J.P. Berkeley	J.P. Berkeley
do	10/6/17		Pt. Worden and Pt. Readman R.A.M.C. returned from leave.	J.P. Berkeley
do	11/6/17		Lt. Roakph R.A.M.C. joined this unit for duty being transferred from 37th Div and was temporarily detailed for duty with 10th Sherwoods	J.P. Berkeley

Army Form C. 2118.

WAR DIARY
or
INTELLIGENCE SUMMARY.
(Erase heading not required.)

Place	Date	Hour	Summary of Events and Information	Remarks and references to Appendices
HANDICOURT	12/6/17		Pte Harrison proceeded for temporary duty to I.O.M. XIIIth Corps. Pte Bellamy promoted to Acting Sgt from 2.6.17. Auth D.Q.M.S. 1450/1003 8/5/17	J.P.Brockley
do	13/6/17		Capt D.A. Laird reported for duty with this unit. Pte Walford returned to duty from temporary duty with 58th San. Sec.	J.P.Brockley
do	14/6/17		Capt J.S. Lewis returned from leave, and assumed command of the unit. Lt H.E. Bunel U.S.R. reported for duty with this unit.	J.P.Brockley
do	15/6/17		Lt Col Gouldland D.S.O. R.A.M.C. proceeded on leave to U.K.	J.P.Brockley
do	16/6/17		Four Military Medals were awarded to this unit M.A.D.R.O. 1764 7/15/6/17. Pte Smith C.A. McHugheson W.W. Pte Phaisell S.G. and H/4 McKeown S.E. Dinsmore returned from leave	J.P.Brockley
do	17/6/17		Lieut Rodolph struck off strength of unit, and proceeded for duty with the 7th Yorkshire Reg.	J.P.Brockley
do	18/6/17		Capt Beaumont struck off strength of unit, and proceeded for duty with the 7th D.g.W. Pte Losey R.A.M.C. proceeded to I.B.D. being no longer for a trade test. Brigade Sports were held	J.P.Brockley

Army Form C. 2118.

WAR DIARY
or
INTELLIGENCE SUMMARY.

(Erase heading not required.)

Instructions regarding War Diaries and Intelligence Summaries are contained in F. S. Regs., Part II. and the Staff Manual respectively. Title pages will be prepared in manuscript.

Place	Date	Hour	Summary of Events and Information	Remarks and references to Appendices
MONDICOURT.	19/6/17		Nothing to report. Capt. Randle R.A.M.C. returned from leave.	
do	20/6/17		Capt. Randle struck off strength and proceeded to 10th Sherwoods for duty as M.O. Capt. Laird R.A.M.C. and 6 stretcher squads proceeded to St Nicholas to take over from 103rd Fld Amb. J.P.Mackey	
do	21/6/17		Unit moved by buses from MONDICOURT to ST NICHOLAS at 10 A.M. CAPT. BARCLAY R.A.M.C. RAMC returned from leave and assumed command of the unit. Transport moved night of 21st/22nd to St Nicholas from MONDICOURT. J.P.Mackey	
ST NICHOLAS	22/6/17		On night of 20th/21st June Capt Laird and detachment took over from 103rd F.A. bearer post and A.D.S at H4 & 3, relay post at Hq 6 and car loading post Hq 27 bearers with each R.A.P. parties on squads of 6 bearers with each R.A.P.	Map 51b 1/40000
		5 a.m.	Notification received from Capt Laird that A.D.S. had been mined & shelled. The and he had withdrawn to relay post.	

Place	Date	Hour	Summary of Events and Information	Remarks and references to Appendices
St Nicholas	23/6/17	—	It was hoped arrange that the A.D.S should be moved to H11a'5, in conjunction with 53 Fd Amb. This was done at dusk. No great was left at front	
- do -	24/6/17	6	Cadre post. Nothing to report	W.M. Barclay
- do -	25/6/17		do	W. M. Barclay
do	26/6/17	7am	Bearers relieved at A.D.S etc.	W.M. Barclay
do	27/6/17		Nothing to report.	W.M. Barclay
		11p	Orders received to clear H.S.W. & P and store marquees etc in Hospice de Vieillards, Amac.	W.M. Barclay
- do -	28/6/17	6	Lt Col F.K. Gourlay D.S.O returned from leave Nothing to report.	W.M. Barclay
- do -	29/6/17	5	Bearers relieved at A.D.S etc	W.M. Barclay
- do -	30/6/17		Nothing to report.	W.M. Barclay

COPY   CONFIDENTIAL

RE-INOCULATION WITH T.A.B. VACCINE

1. With a view to minimising the wastage from Typhoid and the Para-Typhoid Fevers this Summer, it has been decided to inoculate all ranks of the Division who have not been inoculated with T.A.B. Vaccine since 30th. November 1916, as verified by entries in A.B.64.

2. Inoculation will be carried out by Brigade Groups on the following days, commencing at 8-30 am :-
    50th. Inf. Brigade   May 30th.
    52nd.   -do-   June 1st.
    51st.   -do-   June 2nd.
All men inoculated will be rested the day after inoculation and given light duty the following day.

3. The inoculations will be carried out under similar arrangements to those made in May 1916 but it will be for Field Ambulance Commanders to decide whether more than one inoculation centre per Brigade Group is required.
    Officers Commanding Field Ambulances will ensure that suitable accommodation is available at the centre, billets being temporarily taken over for the day, or tents erected, whichever is considered more suitable.
    The possibility of bad weather conditions should be borne in mind and alternative accommodation provided.
    The proportion of each battalion to be inoculated is not at the present known but it is thought that with three Medical Officers working and good organisation it will be possible to dispose of a battalion per hour.
    Two companies should therefore arrive every half-hour.

4. Field Ambulance Commanders will arrange direct with their own Brigades all details as regards times and places at which Units have to arrive for inoculation.
    The O.C. 52nd. Field Ambulance will in addition to his own Brigade Group have to arrange for the inoculation of the 7th. Yorks & Lancs Regt.

5. In working out details of procedure, the following points should be borne in mind:-
    a. As there is a shortage of Field Ambulance Medical Officers the services of Regimental Medical Officers should be taken advantage of and not necessarily exclusively with their own battalions.
    b. The names of all men inoculated should be ticked off on the duplicate nominal rolls brought with them, the original being returned to the Unit, and the duplicate retained by the Field Ambulance.
    c. An entry of all inoculations will be made in the mens paybooks A.B.64. This can easily be done as the men file out through a common exit, the Regimental Medical Officer of the Unit being present there to sign the books.
    d. Men who object to being inoculated should be directed to a place set apart for them in order that they may not get mixed up with the others. When the latter have been dealt with, a special mark should be placed opposite the names of objectors on the nominal rolls.
    e. Units have been instructed to parade every available man whether he requires inoculation or not. Paybooks will have to be scrutinised therefore at the inoculation centres and it is suggested that a warrant officer or senior N.C.O. of the Field Ambulance might be detailed for this purpose.

6. Instructions which have been issued through Brigades to Officers Commanding Battalions are attached.

7. Sufficient T.A.B. Vaccine and extra syringes will be obtained and distributed to Field Ambulances from this Office.

8. Officers Commanding Field Ambulances will render a return to this Office by 12 noon on the day following inoculation showing the numbers, by Units, inoculated the previous day.

SD/ H. BARROW

Colonel
A.D.M.S., 17th. Division

27/5/17   No. R.610

G 1285

Lincolns.
Borders.
Staffords.
Sherwoods.
M.G.Coy.
T.M.Batty.
Fld.Amb.
No 3 Coy.Train

INOCULATION

Inoculation of the Brigade will take place as follows, tomorrow June 2nd at H.Q. 51st.Field Ambulance, MONDICOURT.

Staffords.	1 Coy at 9.a.m. 1 Coy at 9.15.a.m. 1 Coy at 9.30.a.m. 1 Coy at 9.45.a.m.
Borders	1 Coy at 10.15.a.m. 1 Coy at 10.30.a.m. 1 Coy at 10.45.a.m. 1 Coy at 11.0.a.m.
Lincolns.	1 Coy at 11.30.a.m. 1 Coy at 11.45.a.m. 1 Coy at 12 noon. 1 Coy at 12.15.p.m.
Sherwoods.	1 Coy at 2.30.p.m. 1 Coy at 2.45.p.m. 1 Coy at 3.0.p.m. 1 Coy at 3.15.p.m.
M.G.Coy T.M.Batty	3.30.p.m.

O.C.51st.Field Ambulance would like the strongest company of each battalion to parade first, i.e. at 9.a.m., 10.15.a.m., 11.30.a.m., and 2.30.p.m.

One half of the Brigade H.Q. will parade at 51st.Field Ambulance at 11.30.a.m. to be inoculated with the 7th.Lincolns. The other half will parade at 3.30.p.m. and will join the M.G.Coy.

No parades (Church or otherwise) will take place either on Sunday June 3rd or Monday June 4th, and only really light duty will be given on Monday.

The M.O.No.3.Coy.Train will make his own arrangements for inoculation.

(Sd) T.P.C.Wilson
Captain,
Staff Captain, 51st.Inf.Brigade.

1.6.17

War Diary 110/298

51st & Field Ambulance

from 1st July to 31st July, 1917.

Volume VI

COMMITTEE FOR THE
MEDICAL HISTORY OF THE WAR
Date 10 SEP.1917

CONFIDENTIAL

Army Form C. 2118.

WAR DIARY
or
INTELLIGENCE SUMMARY.
(Erase heading not required.)

MEDICAL

Place	Date	Hour	Summary of Events and Information	Remarks and references to Appendices
St. Nicholas	1/7		Nothing to report	WBarclay
do	2/7		— do —	WBarclay
do	3/7	7am	Beavis relieved at A.D.S.	
		5pm	Capt J.P. Blockly, R.A.M.C. proceeded to 10th Sherwood for temporary duty vice Capt Q. Randle, sick	WBarclay
do	4/7		Capt H.N. Matthews R.A.M.C. proceeded to 38th Fld Amb Warlin for temporary duty	WBarclay
do	5/7		Nothing to Report	WBarclay
do	6/7		— do —	WBarclay
do	7/7		Beavis relieved at A.D.S.	WBarclay
do	8/7		Nothing to report	WBarclay
do	9/7		— do —	WBarclay
do	10/7		Lt Bunch. W.S.R. posted to 4th Borders for temporary duty	WBarclay

WAR DIARY
or
INTELLIGENCE SUMMARY.
(Erase heading not required.)

Army Form C. 2118.

Place	Date	Hour	Summary of Events and Information	Remarks and references to Appendices
St Nicolas	11/7		Bearers relieved at A.D.S.	
-do-	12/7		Army preceding 6 days work has been carried at the A.D.S. with a view to forming a dressing room and aeroplane shaft. Nothing to report	W/Bare Co. W/Bare Co.
-do-	13/7		Capt W. Bare Co. proceeded on a two-day course to Boulogne for the purpose of studying work at the Special Fracture Hospital & Hot. Hoyomes. No special features to report.	W/Bare Co.
-do-	14/7		Nothing to report.	W/Bare Co.
-do-	15/7		Bearers relieved at A.D.S.	W/Bare Co.
-do-	16/7		Nothing to report	W/Bare Co.
-do-	17/7		-do-	W/Bare Co.
-do-	18/7		-do-	W/Bare Co.

Army Form C. 2118.

WAR DIARY
or
INTELLIGENCE SUMMARY.
(Erase heading not required.)

Instructions regarding War Diaries and Intelligence Summaries are contained in F. S. Regs., Part II. and the Staff Manual respectively. Title pages will be prepared in manuscript.

Place	Date	Hour	Summary of Events and Information	Remarks and references to Appendices
St Nicholas Rly	19/7		Bearers relieved at A.D.S.	W.D. Barcla[y]
-do-	20/7		Nothing to report	W.D. Barcla[y]
-do-	21/7		Nothing to report	W.D. Barcla[y]
-do-	22/7		Nothing to report	W.D. Barcla[y]
-do-	23/7		Bearers relieved at A.D.S.	W.D. Barcla[y]
-do-	24/7	11pm	Lieut H.M. CLUTE U.S.M.C. attached for duty to this unit.	
			Sgt Bellamy sent to 3rd Fd Amb (Corps Rest Stn) to A.A.A.	
			P.M. TOLMIE Ronnie posted for duty to this unit.	
			Oho Thom 10 on Corps interpreter	
-do-	25/7		Went to Poperin[g]. L. Buick returned 8 day work. his unit.	W.D. Barclay
-do-	26/7		Lt Col G.L. Gorrard D.S.O. proceeded on Special leave to the United Kingdom.	
-do-	27/7		Bearers relieved at A.D.S. Lieut Clute proceeded to A.D.S. relar inspection.	W.D. Barclay

Army Form C. 2118.

WAR DIARY
or
INTELLIGENCE SUMMARY.
(Erase heading not required.)

Instructions regarding War Diaries and Intelligence Summaries are contained in F. S. Regs., Part II. and the Staff Manual respectively. Title pages will be prepared in manuscript.

Place	Date	Hour	Summary of Events and Information	Remarks and references to Appendices
St Nicholas	28/7		Nothing to report.	W.M.Barclay
do	29/7		do	W.M.Barclay
do	30/7		do	W.M.Barclay
do	31/7		Bearers relieved at A.D.S.	W.M.Barclay
			During the last work has been in progress with a view to making stables in the field East of the camp. (G.16.d.1.3.) The present horse standings will be untenable in the event of continued wet weather.	W.M.Barclay

CONFIDENTIAL
Vol 23

140/264.

War Diary

of

51st Field Ambulance

from 1-8-17 to 31-8-17

Volume VII

MEDICAL
Aug 17

COMMITTEE FOR THE
MEDICAL HISTORY OF THE WAR
Date -1 OCT 1917

Army Form C. 2118.

WAR DIARY
or
INTELLIGENCE SUMMARY.
(Erase heading not required.)

"MEDICAL"

Place	Date	Hour	Summary of Events and Information	Remarks and references to Appendices
ST NICHOLAS	1/8/17		Lt Col E Gartlad D.S.O. returned from leave to U.K. and resumed command of this unit.	W/Barala
	2/8/17		1st Lt H.M. Clute, U.S.M.C. attached 12th Manchesters for instruction in regimental duties.	W/Barala W/Barala
	3/8/17		Nothing to report	
	4/8/17		Bearers relieved at A.D.S. Capt J.S. Lavrock & Lt Clate proceeded to A.D.S. for duty Capt De Lara proceeded to 9th Duke of Wellg's for temporary duty vice Capt. E.W. Beaumont proceeding on leave.	W/Barala W/Barala
	5/8/17		Nothing to report	W/Barala
	6/8/17		Nothing to report	W/Barala
	7/8/17		do.	W/Barala
	8/8/17		About 5 a.m. Napier Ambulance car (A9379) was hit by a shell at the forward car post on and had to be removed	

Army Form C. 2118.

WAR DIARY
or
INTELLIGENCE SUMMARY.
(Erase heading not required.)

Place	Date	Hour	Summary of Events and Information	Remarks and references to Appendices
ST NICHOLAS	9/5/17	—	to workshop.	W.Baralay
			Bearer relieved at A.D.S.	W.Baralay
			Lieut. L. Scott U.S.M.C. proceeded to 7th Border for duty.	
	10/5/17	—	Nothing to report	W.Baralay
	11/5/17	—	do	W.Baralay
	12/5/17	7am	Bearer relieved at A.R.S.	
		12 noon	A Court of Enquiry assembled at Headquarters to amount of damage done this unit to de ferme. Amb No A 9379. An officer from No 47 Suffolk Amb Ce was in attendance.	W.Baralay
	13/5/17		Nothing to report	W.Baralay
	14/5/17		do	W.Baralay
	15/5/17		do	W.Baralay

WAR DIARY
or
INTELLIGENCE SUMMARY.

(Erase heading not required.)

Army Form C. 2118.

Place	Date	Hour	Summary of Events and Information	Remarks and references to Appendices
S. Marcus	16/2/17		Bearers relieved at A.D.S.	W.J. Barclay
	17/2/17		Nothing to report	W.J. Barclay
	18/2/17		Capt W. Barclay & Capt Dr Lane Raine attended a lecture on "Poison Gas Poisoning" at 3rd Army Gas School, ALBERT.	
	19/2/17		Capt Dr Lane Raine departed on leave to U.K.	W.J. Barclay
	20/2/17		Bearers relieved at A.D.S.	W.J. Barclay
	21/2/17		Nothing to report	W.J. Barclay
	22/2/17		—do—	W.J. Barclay
	23/2/17		—do—	W.J. Barclay
	24/2/17		Bearers relieved at A.D.S.	W.J. Barclay
	25/2/17		Nothing to report	W.J. Barclay
	26/2/17		—do—	W.J. Barclay
	27/2/17		Capt Dr Lane Raine proceeded on leave to U.K. Bearers relieved at A.D.S.	W.J. Barclay
	28/2/17			W.J. Barclay

Army Form C. 2118.

WAR DIARY
or
INTELLIGENCE SUMMARY.
(Erase heading not required.)

Place	Date	Hour	Summary of Events and Information	Remarks and references to Appendices
St Nicholas	22/4/17		Nothing to report.	W.J.Barclay
do	23/4/17		do	W.J.Barclay
do	24/4/17		Nothing to note	W.J.Barclay
			During h month improvements were carried out in the A.D.S (Hill a central map 51B N.W.) ie a drawing room and ward for the reception) cases was built. Improvements were made to the billets occupied by the unit in St Nicholas, and work was carried on with the winter standings for stretchers.	

Instructions regarding War Diaries and Intelligence Summaries are contained in F. S. Regs., Part II. and the Staff Manual respectively. Title pages will be prepared in manuscript.

Confidential

MEDICAL
Vol 24

War Diary

of

51st Field Ambulance.

From: September 1st-17 To: September 30th 1917.

Volume 8.

140/2438

COMMITTEE FOR THE
MEDICAL HISTORY OF THE WAR
Date -5 NOV. 1917

Army Form C. 2118.

MEDICAL

WAR DIARY
or
INTELLIGENCE SUMMARY.
(Erase heading not required.)

Place	Date	Hour	Summary of Events and Information	Remarks and references to Appendices
St NICHOLAS	1/7	—	Capt J.P. Beasley rejoined this unit for duty, for leave U.K.	
	2/7	—	Beasley relieved at A.D.S. Nothing to report	W.Bare Co
	3/7	—	— do —	W.Bare Co
	4/7	—	Lt Col Gifford WMB k D.A.D.M.S reconnoitred an alternative route for A.D.S to Atheis, via Cam Valley. S.M. Dodd proceeded to 19 Div. before Barn. Beasley relieved at A.B.S.	W.Bare Co W.Bare Co
	5/7	—	Nothing to report	
	6/7	—	Capt Da Rana Rowe returned from leave U.K.	W.Bare Co
	7/7	—	Hon Q.M. H.B. Lee Rowe returned from leave. 2 nursing orderlies were sent to 19 C.C.S. for instruction. I was put to Keane work and forwards under numerous dates 10 P.B. Rana rejoined this unit for duty	W.Bare Co

Army Form C. 2118.

WAR DIARY
or
INTELLIGENCE SUMMARY.
(Erase heading not required.)

Instructions regarding War Diaries and Intelligence Summaries are contained in F. S. Regs., Part II. and the Staff Manual respectively. Title pages will be prepared in manuscript.

Place	Date	Hour	Summary of Events and Information	Remarks and references to Appendices
ST NICHOLAS	8.9.17	12 Noon	O.C. 17 Theatre arranged to have 6 stretcher squads at his tentorary post in preparation for a train to take place at 10 p.m.	
		2 p.m.	4 extra squads were sent to Tank Dump A.D.S. Capt J.S. Keen proceeded to A.D.S. for temporary duty making no W.T.Base a/c	
			affairs in during train	W.T.Base a/c
	9.17		During the night there were 30 wounded passed through the A.D.S. including 21 stretcher cases	
do		7am	The trains were relieved at A.D.S.	W.T.Base a/c
do	10.17		2 mac worning orderlies were sent to No 19 C.C.S. for instruction.	W.T.Base a/c
do	11.17	9am	8 A.S.C. Batmen were despatched Base HT Depot, HAVRE. Nothing to report	W.T.Base a/c
do	12.17	—	Nothing to report	W.T.Base a/c
do	13.17	10am	Bearers relieved at A.D.S.	W.T.Base a/c
do	14.17	—	17th Lieut. U.S.R. proceeded to X" Corps Rest Stn for duty via Le HN Matteo via Roly. Capt J.S. From out to HN Diemero proceeded on leave to U.K. via Base etc	W.T.Base a/c

Army Form C. 2118.

WAR DIARY
or
INTELLIGENCE SUMMARY.
(Erase heading not required.)

Instructions regarding War Diaries and Intelligence Summaries are contained in F.S. Regs., Part II. and the Staff Manual respectively. Title pages will be prepared in manuscript.

Place	Date	Hour	Summary of Events and Information	Remarks and references to Appendices
ST NICHOLAS	15/7	6p	Capt. J.A. Bath. U.S. M.O. joined HQ went for duty	W.P.Barrelay
do	16/7	2p	to the opposite was sent to A.D.S. Tank Dump for temporary duty	
		6pm	Capt J.P. Blackley RAMC proceeded to 6th DORSETS for duty vice Capt Hallperstik who is for the moment performing duty.	W.P.Barrelay
do	17/7	-	During the night of 16/17th & the 12th Manchesters made a raid. Casualties were cleared quickly and without noise, 6 squads being put under charge of N.C.O's Stretcher bearers for this purpose.	
		11p	Capt D.A. Laura RAMC proceeded to RAMC Depot Blackpool for disposal to India and Mesopotamia, and was struck off the strength.	W.P.Barrelay
do	18/7	-	Nothing to report	W.P.Barrelay
do	19/7	-	— do —	W.P.Barrelay

Army Form C. 2118.

WAR DIARY
or
INTELLIGENCE SUMMARY.
(Erase heading not required.)

Instructions regarding War Diaries and Intelligence Summaries are contained in F. S. Regs., Part II. and the Staff Manual respectively. Title pages will be prepared in manuscript.

Place	Date	Hour	Summary of Events and Information	Remarks and references to Appendices
ST NICHOLAS	20/9/17	2p.	The O.C. and 2 officers 57 1/2 Sd. Ambd. and 7d. Amb. inspected the headquarters and ADS of this unit with a view to taking over same.	
	21/9/17	9a.	Lt. Pr. Tolmie, R.A.M.C. reported to this unit for duty.	W/Sage Day
	22/9/17		Nothing to report.	W/Sage Day W/Sage Day
	23/9/17	4p.	The personnel of R.A.O.S. and baggage pt. was relieved by 57 1/2 Sd. Ind. Fd. Amb.; also the Cor at of formed post.	
	24/9/17	—	Capt. W. Barclay. M.C. R.A.M.C. proceeded on leave to the U. Kingdom.	
		—	This unit was relieved at St. NICHOLAS (ARRAS) by 9th S.M. Fd. Amb.	
		—	This unit proceeded to SIMENCOURT.	
SIMENCOURT	24/9/17	11.30am	Arrived SIMENCOURT. Personnel marched well.	Herron Capt. Herron Capt.
	25/9/17	4pm	Nothing to Report.	Herron Capt. Herron Capt.

Army Form C. 2118.

WAR DIARY
or
INTELLIGENCE SUMMARY.
(Erase heading not required.)

Place	Date	Hour	Summary of Events and Information	Remarks and references to Appendices
SIMENCOURT	26/9/17	9 am	Left SIMENCOURT marched to GRAND RULLICOURT. 14 men of this Brigade (51st) were picked up on the line of march, + 41 men were sent to their unit, unable to do the march. JHewis Capt	
	27/9/17	—	Nothing to report. JHewis Capt	
	28/9/17	—	Nothing to report. JHewis Capt	
	29/9/17	—	LIEUT P.M. TOLMIE RAMC proceeded to the United Kingdom on leave. JHewis Capt	
	30/9/17	4 PM	Medical Inspection of P.B. Officers N.C.O.s + men of 51st Brigade. JHewis Capt by A.D.M.S, D.A.D.M.S + Lieut Col Gourland D.I.O R.A.M.C. JHewis Capt	

CONFIDENTIAL

War Diary

of

51st Field Ambulance.

October 1st 1917 — October 31st 1917.

Volume. 9.

COMMITTEE FOR THE
MEDICAL HISTORY OF THE WAR
Date —8 DEC. 1917

B.E.F.

SUMMARY OF MEDICAL WAR DIARIES FOR

51st F.A., 17th Divn. 14th Corps, 5th Army.

19th Corps from 20/10/17.

2nd Corps from 29/10/17.

18th Corps from 2/11/17.

19th Corps from 8/11/17.

2nd Army from 14/11/17.

―――――

WESTERN FRONT Oct.– Nov. 1917.

―――

O.C. Lt. Col. E. Gowlland.

SUMMARISED UNDER THE FOLLOWING HEADINGS.

Phase "D" 1. Passchendaele Operations July–Dec. 1917.

    (b) Operations commencing 1/10/17.
        Canadians attacked Passchendaele Oct. 30th
        Canadians took Passchendaele Nov. 6th.

―――――

B.E.F. 1.

51st F.A., 17th Divn. 14th Corps, 5th Army. WESTERN FRONT

O.C. Lt. Col. E. Gowlland.   Oct. '17.

19th Corps from 20/10/17.

Phase "D" 1. Passchendaele Operations July-Dec. 1917.

(b) Operations commencing 1/10/17.
Canadians attacked Passchendaele Oct. 30th.
Canadians took Passchendaele Nov. 6th.

1917.	Headquarters. At Singapore Camp St. Sixte.
Oct. 4th.	Moves and Transfer. Unit transferred with 17th Divn. from 7th Corps, 3rd Army to 14th Corps, 5th Army, and moved to Singapore Camp St. Sixte.
6th.	Moves Detachment. O and 70 to Canada Farm A.18.a.1.8. (Sheet 28)
7th.	Moves Detachment. O and 4 to 17th Divn. Depot Batt.
8th.	Moves. To Canada Farm and took over C.M.D.S.
13th.	Moves: Medical Arrangements. To Solferino Farm Adv. C.M.D.S. taken over from 10th Field Ambulance.
14th.	Operations Enemy: Casualties. Hostile aircraft bombed camps around Adv. C.M.D.S. Causing about 80 casualties.
18th.	Operations Enemy. Hostile aircraft again bombed surrounding camps.
20th.	Transfer. To 19th Corps.

51st F.A., 17th Divn. 19th Corps. WESTERN FRONT.

O.C. Lt. Col. E. Gowlland. Oct. 1917.

5th Army.

2nd Corps from 29/10/17.

Phase "D" 1. Passchendaele Operations July-Dec. 1917.

    (b) Operations commencing 1/10/17.
        Canadians attacked Passchendaele Oct. 30th.
        Canadians took Passchendaele Nov. 6th.

1917.	Headquarters. Solferino Farm.
Oct. 20th.	Transfer. To 19th Corps.
29th.	Transfer. To 2nd Corps with 17th Divn.

B.E.F. 3.

<u>51st F.A., 17th Divn. 2nd Corps.</u>   <u>WESTERN FRONT.</u>
<u>O.C. Lt. Col. E. Gowlland.</u>   <u>Oct.- Nov. 1917.</u>
<u>5th Army.</u>
<u>18th Corps from 2/11/17.</u>

<u>Phase "D" 1. Passchendaele Operations July-Dec. 1917.</u>

    (b) Operations commencing 1/10/17.
        Canadians attacked Passchendaele Oct. 30th.
        Canadians took Passchendaele Nov. 6th.

1917.	<u>Headquarters.</u>	Solferine Farm.
Oct. 29th.	<u>Transfer.</u>	To 2nd Corps with 17th Divn.
Nov. 2nd.	<u>Transfer.</u>	To 18th Corps with 17th Divn.

B.E.F.

51st F.A., 17th Divn. 14th Corps, 5th Army. WESTERN FRONT

O.C. Lt. Col. E. Gowlland.　　　　　　　　　　Oct. '17.

19th Corps from 20/10/17.

Phase "D" 1. Passchendaele Operations July-Dec. 1917.

　　(b) Operations commencing 1/10/17.
　　　　Canadians attacked Passchendaele Oct. 30th.
　　　　Canadians took Passchendaele Nov. 6th.

1917.	Headquarters. At Singapore Camp St. Sixte.
Oct. 4th.	Moves and Transfer. Unit transferred with 17th Divn. from 7th Corps, 3rd Army to 14th Corps, 5th Army, and moved to Singapore Camp St. Sixte.
6th.	Moves Detachment. O and 70 to Canada Farm A.18.a.1.8. (Sheet 28)
7th.	Moves Detachment. O and 4 to 17th Divn. Depot Batt.
8th.	Moves. To Canada Farm and took over C.M.D.S.
13th.	Moves: Medical Arrangements. To Solferino Farm Adv. C.M.D.S. taken over from 10th Field Ambulance.
14th.	Operations Enemy: Casualties. Hostile aircraft bombed camps around Adv. C.M.D.S. Causing about 80 casualties.
18th.	Operations Enemy. Hostile aircraft again bombed surrounding camps.
20th.	Transfer. To 19th Corps.

51st F.A., 17th Divn. 10th Corps.   WESTERN FRONT.

O.C. Lt. Col. E. Gowlland.   Oct. 1917.

5th Army.

2nd Corps from 29/10/17.

Phase "D" 1. Passchendaele Operations July-Dec. 1917.

   (b) Operations commencing 1/10/17.
       Canadians attacked Passchendaele Oct. 30th.
       Canadians took Passchendaele Nov. 6th.

1917.	Headquarters.	Solferino Farm.
Oct. 20th.	Transfer.	To 19th Corps.
29th.	Transfer.	To 2nd Corps with 17th Divn.

WAR DIARY
or
INTELLIGENCE SUMMARY.
(Erase heading not required.)

Army Form C. 2118.

MEDICAL ①

Place	Date	Hour	Summary of Events and Information	Remarks and references to Appendices
G.A. RULLICOURT	1/10/17	—	C.O. proceeded to E.G.A.W. on leave	
"	2/10/17	—	with 1 officer *Stew*	
"	2/10/17	—	Capt HERPLEWHITE + 3 O.R. proceeded to PROVEN as billeting party *Stew*	
"	3/10/17	—	51st Field Ambulance entrained at MONDICOURT for PROVEN *officers Stew*	
"	4/10/17	—	Arrived at PROVEN at 10 noon + proceeded to SINGAPORE Camp ST SIXTE	
PROVEN	5/10/17	—	Working to report *officers Stew*	
"	6/10/17	—	Working to report *officers Stew* 70 O.R. proceed to CANADA FARM $A.18 & 2.18 (B21 28/7) *Stew*	
"	7/10/17	10a	Capt W. BARR Co. returned from leave and assumed command of unit.	
"	"	2p.	Capt BATIN M.O. R.C. U.S.A. and 4 O.R. proceeded to 17 Div for duty.	
"	"	"	Capt BARR MO attached POLEZEELE for duty. 10 O.R. proceeded to RV Camp POPERINGHE for duty.	
"	"	1.30p	OC and 3 officers proceeded to CANADA FARM to interview OC No 10 F.A. with a view to taking over CANADA FARM as advance	W.J. BARR Capt
CANADA FARM	8/10/17	10a.	2 officers and 6 OR proceeded to CANADA FARM as advance	W.J. BARR Capt
"	"	2p.	2 officers proceeded to SOLFERINO FARM for duty remainder of unit marched for CANADA FARM arrived 4pm Comm.	W.J. BARR Capt

Army Form C. 2118.

WAR DIARY
or
INTELLIGENCE SUMMARY.
(Erase heading not required.)

Place	Date	Hour	Summary of Events and Information	Remarks and references to Appendices
CANADA FARM	9/7/17	9a.	20 O.R. proceeded to SOLFERINO FARM	
		6p.	3 Officers and 60 O.R. proceeded to SOLFERINO FARM for night duty at X Corps Adv. Dressing Station (No 10 F.A. A.D.S.)	W. Baradon
-do-	10/7	8a.	During the night of the 9/10 the 52nd and 53rd Field Ambulances were evacuated at CANADA FARM. 20 O.R. proceeded to SOLFERINO FARM for day duty.	
-do-	11/7	6p.	18 Officers and 31 O.R. proceeded to SOLFERINO FARM for night duty.	W. Baradon
-do-	12/7	—	Nothing to report.	W. Baradon
		8a.	Capt. W.G.T. Applewhite R.A.M.C. departed for England on expiration of contract.	W. Baradon
		8p.	60 1 Officer and 0 OR reported to No 10 Fd Amb. Solferino Farm for night duty.	W. Baradon
SOLFERINO FARM	13/7	8p.	51st 3rd Fd. Amb. relieved No 10 Fd Amb. at SOLFERINO FARM XIV Corps Main Advanced Dressing Station.	W. Baradon

WAR DIARY
or
INTELLIGENCE SUMMARY.
(Erase heading not required.)

Army Form C. 2118.

Place	Date	Hour	Summary of Events and Information	Remarks and references to Appendices
PERINO 14 FARM	14/9	11.15a	The O.C. V Corps. and Surgeon of D.M.S. V Corps accompanied by D.D.M.S. XIV Corps. visited this	
		noon	draw station. A number of doubled arcs put, tented the camps around this station. Casualty about 80 admissions.	
		4.30p	The A.D.M.S. 17 Divn. visited this dressing station.	
		6p.m	St Davis. U.S.M.O.R.C. returned for duty to 52 C.C.S.	W.P.Barclay
	15/9	—	Nothing to report.	W.P.Barclay
	16/9	—	Nothing to report.	W.P.Barclay
	17/9	3p	Stge Sgt A.O.R. on leave any any with 53 Fd Amb returned to the unit.	
		9.10.a.m	Pte A/Cear returned to unit this day.	
		1p	Lt. Col. E.R. Rowland S.S.O. returned from leave to United Kingdom	W.P.Barclay

Army Form C. 2118.

WAR DIARY
or
INTELLIGENCE SUMMARY
(Erase heading not required.)

Place	Date	Hour	Summary of Events and Information	Remarks and references to Appendices
St. FERINO FARM	18/10/17	—	2 O.R. (clerks) arrived for temporary duty from 53rd Tr. Mtr. Battle aircraft started surrounding camps and barracks	W.P. Barclay
do	19/10/17	11 a.m.	2. P.M. 2 Lieut. Rawe returned from leave 6 U.K.	W.P. Barclay
do	20/10/17		2. BB. 2 Lieut. Osmore was posted for temporary duty with this unit.	W.P. Barclay
do	21/10/17		Nothing to report	W.P. Barclay
do	22/10/17		A busy day as a result of attack on Corps front	W.P. Barclay
do	23/10/17		A wireless hut has been erected and furnished as a orderly room for use at night, to obviate the inconvenience caused when hostile aircraft are in the vicinity.	W.P. Barclay
do	24/10/17		Nothing to report	W.P. Barclay

WAR DIARY
or
INTELLIGENCE SUMMARY
(Erase heading not required.)

Army Form C. 2118.

Place	Date	Hour	Summary of Events and Information	Remarks and references to Appendices
SOLFERINO FARM	25/10/17		6 marquees were blown down by gale during the night. W.W.Barclay	
-do-	26/10/17		Nothing to report. W.W.Barclay	
-do-	27/10/17		Nothing to report. W.W.Barclay	
-do-	28/10/17	1pm	A.D.M.S. 1st Div. visited the Dressing Station. W.W.Barclay	
-do-	29/10/17		Nothing to report. W.W.Barclay	
-do-	30/10/17		D.D.M.S. 19 tCorps visited this A.D.S. and informed O.C. that 19 tCorps had taken over from 14 t. W.W.Barclay	
-do-	31/7		Nothing to report. W.W.Barclay	

CONFIDENTIAL

WAR DIARY

OF

51st FIELD AMBULANCE

From Nov. 1st To. Nov. 30th.

VOLUME 10

COMMITTEE FOR THE
MEDICAL HISTORY OF THE WAR
Date 17 JAN. 1918

B.E.F.

SUMMARY OF MEDICAL WAR DIARIES FOR

51st F.A., 17th Divn. 14th Corps, 5th Army.

19th Corps from 20/10/17.

2nd Corps from 29/10/17.

18th Corps from 2/11/17.

19th Corps from 8/11/17.

2nd Army from 14/11/17.

WESTERN FRONT Oct.- Nov. 1917.

O.C. Lt. Col. E. Gowlland.

SUMMARISED UNDER THE FOLLOWING HEADINGS.

Phase "D" 1. Passchendaele Operations July-Dec. 1917.

(b) Operations commencing 1/10/17.
Canadians attacked Passchendaele Oct. 30th
Canadians took Passchendaele Nov. 6th.

51st F.A., 17th Divn. 18th Corps.   WESTERN FRONT.
O.C. Lt. Col. E. Gowlland.   Nov. 1917.
5th Army.
19th Corps from 8/11/17.

Phase "D" 1. Passchendaele Operations July-Dec. 1917.

       (b) Operations commencing 1/10/17.
           Canadians attacked Passchendaele Oct. 30th.
           Canadians took Passchendaele Nov. 6th.

1917.	Headquarters. At Solferine Farm.
Nov. 2nd.	Transfer. To 18th Corps with 17th Divn.
7th.	Medical Arrangements. C.M.D.S. handed over to 52nd Field Ambulance..
	Moves Detachment. 2 and 18 stretcher squads to 53rd Field Ambulance Pelissier Farm.
8th.	Moves and Transfer. To Proven (19th Corps) and took over 19th Corps Aux. R.S. from 3/2nd W. Lancs. F.A.

B.E.F. 5.

51st F.A., 17th Divn. 19th Corps.   WESTERN FRONT.

O.C. Lt. Col. E. Gowlland.   Nov. 1917.

5th Army.

2nd Army from 14/11/17.

Phase "D" 1. Passchendaele Operations July-Dec. 1917.

    (b) Operations commencing 1/10/17.
        Canadians attacked Passchendaele Oct. 30th.
        Canadians took Passchendaele Nov. 6th.

1917.   Headquarters. At Proven.

Nov. 8th.   Moves and Transfer. To Proven (19th Corps) and took over 19th Corps Aux. R.S. from 3/2nd W. Lancs. F.A.

14th.   Transfer. Unit transferred with 17th Divn. and 19th Corps to 2nd Army.

51st F.A., 17th Divn. 18th Corps.   WESTERN FRONT.

O.C. Lt. Col. E. Gowlland.   Nov. 1917.

5th Army.

19th Corps from 8/11/17.

Phase "D" 1. Passchendaele Operations July-Dec. 1917.

(b) Operations commencing 1/10/17.
Canadians attacked Passchendaele Oct. 30th.
Canadians took Passchendaele Nov. 6th.

1917.	Headquarters. At Solferine Farm.
Nov. 2nd.	Transfer. To 18th Corps with 17th Divn.
7th.	Medical Arrangements. C.M.D.S. handed over to 52nd Field Ambulance.
	Moves Detachment. 2 and 18 stretcher squads to 53rd Field Ambulance Pelissier Farm.
8th.	Moves and Transfer. To Proven (19th Corps) and took over 19th Corps Aux. R.S. from 2/2nd W. Lancs. F.A.

B.E.F.   5.

51st F.A., 17th Divn. 19th Corps.   WESTERN FRONT.

O.C. Lt. Col. E. Gowlland.   Nov. 1917.

5th Army.

2nd Army from 14/11/17.

Phase "D" 1. Passchendaele Operations July-Dec. 1917.

    (b) Operations commencing 1/10/17.
        Canadians attacked Passchendaele Oct. 30th.
        Canadians took Passchendaele Nov. 8th.

1917.	Headquarters. At Proven.
Nov. 8th.	Moves and Transfer. To Proven (19th Corps) and took over 19th Corps Aux R.S. from 3/2nd W. Lancs. F.A.
14th.	Transfer. Unit transferred with 17th Divn. and 19th Corps to 2nd Army.

Army Form C. 2118.

MEDICAL

WAR DIARY
or
INTELLIGENCE SUMMARY
(Erase heading not required.)

Instructions regarding War Diaries and Intelligence Summaries are contained in F.S. Regs., Part II. and the Staff Manual respectively. Title Pages will be prepared in manuscript.

Place	Date	Hour	Summary of Events and Information	Remarks and references to Appendices
SOLFERINO FARM	1/11/17	—	Nothing to report	W.S. Barclay Capt
do	2/11/17	11:30 am	D.D.M.S. 19th Corps visited this Dressing Station	W.S. Barclay Capt
do	3/11/17		O.C. 51st Fld Amb. was summoned by wire to meet A.D.M.S. 17th Divn at ZUYTKERKE	
			Lt H.M. Clune U.S.M.R.C. proceeded on leave to United Kingdom 7/days	W.S. Barclay Capt
do	4/11/17	2 am	J.W. Lester R.A.M.C. joined this unit for duty	W.S. Barclay Capt
do	5/11/17	1 pm	17th Divn R.A.M.C. O.O. 51 to 57 received	Enno Gaskond Lieut Col R.A.M.C.
	6/11/17		Nothing to report	
	7/11/17	4 p.m.	52nd Field Ambulance arrived at SOLFERINO FARM and take over XIX Corps Main Dressing Station from this Unit.	
		6 p.m.	Capt W. BARCLAY M.C. and Lieut H.N. MATTHEWS R.A.M.C. with 18 stretcher Squads report to O.C. 52nd Field Ambulance PELISSIER FARM for Duty. Lieuts DRANE & TILLERY U.S.R.M.C. 7/from 52nd Field Ambulance.	Enno Gaskond Lieut Col R.A.M.C.

Wt. W14957/M90 750,000 1/16 J.B.C. & A. Forms/C.2118/12.

Army Form C. 2118.

WAR DIARY
or
INTELLIGENCE SUMMARY
5/2½ Field Ambulance
(Erase heading not required.)

Place	Date 1917 Nov.	Hour	Summary of Events and Information	Remarks and references to Appendices
PROVEN	8th		Tent Division of this Unit proceed to Proven and take over the XIX Corps Auxiliary Rest Station from 3/2 West Lanc. Fd Amb. Bill No	
"	9th		Nothing to report	
"	10th		Lieut TOLMIE detailed to visit HQ + the 3 companies 17 Div¹ Train Daily whilst they are in this area, and supervise the sanitation of camps.	
"	11th		D.D.M.S. XIX Corps called inspected Hospital, and site for Convalescent Camp.	
"	12th		Nothing to report	
"	13th		" "	
			Capt. BATTIN U.S.R.M.C. returned to duty with this Unit from No 47. C.C.S.	
			Colonel S. MAYNARD-SMITH Consulting Surgeon Fifth Army called	

Edward Ironside
Lieut Col R.A.M.C.

Army Form C. 2118.

WAR DIARY
or
INTELLIGENCE SUMMARY

(Erase heading not required.)

Instructions regarding War Diaries and Intelligence Summaries are contained in F. S. Regs., Part II. and the Staff Manual respectively. Title Pages will be prepared in manuscript.

Place	Date 1917	Hour	Summary of Events and Information	Remarks and references to Appendices
PROVEN	Nov. 14th		Nothing to report	
	15th		A.D.M.S. 17 Div. visited Rest. Station & inspected Convalescent Camp	
	16th		Capt. J.A. BATTIN M.O.R.C., U.S.A. & 1 O.R. ordered to report to A.D.M.S. 7th Div.	
	17th		Nothing to report	
	18th		" " "	
	19th		" " "	
	20th		LIEUT. TOLMIE R.A.M.C. reports to O.C. 53rd Field Ambulance for temporary duty	
	21st		One Corporal and five stretcher Bearers wounded at duty near "CEMENT HOUSE"	
	22nd		17 O.R. gassed (wounded) Enemy shell; & were evacuated to C.C.S.	
	23rd		Nothing to report	
	24th		" " "	
	25th		" " "	
	26th		" " "	
	27th		R.S.M. DODD R.A.M.C. returned to Duty from 17 Div. Depot. Bn.	
	28th		Sergt. HANCOCK A.S.C. sent to ABBEVILLE for course of instruction in Transport Duties.	
	29th			
	30th		Capt. M.E. GORMAN R.A.M.C. returned to this Unit for Duty	

Edward Rowland
Lt. Col. R.A.M.C.

CONFIDENTIAL

WAR DIARY

OF

51st FIELD AMBULANCE

From Dec^{br} 1st To Dec^{br} 31st

VOLUME II

COMMITTEE FOR THE
MEDICAL HISTORY OF THE WAR
Date. -1 FEB. 1918

Army Form C. 2118.

WAR DIARY
or
INTELLIGENCE SUMMARY
(Erase heading not required.)

MEDICAL

Instructions regarding War Diaries and Intelligence Summaries are contained in F. S. Regs., Part II and Staff Manual respectively. Title Pages will be prepared in manuscript.

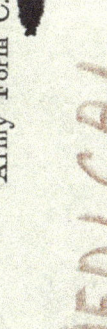

Place	Date	Hour	Summary of Events and Information	Remarks and references to Appendices
PROVEN	1/12/17		Nothing to note	
	2/12/17		Lt Tolmie R.A.M.C. proceeded to 9th D.T.W. for Carpentry duty	
	3/12/17		Nothing to note	
	4/12/17		Nothing to note	
	5/12/17		Nothing to note	
	6/12/17		Beaver division returned from 53rd Fd Amb.	csy Bara Ca
	7/12/17		Nothing to note	
			Lt Matthews R.A.M.C. proceed to 6 Forces to take up Sup Bara Ca duties — do — 7 Cyphs — do —	csy Bara Ca csy Bara Ca
	8/12/17		Nothing to note	csy Bara Ca
	9/12/17		Nothing to note	csy Bara Ca

Army Form C. 2118.

WAR DIARY
or
INTELLIGENCE SUMMARY.
(Erase heading not required.)

Instructions regarding War Diaries and Intelligence Summaries are contained in F. S. Regs., Part II. and the Staff Manual respectively. Title pages will be prepared in manuscript.

Place	Date	Hour	Summary of Events and Information	Remarks and references to Appendices
PROVEN	10/9/17	—	Nothing to note	W/T Barraclay
–do–	11/9/17		do	W/T Barraclay
MONNECOVE	12/9/17	7am.	Gr. relief by 106th Fd. Amb. diversion personnel. This unit proceeded to MONNECOVE by lorry arriving at noon.	
		8am.	Transport proceeded en route for MONNECOVE	W/T Barraclay
–do–	13/9/17	1pm.	Transport arrived at MONNECOVE. Warning order received for 5/3 By Bde to be ready. Unit in at WIZERNES	
		11am.		W/T Barraclay
	14/9/17	5.30pm.	Transport proceeded to WIZERNES to entrain.	
		8pm.	Dismounted personnel to do	W/T Barraclay
	15/9/17	4pm.	Entrainment was complete by 3am. and train started at 4 noon	
		noon	Unit detrained at BARAUNE and marched to BARASTRE arriving at Camp O.16.D at 4.15p.	W/T Barraclay

WAR DIARY
or
INTELLIGENCE SUMMARY
(Erase heading not required.)

Army Form C.2118.

Place	Date	Hour	Summary of Events and Information	Remarks and references to Appendices
BARASTRE	16/7/17		2/Lt E. Gosford R.A.M.C. proceeded on special leave to United Kingdom	
- do -	17/7/17		Notification received that division was in Army Reserve and at 2 hours notice. Nothing to report.	C.W.Barada C.S.W.Barada
- do -	18/7/17		Nothing to report	C.W.Barada C.S.W.Barada
- do -	19/7/17		Capt Barada with A.D.M.S. 17th Div. inspected A.D.S. and system of evacuation of wounded of 59 Brig. Capt J.S. Livin and Capt R.E. Jones carried on the one in Pairs	C.W.Barada C.S.W.Barada
- do -	20/7/17		A.H.R. Lee proceeded on leave to U.K. Lt Wiseman, 57th Fd Amb. reported for duty. This unit took over from 59th Div. (2/2 no Midland Fd Amb) Beaver Post at FLESQUIÈRES (+ 15 OR)	
- do -	21/7/17		(1) A.D.S. + Beaver Post at FLESQUIÈRES (+ 15 OR) (2) A.D.S. at RIBECOURT (1 M.D. 15 OR)	

WAR DIARY
INTELLIGENCE SUMMARY.
(Erase heading not required.)

Army Form C. 2118.

Place	Date	Hour	Summary of Events and Information	Remarks and references to Appendices
			(3) A.D.S at HAVRINCOURT (1 M.O. 15 O.R)	
			(4) N.W.C.P. at TRESCAULT (1 M.O. 9 O.R)	
			The nights previously to 22 proceed from the	
			S/B deans R.A.Ps Kings HAVRINCOURT A.D.S to	
			V.C.M.D.S by car or train at RUYALCOURT:	
			from the night Brigade Kings A.D.S FLESQUIERES and	
			RIBECOURT by car to V.C.M.D.S.	
			from TRESCAULT by car or train to V.C.M.D.S	
			Cars run Rgt at FLESQUIERES & one at RIBECOURT	
			But HAVRINCOURT with the unit US Bar Co	
			Lt Toulmie returned to duty with Q.Im.C.S.S. (Aux 57e) in relief.	
METZ	22/11/17	9a	Headquarters moved to RIBECOURT for duty.	
		1.27p	No MID. Fd. AMB.	
			Capt the Lt TOULMIE proceeded to RIBECOURT for duty	
			Capt. R. E. Gowa moved to FLESQUIERES	
			2 Officers and 58 O.R. Rear Det. 32nd field Amb	
		4.30p	of Troops reported for duty US Bar Co	

WAR DIARY
or
INTELLIGENCE SUMMARY.
(Erase heading not required.)

Army Form C.2118.

Place	Date	Hour	Summary of Events and Information	Remarks and references to Appendices
METZ	23/12/17	—	Nothing to report.	W. Bare Coy
-do-	24/12/17		A.D.M.S. 17th Div. inspected a proposed A.D.S at CHALK PITS, HAVRINCOURT	W. Bare Coy
-do-	25/12/17		It was impossible to do much towards entertaining the personnel of this unit, but each detached Body of bearers etc. made the best of things and spent a moderately enjoyable Christmas.	W. Bare Coy
	26/12/17		A.D.M.S. 17th Div. inspected RAPs and A.D.S. in right sector.	W. Bare Coy
-do-	27/12/17	10.30am	The whole of the Bearer Divn. 51st & 52nd F.A.s. in the line by Kent of FRESNOIRES and Lt DRANE to HARMIGNIES proceeded to relief of Capt. G. ma and Lt WISEMAN on departure on Capt. J.C. Jackson. 27 Base Hosp. US army reported for instruction.	Capt. Baker W. Bare Coy
-do-	28/12/17		Nothing to report	W. Bare Coy

WAR DIARY
or
INTELLIGENCE SUMMARY.

(Erase heading not required.)

Army Form C. 2118.

Place	Date	Hour	Summary of Events and Information	Remarks and references to Appendices
M.S. 2	29/7/17		Rothery Capt Simpson, USMORC proceeded to HAVRINCOURT for maturation W. Barcelar	
do	30/7/17		Lt Toumie relieved at RIBECOURT. Return reader to be an A.D.S. and is being held as a cav. post. Lt Toumie proceeded to 7th F.A.B. for duty W. Barcelar	
do	31/7/17		Lt MATTHEWS returned to the unit from 6th Brokes Lt SENTER, R.A.M.C. returned to the unit from 7 F. Yorks. Reconnaissance of 2nd Div system of evacuation carried out by A.D.M.S. 17th Div. and O.C. 9th Fd Amb. W. Barcelar	

MEDICAL

CONFIDENTIAL

War Diary

Of

51st Field Ambulance

From January 1st 1918 To January 31st 1918.

Volume 12.

MEDICAL

Army Form C. 2118.

WAR DIARY
or
INTELLIGENCE SUMMARY.
(Erase heading not required.)

Instructions regarding War Diaries and Intelligence Summaries are contained in F. S. Regs., Part II. and the Staff Manual respectively. Title pages will be prepared in manuscript.

Place	Date	Hour	Summary of Events and Information	Remarks and references to Appendices
METZ	1/8	—	Nothing to report	W.R.Banks
do -	2/8		Recces at HARRINCOURT A.D.S. were relieved.	W.R.Banks
do	3/8		A portion of 2nd Div. Troops were taken over by 17th Div. It was arranged that cases should be cleared to A.D.S. Havrincourt.	W.R.Banks
do	4/8		Personnel at FLESQUIERES and RIBECOURT relieved.	W.R.Banks
do	5/8		Personnel of 52nd F.Amb. Rear Div. proceeded by lorry from Roclincourt to HERMIES to report to A.D.S.	W.R.Banks
VELU	6/8	10a.	Headquarters of this unit moved from Q.14.c.5.8. to P.1.c.9.9. (map 57D), & relief by 6th London Fd. Amb. and took over.	W.R.Banks
		11.30	Camp occupied by 105th Fd. Amb. Rear Div. 53rd F. Amb. joined this unit for duty.	W.R.Banks
- do -	7/8		Nothing to note	W.R.Banks
—	8/8		— do —	W.R.Banks
—	9/8		— do —	W.R.Banks

Army Form C. 2118.

WAR DIARY
or
INTELLIGENCE SUMMARY.
(Erase heading not required.)

Instructions regarding War Diaries and Intelligence Summaries are contained in F. S. Regs., Part II. and the Staff Manual respectively. Title pages will be prepared in manuscript.

Place	Date	Hour	Summary of Events and Information	Remarks and references to Appendices
VELU	10/6	—	Working party of 1 it ER & 33rd the are proceeded to A.D.S. Haminicourt for duty at new A.D.S. Clock Pub. C.W.Barnes Ca	
"	11/6		Near of scene division 35. 7th ans reconnoitred the afternoon & evacuation. Beacon w—Cayl sector of the Canal Bank and Chinese Wall of relieved. C.W.Barnes Ca	
"	12/6		A large car was taken up to the Canal du Nord at dusk and visited at Relay Post at Kisa Or. Hee 19th. This is a excellent way of evacuating cases from left flanque to Hennois. C.W.Barnes Ca	
"	13/6		Lt R. DEANE 59th Fd Amb. proceeded for mptn duty to 15th W. Yorks via Corps Divl. Hamlin, D.S.O. C.W.Barnes Ca	
"	14/6		Officers and O.R. at A.D.S. Haminicourt were relieved from H.Q. C.W.Barnes Ca	

Army Form C. 2118.

WAR DIARY
or
INTELLIGENCE SUMMARY.
(Erase heading not required.)

Place	Date	Hour	Summary of Events and Information	Remarks and references to Appendices
VELU	[1918]	—	Capt. Z.B. ADAMS and G. FAY, U.S.M.O.R.C. were attached for temporary duty as Chaplains. They proceeded to HAVRINCOURT and HERMIES A.D.Ss. respectively and were nominated to the works of A.D.S., R.A.P. and bearer work. W.P. Barrett	
do	15/12		nothing to report	
do	16/12		Capts. ADAMS and FAY returned to H.Q. Lt MATTHEWS relieved proceeded to A.D.S. Hermies for duty vice Lt SENTER. W.P. Barrett	
do	17/12		Capts. ADAMS and FAY USMORC proceeded to regain their units. Acason in Capt. Cector relieved Lt Col F.L. GOWLAND DSO returned from leave to UK. W.P. Barrett	
do	18/12	10 a	Lt WISEMAN sent to AMB proceeded to regain his unit.	

Army Form C. 2118.

WAR DIARY
or
INTELLIGENCE SUMMARY.
(Erase heading not required.)

Instructions regarding War Diaries and Intelligence Summaries are contained in F. S. Regs., Part II. and the Staff Manual respectively. Title pages will be prepared in manuscript.

Place	Date	Hour	Summary of Events and Information	Remarks and references to Appendices
VF-W	18/8		Capt. Taylor U.S.M.O.R.C. joined this unit for temp. duty from 52nd Fd Amb. W.Barclay	
-do-	19/8		Capt. Taylor U.S.M.O.R.C. proceeded to A.D.S. Havrincourt for duty. W.Barclay	
-do-	20/8		Nothing to note W.Barclay	
-do-	21/8		Nothing to note W.Barclay	
-do-	22/8		Nothing to note W.Barclay	
-do-	23/8		Lt J.S. Senter R.A.M.C. proceeded to 3rd Army School of Sanitation, ARRAS on a course. W.Barclay	
-do-	24/8		Nothing to report. E.G.	
"	25/8		Nothing to report. E.G.	
"	26/8		Braces relieves at HAVRINCOURT. Lieut. SENTER returned from 3rd Army School of Sanitn. E.G.	
"	27/8		Lieut SENTER (Hawks) Lieut H.N. MATTHEWS R.A.M.C. as O/c A.D.S. HERMIES. Capt. N.E. GORMAN R.A.M.C. relieved Capt. J.S. LEWIS M.C. R.A.M.C. at A.D.S. HAVRINCOURT E.G.	
"	28/8		Capt. W. Barclay M.C. R.A.M.C. relieved Capt. L.M. TAYLOR M.O.R.C. U.S.A. at HAVRINCOURT. Edwin Gorland Lieut Col R.A.M.C.	

Army Form C. 2118.

WAR DIARY
or
INTELLIGENCE SUMMARY
(Erase heading not required.)

Instructions regarding War Diaries and Intelligence Summaries are contained in F. S. Regs., Part II. and the Staff Manual respectively. Title Pages will be prepared in manuscript.

Place	Date	Hour	Summary of Events and Information	Remarks and references to Appendices
VELU	1918 JANY 29		Barrage observed at HERMIES. Hostile shell gas barrage on HAVRINCOURT, 23 other tanks gassed, one gas shell made direct hit on A.D.S. Ef.	
	30		Capt. L. M. TAYLOR M.O.R.C. U.S.A. to ARRAS 3rd Army School of Sanitation for short course Ef	
	31st		Nothing to report.	
	31		During the month one 3rd Army Hut. for hospital purposes, & four Small Nissen Huts have been erected (horse standings). Deep dug-outs are under construction at the Quarry Havrincourt, to be used as A.D.S. when completed as the present A.D.S. HAVRINCOURT is not well protected.	

Edward Stanland
Lieut Col R.A.M.C.

MEDICAL
Vol 29

CONFIDENTIAL

WAR DIARY

OF

51st FIELD AMBULANCE

FROM FEBRUARY 1st 1918 TO FEBRUARY 28th 1918.

VOLUME 13

COMMITTEE FOR THE
MEDICAL HISTORY OF THE WAR
Date -8 APR. 1918

Army Form C. 2118.

WAR DIARY or INTELLIGENCE SUMMARY

"MEDICAL"

(Erase heading not required.)

Instructions regarding War Diaries and Intelligence Summaries are contained in F.S. Regs., Part II. and the Staff Manual respectively. Title Pages will be prepared in manuscript.

Place	Date 1918	Hour	Summary of Events and Information	Remarks and references to Appendices
VELU	FEB 1st		Capt. L.M. TAYLOR U.S. R.M.C. returned from 3rd Army School of Sanitation. Eg.	
	2nd		Nothing to report Eg	
	3rd		Capt. R. DRANE U.S. R.M.C. reported for duty	
	4th		Capt. R. DRANE U.S. R.M.C. sent to Corps Rest Station Graces Sucary Sherry	
	5th		nothing to report Eg	
	6th		Capt. H.N. MATTHEWS R.A.M.C. to short course at Third Army School of Sanitation Eg.	
	7th		Bearers rehearsed at Canal Bank Posts Eg.	
	8th & 9th		nothing to report.	
	10th		Capt. H.N. MATTHEWS returned from Sanitation Course Eg	
	11th & 12th		Nothing to report.	
	13th		Captain W. BARCLAY M.C. + Capt. M.E. GORMAN R.A.M.C. relieved by Capt. L.M. TAYLOR U.S.R.M.C. at A.D.S. HAVRINCOURT.	
	14th		Captains Barclay & Gorman proceeded on leave to U.K. Eg.	
	15th		Bearers at A.D.S. HAVRINCOURT relieved. Henry Shelling about A.D.S. for 24 hours. Geo + H.E. Destroying patients bathing dug out. Damaging water cart + Motor cycle also Miller James Wheeler stretcher carrier. Only one O.R. was wounded. E Sutherland Col R.A.M.C. ...	

2449 Wt. W14957/M90 750,000 1/16 J.B.C. & A. Forms/C.2118/12.

WAR DIARY
INTELLIGENCE SUMMARY
(Erase heading not required.)

Army Form C. 2118.

Place	Date 1918	Hour	Summary of Events and Information	Remarks and references to Appendices
VELU	Feb 16th	6 am	A.D.S. HAVRINCOURT returned to the QUARRY in TRESCAULT Road to place known as BOGGART$ HOLE. Map ref - Sheet 57c N.E.3. K.33.b.2.6.	
		noon	Capt. A. GASTON M.O. R.A.M.C. reported for duty & was sent to 7th BORDER Regt for duty during the absence "sick" of Capt. H.E. BUNCH U.S.R.M.C.	Eg
	17.		Lieut. H.H. MATTHEWS R.A.M.C. relieved LIEUT. J.W. SENTER. R.A.M.C at A.D.S. HERMIES. Capt. J.S. LEWIS M.O. R.A.M.C. returned from leave	Eg
	18. 19.		Capt. J.S. LEWIS M.C. R.A.M.C. sent to A.D.S. QUARRY in command. Lieut SENTER to 7. York & Lancs Regt.	Eg
	20.		Capt. TAYLOR M.O R.C. U.S.A. returned from Havrincourt A.D.S. Lieut H.N. MATTHEWS R.A.M.C was relieved at HERMIES by Capt TAYLOR M.O.R.C. U.S.A. & proceeded to report to D.D.M.S. V th Corps for duty	
	21st		LIEUT. W.J. MIEHE M.O.R.C. U.S.A. reported for duty Nothing to report.	

Edward Renshaw Capt
Lieut. Col. R.A.M.C.

WAR DIARY
or
INTELLIGENCE SUMMARY
(Erase heading not required.)

Army Form C. 2118.

Place	Date 1918	Hour	Summary of Events and Information	Remarks and references to Appendices
VELU	21st FEB		Lieut. J. W. SENTER R.A.M.C. returns to this Unit from J. Yates & Lancs. Regt.	
			Lieut. MIEHE M.O.R.C. U.S.A. relieves Capt Taylor at HERMIES A.D.S. Eq	
	23rd		Gotty to report Eq	
	24th		Captain L.M. Taylor M.O.R.C. U.S.A. to A.D.S. HAVRINCOURT Eq	
	25th 26		nil report Eq	
	27		Lieut Miehe relieved by Lieut Suita at A.D.S. Hermies & proceeded to Third Army School of Sanitation for a short practical course	
	28th		Capt. C.G. SCHURR. R.A.M.C. (S.R.) reports for duty with this Unit Nothing to report Eq	

Edmond Rowland
Lieut. Col. R.A.M.C.

MEDICAL

CONFIDENTIAL. WO 30

140/284 Q

COMMITTEE FOR THE
MEDICAL HISTORY OF THE WAR
Date 12 MAY 1918

WAR DIARY

OF

51st FIELD AMBULANCE

FROM MARCH 1st 1915 TO MARCH 31st 1915

VOLUME 14

Army Form C. 2118.

WAR DIARY
or
INTELLIGENCE SUMMARY
(Erase heading not required.)

MEDICAL

Instructions regarding War Diaries and Intelligence Summaries are contained in F. S. Regs., Part II. and the Staff Manual respectively. Title Pages will be prepared in manuscript.

Place	Date 1918	Hour	Summary of Events and Information	Remarks and references to Appendices
VELU	MARCH 1st		Lieut. L.T. MIEHE M.O.R.C. U.S.A. to School of Sanitation ARRAS for course. Capt. C.G SCHURR R.A.M.C. S.R. to 70th Lanc. Fus. for temporary duty. Capt. GORMAN returned from leave Eg.	
	2nd	6.45 p.m.	Captain A. GALLETLY M.C., R.A.M.C. reported for duty. 305, B1 & B2 reinforcements arrived almost all in an exhausted condition having marched from FREMICOURT a distance of only 3½ miles taking five hours to cover this distance. A protest was sent to A.D.M.S. pointing out that B1 & B2 Health Catgy. 7 men are useless & positively dangerous as Feb. Ambulance Stretcher Bearers. Eg. Lieut MIEHE M.O.R.C. U.S.A. returned from 3rd Army School of Sanitation Eg.	Ernest Forsland Lieut Col. RAMC
	3rd 4th		Nothing to report.	

2449 Wt. W14957/M90 750,000 1/16 J.B.C. & A. Forms/C.2118/12.

WAR DIARY or INTELLIGENCE SUMMARY

Place	Date	Hour	Summary of Events and Information	Remarks and references to Appendices
VELU	1918 MARCH			
	5th		Nothing to report. EJ.	
	6th		D.D.M.S. VIIth Corps visited & inspected Camps: also inspected individually the new draft of class B men sent no obstetrian trainers nothing to report. EJ	
	7th		" " EJ	
	8th		" " EJ	
	9th		Lieut. A.T. MIETHE M.O.R.C. U.S.A. to 7th E. Yorks Regt for temporary duty. EJ	
	10th		Capt. L.M. TAYLOR M.O.R.C. U.S.A. granted 4 days special leave. One N.C.O sent to VIIth Corps Gas School for 6 days Course. Capt. A. GALLETLY M.C. R.A.M.C. to A.D.S. HAVRINCOURT. EJ	
	11th		Nothing to report. EJ	
	12th 13th 14th 15th		Capt. L.M. TAYLOR U.S.R.M.C returned from short leave. EJ Capt. GALLETLY at A.D.S. HAVRINCOURT. Major LT BARCLAY M.C. R.A.M.C.	
	16th		Capt L.M. Taylor relieved Capt GALLETLY at duty with 2nd DSS. Capt. GALLETLY proceeded on duty with 2nd DSS. EJ	
	"		Lieut. J.W. SENTER R.A.M.C. proceeded on ordinary leave. EJ	

Army Form C. 2118.

WAR DIARY
or
INTELLIGENCE SUMMARY
(Erase heading not required.)

Place	Date	Hour	Summary of Events and Information	Remarks and references to Appendices
VELU	1918 March 17th 18th 19th 20th		Nothing to report.	
	21st	5 a.m.	Heavy hostile barrage. Major W. Barclay M.C. sent to HERMIES A.D.S. to assist Capt. GORMAN. A.D.S. opened by 8.30 a.m. at SLAG HEAP HERMIES. Original A.D.S. near WINDY CORNER Hermies destroyed by shell fire & evacuated to HERMIES. Struck & destroyed by shell. The Beaumetz railway at HERMIES wounded impossible by this means. The evacuation. A.D.S. Slag Heap has held until 19 lying and 1 up to 6 p.m. 2 pt. mots. 81 Sitting Cases – Transport (Horsed) has all been sent back to BEAULENCOURT.	
		7.30 p.m.	Orderly O.C. A.D.S. HERMIES to return to SLAG HEAP in view of situation	
	22nd	2.30 P.M.	Evacuated SLAG HEAP A.D.S. leaving Capt McGORMAN & 12 O'Ranks to run same as Car Loading Post, remainder of personnel proceeded to Bus opened A.D.S. stayed there one night.	E. Barclay Lt. Col R.A.M.C.

2449 Wt. W14957/M90 750,000 1/16 J.B.C. & A. Forms/C.2118/12.

Army Form C. 2118.

WAR DIARY
or
INTELLIGENCE SUMMARY
(Erase heading not required.)

Instructions regarding War Diaries and Intelligence Summaries are contained in F. S. Regs., Part II. and the Staff Manual respectively. Title Pages will be prepared in manuscript.

Place	Date	Hour	Summary of Events and Information	Remarks and references to Appendices.
	23/3/18	11 am	Left BUS for BEAULENCOURT, reported arrival to ADMS 17th Division stayed there 3 hours, and then proceeded to LOUREELETTE with 53rd & 52nd Field Ambulances. MAJOR J.S. LEWIS. MC opened ADS Station at BUS, & remained there with stretcher bearers until the shelling was so bad that caused him to evacuate the place. Main body arrived LOUREELETTE 8 pm reported arrival to OC 17th Div Train as instructed by ADMS 17th Division. E.g.	
	24/3/18		Unit proceeded to LA BOISSELLE. 53rd Fld Ambce Stretcher bearers joined their unit. 6.20 pm main body less transport proceeded to HENENCOURT. Pitched Camp at 10.30 pm when transport arrived under CAPT ABRAHAMS. E.g.	
	25/3/18	2.30 pm	Opened 17th Div Main Dressing Station at HENENCOURT. E.g.	
	26/3/18	3.30	13th Div Fld Ambce took over Div Dressing Station. Unit moved to SENLIS arrived 6 pm opened ADS. moved at 11.15 pm, proceeded to WARLOY. Opened 17th Div main Dressing Station. CAPT. C.G. SCHURR RAMC proceeded to 10 West Yorks Regt for temp duty as R.M.O. E.g.	
	27/3/18	noon	CIVIL HOSPICE evacuated by Mother Superior & patients [signature]	

2449 Wt. W14957/M90 750,000 1/16 J.B.C. & A. Forms/C.2118/12

WAR DIARY or INTELLIGENCE SUMMARY

Army Form C. 2118.

Place	Date	Hour	Summary of Events and Information	Remarks and references to Appendices
	28/3/16	11am	Two Bearer squads reported for duty to 7th Lincs 10th Sher Foresters 10th & 9th Yorks & 7/6 Yorks respectively. 2 officers + 7.5 Other Ranks passed through this Divisional Dressing Station. E.S.	
	29/3/16	10 pm	1 officer + 84 Other Ranks passes through this Dressing Station. E.S.	
	30/3/16	10 pm	3 officers + 130 other Ranks passed through this Dressing Station. E.S. Otherwise everything quiet.	
	31/3/16	10 pm	19 officers + 141 Other Ranks passed through this M.D.S. CAPT A RANDLE M.C. R.A.M.C. and CAPT A GASTON M.C. R.A.M.C. returned from leave.	

Edward Rowland
Lieut. Col. R.A.M.C.

MEDICAL
96 31
140/2902

CONFIDENTIAL

WAR DIARY

OF

51st FIELD AMBULANCE

FROM APRIL 1st TO APRIL 30th 1918

VOLUME 15

COMMITTEE FOR THE
MEDICAL HISTORY
Date 6 JUN 1918

Army Form C. 2118.

WAR DIARY
or
INTELLIGENCE SUMMARY.
(Erase heading not required.)

MEDICAL

Place	Date	Hour	Summary of Events and Information	Remarks and references to Appendices
MARIEUX	1/4/18		Nothing to report. W.Barclay	
- do -	2/4/18		Capt A. Riddle McRainie proceeded to 10th Wds for duty on relief of Capt R.G. Abraham. W.Barclay	
VILLERS-BOCAGE	3/4/18	9.15a	On relief of 52nd FdAmb. This unit proceeded to VILLERS-BOCAGE. Capt a gawn, a/a Capt. R.G. Abraham, handed over 52nd FdAmb.	
		7.30p	Transport regimen for PIERREGOT. W.Barclay	
FLESSELLES	4/4/18	2.15p	Unit marched from VILLERS BOCAGE to FLESSELLES. Lt J.W. Sitter Rainie proceeded to 6th Dpot for duty. W.Barclay	
- do -	5/4/18	6p		
		9a	Orders received from 37th Dy. Bde to move to MONTONVILLERS but owing to the state of the roads this village to be ordered was cancelled. W.Barclay	
	6/4/18		Nothing to report. W.Barclay	
FRANQUEVILLE	7/4/18	10.0a	Unit marched to FRANQUEVILLE arriving at 12.30p. W.Barclay	
- do -	8/4/18		Capt. H.L. REAZIN CAMC reported for duty. W.Barclay	
	9/4/18		Nothing to report. W.Barclay	

Army Form C. 2118.

WAR DIARY
or
INTELLIGENCE SUMMARY.
(Erase heading not required.)

Instructions regarding War Diaries and Intelligence Summaries are contained in F.S. Regs., Part II. and the Staff Manual respectively. Title pages will be prepared in manuscript.

Place	Date	Hour	Summary of Events and Information	Remarks and references to Appendices
FRANQUE-VILLE	10/7/18	10 a.	Received shipment of Battery of 51st Inf Bde. inspected by Major Whiteley and Capt Qr M.B. Lee. Lt. Col. F. Goodall, D.S.O. proceeded to LE TOUQUET by air conveyance.	
		3 p.	Classes were held for the Regimental Stretcher Bearer. Water duty man, and Cooks of the Battalion of 51st Inf Bde.	
LAVICOGNE	11/7/18	12.30 p.	Bn marched from FRANQUEVILLE	
FRANQUEVILLE	11/7/18	3 p.	Clearing Station of B/51 Inf Bde Shrapnel staked [?]	
LAVICOGNE	11/7/18	12.15 p.	Bn proceeded by march route in rear of 51st Inf Bde from FRANQUEVILLE to LAVICOGNE arriving 6.30 p.	C.W. Bazo Cay 51st Inf Bde
CLAIREYE	12/7/18	9.15 a.	Bn proceeded by march route in rear of 51st Inf Bde from LAVICOGNE arriving CLAIREYE 2 p.	C.W. Bazo Cay 51st Inf Bde The OC.
			H.Q. 2nd A.L.B. (R.N.D.) offered every assistance and the utmost confidence declared in Camp by 3 p.	C.W. Bazo Cay
		H.R	Capt. H. Reaney C.N.9 proceeded to (?) BN8 for duty.	

WAR DIARY
or
INTELLIGENCE SUMMARY

Army Form C. 2118.

Place	Date	Hour	Summary of Events and Information	Remarks and references to Appendices
CLAIRFAYE	13/4/18		Nothing to note	W. Barclay
do	14/4/18		— do —	W. Barclay
do	15/4/18	10.30a	The unit took over accommodation to H.9 at AERODROME, CLAIRFAYE	W. Barclay
do	16/4/18		Nothing to note	W. Barclay
do	17/4/18	3p	Capt. E. Gona, R.A.M.C. proceeded to 17th D.A.C. for duty. was Capt. at FREAZIN, C.A.M.C.	W. Barclay
do		8p	Lieut. Sinclair, D.S.O., R.A.M.C. returned from 3rd Army Officers Convalescent Home and resumed command of the unit.	W. Barclay
do	18/4/18	10a	1 H.D. Horse and 3 mules remounts arrived.	W. Barclay
do	19/4/18		Nothing to report	W. Barclay
do	20/4/18		do	W. Barclay
do	21/4/18		A.D.M.S. 17th Div. inspected the camp and transport of this unit.	W. Barclay

WAR DIARY
or
INTELLIGENCE SUMMARY.
(Erase heading not required.)

Army Form C. 2118.

Place	Date	Hour	Summary of Events and Information	Remarks and references to Appendices
CLAIRFAYE	22/4/18		GO 1st Div Train proposed transport of the unit	W.J.Barclay
do	23/4/18		Nothing to report	W.J.Barclay
do	24/4/18		- do -	W.J.Barclay
do	25/4/18		- do -	W.J.Barclay
do	26/4/18	6 p.m.	Capt. R.E. Gorman Reame returned to duty with this unit	W.J.Barclay
HALLOY-L-PERNOIS	27/4/18	9 a.m.	1st division of this unit proceeded by road route from CLAIRFAYE to HALLOY-LES-PERNOIS. A lot of men and horses finished proved en route and the men and horses arrived in excellent shape. The leave division (left troops) were attached to 53rd Fd Amb for rations. To carry out I find out 1 Motor Ayre with personnel attached to 53rd Fd Amb.	W.J.Barclay

Army Form C. 2118.

WAR DIARY
or
INTELLIGENCE SUMMARY.
(Erase heading not required.)

Instructions regarding War Diaries and Intelligence Summaries are contained in F. S. Regs., Part II. and the Staff Manual respectively. Title pages will be prepared in manuscript.

Place	Date	Hour	Summary of Events and Information	Remarks and references to Appendices
HALLOY-LÈS-PERNOIS	28/4/18		A series of moves at the west end of the village was taken over with a view to making a Divisional Rest Station. The huts are in a bad state of repair.	
	29/4/18		Work carried on on the huts. W.J.Barrow Lt. W.J.Barrow	
	30/4/18		A.D.M.S. 17th Div. inspected the hospitals and passed W.S.B. by the unit. W.J.Barrow Major R.A.M.C. for O.C. 51st Field Ambulance.	

MEDICAL

Vol 32
140/2983

CONFIDENTIAL

WAR DIARY

OF

51st FIELD AMBULANCE

FROM MAY 1st 1918 TO MAY 31st

VOLUME 16.

COMMITTEE FOR THE
MEDICAL HISTORY OF THE WAR
Date 9 JUL 1918

Army Form C. 2118.

MEDICAL

WAR DIARY
or
INTELLIGENCE SUMMARY.
(Erase heading not required.)

Instructions regarding War Diaries and Intelligence Summaries are contained in F. S. Regs., Part II. and the Staff Manual respectively. Title pages will be prepared in manuscript.

Place	Date	Hour	Summary of Events and Information	Remarks and references to Appendices
HALLOY-L-PERNOIS	1/5/18		Nothing to note	Capt. Barn Coy
do	2/5/18		— do —	Capt. Barn Coy
do	3/5/18		— do —	Capt. Barn Coy
do	4/5/18		— do —	Capt. Barn Coy
do	5/5/18	6 p.m.	Lt. Col. E.T. Gulland D.S.O. departed on 2 months leave to UNITED KINGDOM. Nothing to note	Capt. Barn Coy
do	6/5/18			Capt. Barn Coy
do	7/5/18		2nd H.Q. Horses commenced entr.	Capt. Barn Coy
do	8/5/18		Baser entrainment moved for CLAIRFAYE & HALLOY-LES-PERNOIS. Capt. J.R. JOHN, Rank S.R. joined for duty Lt. E. CAMSFIELD R.A.M.(T.C.) do	Capt. Barn Coy
do	9/5/18		Nothing to note	Capt. Barn Coy
do	10/5/18	100	Under instructions from M.D.M.S. 10th Div., E.F.A. RAINCHEVAL and SARTON and at VALVION are reorganised into rece & entrie 18	W. Barn Coy

A1091 Wt. W128-9/M1293 750,000. 1/17. D.D & L. Ltd. Forms/C2118/14.

Army Form C. 2118.

WAR DIARY
or
INTELLIGENCE SUMMARY.
(Erase heading not required.)

Instructions regarding War Diaries and Intelligence Summaries are contained in F.S. Regs., Part II. and the Staff Manual respectively. Title pages will be prepared in manuscript.

Place	Date	Hour	Summary of Events and Information	Remarks and references to Appendices
HALLOY LES PERNOIS	11/2/18		Nothing to note	W.J.Barclay
do	12/2/18		do	W.J.Barclay
do	13/2/18		do	W.J.Barclay
do	14/2/18		do	W.J.Barclay
do	15/2/18		do	W.J.Barclay
do	16/2/18		do	W.J.Barclay
do	17/2/18		Unit moved from HALLOY at 7.30a.m. en route for BEAUQUESNE. Arrived at 5p.m. Patients were transferred to 52nd Ja.Aid at FRANQUEVILLE. Scabies patients Nos 52 to 64 incl. were transferred to the unit. A scabies hospital was opened on the unit. kept in a separate part of BEAUQUESNE in relief of Capt J.R.JOHN Raine proceed to BEAUQUESNE & 10=Skinwood G.F. OUSER M.O.R.C U.S.A	W.J.Barclay
BEAUQUESNE	17/2/18 6/1.			W.J.Barclay

Army Form C. 2118.

WAR DIARY
or
INTELLIGENCE SUMMARY.
(Erase heading not required.)

Instructions regarding War Diaries and Intelligence Summaries are contained in F.S. Regs., Part II. and the Staff Manual respectively. Title pages will be prepared in manuscript.

Place	Date	Hour	Summary of Events and Information	Remarks and references to Appendices
BEAUQUESNE	19/16		No M.T. here. W. Barea Cy.	
do	20/16		Day spent in cleaning weapons etc in preparation for inspection by T. Corps Commander. W. Barea Cy	
do	21/16 10.30		Unit inspected by T. Corps Commander do 51st Bn Ada Group	
		3t.	Lt W. OORSTER, U.S.M.C.R.C. evacuated sick. W.M.Barea Cy	
do	22/16		No M.T. to note. W.M.Barea Cy	
do	23/16		Capt. A. E. Graham, R.E. departed for United Kingdom on Campaign of Covenant W.M.Barea Cy	
	24/16		No M.T. to note. W.M.Barea Cy	
	25/16 5		Advance Party (N.C.O. 3 O.R.) — 1 to ARQUEVES to take over Camp B. 53 from Bn R.E. W.M.Barea Cy	
ARQUEVES	26/16 08.30		Unit moved from BEAUQUESNE to ARQUEVES by road arriving at 10.30 a.m. Billets in BEAUQUESNE were handed over to 2/7 A. & S. H. 127 Bn. W.M.Barea Cy	

WAR DIARY
or
INTELLIGENCE SUMMARY.
(Erase heading not required.)

Army Form C. 2118.

Place	Date	Hour	Summary of Events and Information	Remarks and references to Appendices
ARQUEVES	27/5/18	9pm	Major J S Lemon M.C. with 1 Sgt and 22 O.R. proceeded to 53rd Field Amb. at ACHEUX for temporary duty. Lt E CANSFIELD proceeded to 7th Queens for temp. duty.	
do	28/5/16		Nothing to note	W. Barala Capt
do	29/5/16		do	W. Barala Capt
do	30/5/16		do	W. Barala Capt
do	31/5/16		do	W. Barala Capt

31/5/18.
Major R.A.M.C.
for O.C., 51st Field Ambce.

MEDICAL

60/3076.

June 1918.

CONFIDENTIAL

WAR DIARY

OF

51st FIELD AMBULANCE

FROM JUNE 1st TO JUNE 30th 1918

VOLUME 14.

COMMITTEE FOR THE
MEDICAL HISTORY OF THE WAR
Date 7 AUG 1918

Army Form C. 2118.

WAR DIARY
or
INTELLIGENCE SUMMARY.
(Erase heading not required.)

MEDICAL 96/3

Place	Date	Hour	Summary of Events and Information	Remarks and references to Appendices
ARQUEVES	1/9/18		Instructions received from ADMS 17 Div that the CO	
	2/9/18		Lt Gen'l and DSO came about of the unit from 20, 57, 18. Nothing to note.	W.J. Barnes OC
	3/9/18		Nothing to note. Lecture delivered by 57, 59 & 60 Fld SANITATION to NCO. Amb. re Service.	W.J. Barnes OC W.J. Barnes OC
	4/9/18		Nothing to note.	W.J. Barnes OC
	5/9/18		Nothing to note.	W.J. Barnes OC
	6/9/18		2 NCO and 7 OR's of bearers sent to 57 & 58 via 3d Amb at ACHIEUX for temporary duty	W.J. Barnes OC
	7/9/18		Lt W.J. OURSLER OSMORE reported for duty from 2/10 Genl Hospital.	W.J. Barnes OC W.J. Barnes OC
	8/9/18		Nothing to note.	W.J. Barnes OC
	9/9/18		18 ORs sent to 53 Fd Amb. returned safely and received a message of thanks from O.C. 53 Fd Amb.	W.J. Barnes OC

Army Form C. 2118.

WAR DIARY
or
INTELLIGENCE SUMMARY.
(Erase heading not required.)

Instructions regarding War Diaries and Intelligence Summaries are contained in F. S. Regs., Part II. and the Staff Manual respectively. Title pages will be prepared in manuscript.

Place	Date	Hour	Summary of Events and Information	Remarks and references to Appendices
ARQUEVES	10/6/16		1/Lt D.C. KELLEY, USMORC reported for duty, memorandum from A.D.A.S. 17th Div.	W.P.Barclay
do	11/6/16		Nothing to note	W.P.Barclay
do	12/6/16		do	W.P.Barclay
do	13/6/16		1 Cook sent for temporary duty to 52nd Fd. Amb. at TALMAS to replace a cook that went at 3rd ARMY COOKERY COURSE !!!	W.P.Barclay
do	14/6/16		Nothing to report	W.P.Barclay
do	15/6/16		2 H.D. horses and 1 mule received from 29th M.V.S. Good animals.	W.P.Barclay
do	16/6/16		Nothing to report.	W.P.Barclay
RAINNEVAL N8d chap 57.d.	17/6/16	9.30am	Lt OURSLER 1 Mgt and 12 O.R. proceeded to CLAIRFAYE to take over W.W. Gallaghy Park fm 12th Div.	

Army Form C. 2118.

WAR DIARY
or
INTELLIGENCE SUMMARY.
(Erase heading not required.)

Instructions regarding War Diaries and Intelligence Summaries are contained in F. S. Regs., Part II. and the Staff Manual respectively. Title pages will be prepared in manuscript.

Place	Date	Hour	Summary of Events and Information	Remarks and references to Appendices
RAINCHEVAL	17/9/16	9 a.m.	Remainder of unit proceeded to RAINCHEVAL (N.18.d central) Transport Vanford Wackny Wounded Drewery Stokes Cpr 12 q.m.s. Wounded and sick are collected at Acheux Clairfays and Forceville Know 6 Horse wagons to N16d central Big enough for 35 C.C.S.	
- do -	18/9/16		Rtd. RAINCHEVAL Kay are evacuated & 38 CCS FIENVILLERS.	
			The Work was carried out on the wagons at Overseep and by Pagt. Lt OVRSEEP on duty 130 Fd. Amb. received by	W.S. Barnes Co.
- do -	20/9/16		Major J.S. Kane D.M.C. Rane proceeded to 36 CCS to perform duty O D.M.S.T. Corps inspected Camp.	W.S. Barnes Co.
- do -	21/9/16		Nothing to report	W.S. Barnes Co.
			do	W.S. Barnes Co.

Army Form C. 2118.

WAR DIARY
or
INTELLIGENCE SUMMARY. 51st Field Ambulance.
(Erase heading not required.)

Place	Date June	Hour	Summary of Events and Information	Remarks and references to Appendices
RAINCHEVAL	22		Major W.F. Nicolson M.C. R.A.M.C. reported for duty and assumed command of the unit.	
HÉRISSART	23		Under orders from A.D.M.S. the unit marches to W. Barala established Collecting Post at N.18.d. Central (Sheet 57D) to new billets R.A.M.C team at HÉRISSART located by 148 F. Field Ambulance. There has been a great deal of influenza in HERISSART. 51st Bde. marched in to HÉRISSART in the afternoon.	
"	24		Visited the Medical Officers of 7th Lincolns, 7th Borders, & 10th Notts & Derbys. Visited 51st Bde. H.Q. The equipment of the unit is being checked by the Q.M. today. Second Called with reference to 17th Division Defence Scheme. This unit is to be in charge of the evacuation of casualties from the front during the next time. A.D.M.S. No. X.762 - (Provisional medical arrangements in connection with 17th Division Defence Scheme) received	W/Bn

Army Form C. 2118.

WAR DIARY
or
INTELLIGENCE SUMMARY. 51st Ot Field Ambulance.

(Erase heading not required.)

Place	Date	Hour	Summary of Events and Information	Remarks and references to Appendices
HÉRISSART	JUNE 25.		Visited O.C. 52nd Field Ambulance & arranged for him to attach 1 Squad of Stretcher-bearers to each battalion of the 52nd Bde. in the event of that Bde. being ordered to move forward ahead of the Enemy attack. The remainder of his Division is to march to an appointed (undergrowth) Rendezvous till he meets no circumstanced regime. Reconnoitred roads & tracks in the TOUTENCOURT - CONTAY - HÉRISSART area. The road from CONTAY to HÉRISSART is very bad. Inspected the whole unit - Physique & appearance of the men is on the whole, good. Attended a lecture on P.U.O. & Dysentery by the Assistant Advisor in Pathology, this Army.	H.M.
"	26.		Reconnoitred tracks & roads to CLAIRFAYE M.D.S. arranged with O.C. him that if necessary 51st Field Ambulance Bearer H.Q. would be established there. About called with reference to Defence Scheme.	H.M.

Army Form C. 2118.

WAR DIARY
or
INTELLIGENCE SUMMARY. 51st Field Ambulance

(Erase heading not required.)

Instructions regarding War Diaries and Intelligence Summaries are contained in F.S. Regs., Part II. and the Staff Manual respectively. Title pages will be prepared in manuscript.

Place	Date	Hour	Summary of Events and Information	Remarks and references to Appendices
HÉRISSART	JUNE 27		Visited A.D.M.S. to discuss plans for Evacuation of wounded in the event of a heavy battle attack. Horse transport for the unit did very well in 51st Div. Bde. Horse show today.	K McL
"	28		Conference at D.D.M.S. office of Field Ambulance Commanders to arrange R.A.M.C. sports. Reconnoitred roads & tracks round SENLIS, HÉDAUVILLE, VARENNES, HARPONVILLE, WARLOY nr & return.	K McL
"	29		Visited M.D.S. and 1st Lincolns & 10th Sherwood Foresters - inspected latrines &c. Reconnoitred area HÉRISSART- RUBEMPRE for site for M.D.S. if it were necessary to open here.	K McL
"	30		Reconnoitred tracks from BUZINCOURT & SENLIS backwards. Practically all tracks are at present fit for motor Ambulances when today fitted with new eye-restrictors & M.O.S. in this Bde. Influenza is very prevalent but present not present in this area.	K McL

K McLean Lieut Colonel
O.C. 51st Field Ambulance

MEDICAL Vol 34
140/3/31.

CONFIDENTIAL

WAR DIARY

OF

51st FIELD AMBULANCE

FROM JULY 1st 1918 TO JULY 31st 1918.

(VOLUME 18)

MEDICAL

Army Form C. 2118.

WAR DIARY
or
INTELLIGENCE SUMMARY. 51st Field Ambulance.
(Erase heading not required.)

Instructions regarding War Diaries and Intelligence Summaries are contained in F. S. Regs., Part II. and the Staff Manual respectively. Title pages will be prepared in manuscript.

Place	Date	Hour	Summary of Events and Information	Remarks and references to Appendices
HÉRISSART	JULY 1.		Reconnoitred tracks in the area HÉRISSART - CONTAY - TOUTENCOURT.	BMcJean
"	2		Visited 7th Battn. Yorks & Lancs. (Ribemont) who have had a great many cases of influenza. This is now dying down.	AMcM
"	3		A.D.M.S. inspected this unit. Transport fairly satisfactory. Killed. Good.	AMcM
"	4		Visited 53rd Field Ambulance at D.R.S., TALMAS, & 17th Div. M.T. Coy. Paid this unit. A.D.M.S. called with reference to clearance of wounded from the right divisional front (CAVELUY Arras sector?).	AMcM
"	5		Nothing to report.	AMcM
"	6		17th Division Field Ambulance Sports held near RUBEMPRE.	AMcM
"	7		Visited V Corps M.D.S. at CLAIRFAYE, & arranged details & relief & forward posts & M.D.S. with O.C. 37th Field Ambulance - relief to be completed by 6am on 11th.	AMcM

Army Form C. 2118.

WAR DIARY
or
INTELLIGENCE SUMMARY. 51st Field Ambulance

(Erase heading not required.)

Instructions regarding War Diaries and Intelligence Summaries are contained in F. S. Regs, Part II. and the Staff Manual respectively. Title pages will be prepared in manuscript.

Place	Date	Hour	Summary of Events and Information	Remarks and references to Appendices
HÉRISSART	JULY 8		Received warning to "stand to" at 11.30 p.m. last night. "Assembly" (practice) ordered at 11.45 p.m. Division moved to assembly area at U.11.a (Sheet 57D) at 1.45 a.m. on way of 51st Inf. Bde., & arrived at assembly area at 4 a.m. Signature parties to all Battalions of 50th & 51st Inf. Bdes. on arrival, & went back to Concentration Assembly at 5.45 a.m. The heavy Battalions inspected. Major W. BARCLAY, M.O., visited D.C. 37th marched back to HÉRISSART. Major W. BARCLAY, M.O., visited the A.D.S. & learnt Field Ambulance to arrange about taking over 2 squads Ammo moves up to posts & Construction work in forward area of 51st Bde., which moves up to attacks to each battalion of 51st Bde. tomorrow morning. Where the left Bde. of 12th Div.	hm
"	9.		Arranged with D.R.S., to send Railhead personnel at LOUVEN COURT for 17th Division leaving sick for TALMAS to be conveyed on the train leaving LOUVEN COURT at 5 p.m. daily for BEAUVAL. 2 squads attached to Each sight the battalions of 51st Bde., which moves up to relieve the right Bde. of the 12th Div. tomorrow morning. Major W. BARCLAY, M.C. went round the R.A.P.s tomorrow morning. Bearer division moves up to CLAIR FAYE M.D.S. this afternoon.	khm
CLAIRFAYE O.30.a.99 (Sheet 57D)	10.		Tent Division of 51st Field Ambulance marched from HÉRISSART to CLAIRFAYE at 8.30 a.m. & arrived at 11.20 a.m. relieved 37th Field Ambulance the Bearer Division Clair of 37th Field Ambulance in the line this morning. Limited A.D.S. by. (Other)	

Army Form C. 2118.

WAR DIARY
or
INTELLIGENCE SUMMARY. 51st Field Ambulance.
(Erase heading not required.)

Place	Date	Hour	Summary of Events and Information	Remarks and references to Appendices
CLAIRFAYE O.30.a.9.9 (Sheet 57D)	JULY 10	(Contd)	at HEDAUVILLE in the afternoon with A.D.M.S. and inspected the A.D.S. made arrangements at P.33.d.6.9. & at V.16.b.1.9. (Sheet 57 D). Working parties out to commence work tomorrow.	6pm.
"	11.		Spent the whole day going round the M.D.S. at CLAIRFAYE, which afforded a great deal of cleaning up &c. The men were standings in particular are filthy & will have to be gutted. Removed Capt Wallis.	10pm.
"	12.		Horse A.D.S. & R.A.P's & bearer posts & left section of the front. Everything satisfactory except latrine arrangements. D.D.M.S. V work at new R.D.S. HEDAUVILLE is progressing satisfactorily. Capt Wallis CLAIR FAYE.	10pm
"	13.		Visited A.D.S. & H.Q. of Sec. 51st & 52nd Inf. Bdes. Everything satisfactory.	10pm
"	14.		Visited A.D.S. & went round R.A.P's & bearer posts & took Major W. BARCLAY. Bearers & left section and to section. The line has been Relieved tomorrow morning. So far the weather is very changeable & fairly quiet. At present	10pm.

Army Form C. 2118.

WAR DIARY
of
INTELLIGENCE SUMMARY. 51st Field Ambulance.
(Erase heading not required.)

Place	Date	Hour	Summary of Events and Information	Remarks and references to Appendices
CLAIRFAYE O.30.a.9.9. (Sht 57 D)	JULY 15		A.Q.M.G. & D.A.D.M.S. & Capt. visited M.D.S. & paid that the Messes huts have all to be shifted to another site further back on the LEALVILLERS-TOUTENCOURT road. Clearing up of camp proceeding satisfactorily.	ASM
"	16.		Visited A.D.M.S. with reference to distant F.D.R.S. Cases no 1st daily train from LOUVEN COURT is not to turn under his cases gentry as it has been decided to send the cases to D.R.S. by for, as it is inadvisable to collect sick here.	ASM
"	17.		50th Inf. Bde. relieved 52nd Inf. Bde. in the right sector of the front last night. Visited A.D.S. near road bridge Enchinctre at HEDAUVILLE. 6 brightest battalion 55th Bde. - SENLIS, 6 brightest of right Bde. of 55th with reference to which to take place on 18th/19th at A/DN. Bde. visited A.D.M.S. which is to take place on 18th/19th at A/DN. 38th Division by 52nd Bde.	ASM
"	18		Visited A.D.S. HEDAUVILLE & 30th Div. Wine reductions being held in view of emergency, beaducumbs R.A.P.s & Bearer posts of the MESNIL sector.	ASM
"	19.		Visited ADS HEDAUVILLE & went round R.A.P. of Lancs Fusiliers Manchester Lancs & Yorks, visited 50th Fld. 52nd Bde. H.Q.	ASM

Army Form C. 2118.

WAR DIARY
of
INTELLIGENCE SUMMARY. 51st Field Ambulance
(Erase heading not required.)

Instructions regarding War Diaries and Intelligence Summaries are contained in F. S. Regs., Part II. and the Staff Manual respectively. Title pages will be prepared in manuscript.

Place	Date	Hour	Summary of Events and Information	Remarks and references to Appendices
CLAIRFAYE O.30.a.9.9. (Sheet 57 D)	JULY. 20		Visited A.D.S. HEDAUVILLE. Motor Ambce Car damaged by shellfire on the BOUZINCOURT – HEDAUVILLE road, near HEDAUVILLE. Running repairs effected of the front, Called at M.D.S.	A/M.
"	21.		Working at M.D.S. all day. A.D.M.S. presented "Parchments" to several men of R.A.M.C. & A.S.C. M.T. of this unit for gallantry & devotion to duty during the fighting 21st – 27th March 1918.	A/M.
"	22.		Held A.D.S. HEDAUVILLE. Arranged for a Car shelter to be dug near ENGLEBELMER crossroads at P.24.d.3.2.	A/M.
"	23.		Very hot & stormy. Lost of Engine & damage to a Motor Ambce. Car. D.D.M.S. & D.A.D.M.S. I Corps visited M.D.S. Placed all available men & admcs investment in war Service Certificates. Lieut. SUTCH, U.S.M.O.R.C. (C.D.) attached for instruction.	A/M.
"	24.		Visited A.D.S. at HEDAUVILLE. Renewed but more construction at P.24.d.3.2. Enemy shelling of HEDAUVILLE – VARENNES road last night. New A.D.S. at HEDAUVILLE is in rather an unhealthy spot.	A/M.

Army Form C. 2118.

WAR DIARY
or
INTELLIGENCE SUMMARY. 51st Field Ambulance

(Erase heading not required.)

Instructions regarding War Diaries and Intelligence Summaries are contained in F. S. Regs., Part II. and the Staff Manual respectively. Title pages will be prepared in manuscript.

Place	Date	Hour	Summary of Events and Information	Remarks and references to Appendices
CLAIRFAYE JULY O.30.a.9½ (Sht 57D)	25		Visited A.D.S. HEDAUVILLE, & R.A.P. of 12th Manchesters & Border Regts & the left sector of the Divisional front.	½hr
	26.		Pay Parade. hay & straw. Veterinary Officer inspected the horses of the unit.	½hr
	27.		Visited A.D.S. HEDAUVILLE & finished advisability shifting the A.D.S. to the A.D.S. until recently occupied by the 38th Division. this late A.D.S. appears somewhat slaughtering to make a Sphinx group dressing room above ground.	½hr
	28.		Visited A.D.S. HEDAUVILLE & R.A.P.s of 6th Dorsets & 15th W. Yorks. Everything satisfactory. R.E. Office inspected the new A.D.S. in HEDAUVILLE & agrees to commence work immediately.	½hr
	29.		Materiel for new A.D.S. work drawn that & R.O.D	½hr
	30.		Nord calls sick upon to slightly gases case of the Division who are to be admitted by this unit. Tent to 17½ D.R.S.	½hr
	31.		Visited A.D.S. HEDAUVILLE, see def. Base. H.Q. & new A.D.S. site at SENLIS. Everything satisfactory. Glorious weather.	½hr

R W McKean Lieut Col
Comdg. 51st Field Ambulance

Vol 35
140/3200.

Aug 1918.

CONFIDENTIAL
WAR DIARY
OF
51st FIELD AMBULANCE
FROM AUGUST 1st 1918 TO AUGUST 31st 1918.
VOLUME 19.

MEDICAL

Army Form C. 2118.

WAR DIARY
or
INTELLIGENCE SUMMARY. 51st Field Ambulance

(Erase heading not required.)

Instructions regarding War Diaries and Intelligence Summaries are contained in F. S. Regs., Part II. and the Staff Manual respectively. Title pages will be prepared in manuscript.

Place	Date	Hour	Summary of Events and Information	Remarks and references to Appendices
CLAIRFAYE Q.30.a.99. (Sheet 57D)	AUGUST 1.		A.D.M.S. Corps inspected the unit & recommended erection of an extra dressing room. Roy's went the mail.	A/Major Hamilton
"	2		Raid last night by 10 Heavy guns & Lincolns - Renaths very light. HEDAUVILLE was very heavily shelled after the raid. Visited A.M. HEDAUVILLE & ENGLE BELMER. Car of 53rd Field Ambulance knocked out by a shell last night & sent to workshops today.	A/M
"	3		Enemy retired across the ANCRE last night. A.D.M.S. worked visited A.D.S. at Beaumont R. & R.A.P. of right sector. M.D.S. moved to the autobus on the 5th. Got warning that the unit to TALMAS on the 6th. 6.15 to march to TALMAS on 6th.	A/M
"	4	6.15	Visited 53rd Field Ambulance & 130th Field Ambulance. O.C. 131st Field Ambulance called with reference both about relief. A whiff of M.D.S. to arrange	A/M

Army Form C. 2118.

WAR DIARY
or
INTELLIGENCE SUMMARY.
(Erase heading not required.)

51st Field Ambulance

Instructions regarding War Diaries and Intelligence Summaries are contained in F. S. Regs., Part II. and the Staff Manual respectively. Title pages will be prepared in manuscript.

Place	Date	Hour	Summary of Events and Information	Remarks and references to Appendices
CLAIRFAYE O.30.a.9.9. (Sheet 57 D)	AUGUST 5.		Born division relieved on the forward front. Rcd by horse division of 130th Field Ambulance. Park of 52nd Field Ambulance who had been working on the new front at BENLIS reformed their HQ. DADVS inspected the horses & paid a visit. Bodies in splendid condition and collers. Advanced party sent to TALMAS to take over.	S/M S/M
TALMAS	6.		Unit marched from CLAIRFAYE to TALMAS in relief of 4th. 53rd Field Ambulance took over the D.R.S. Men marched very well.	4th
"	7.		Visited 38 CCS at FIENVILLERS to arrange about an R.A.M.C. man to be attached for duty on the hairdressing saw to 4 CCS. Visited RTO at BEAUVAL & ROSEL trailheads to arrange about trains.	4th
O.25.central (Sheet 62 D)	8		Got orders to move at once to the VECQUEMONT area via 50th Inf. Bde. Capt. A. RANDLE & party of 28 men left to take after D.R.S. at TALMAS. Remainder of unit marched to O.25.central. (Sheet 62 D)	(over)

Army Form C. 2118.

WAR DIARY
or
INTELLIGENCE SUMMARY.

(Erase heading not required.)

Army Form C. 2118.

51st Field Ambulance

Instructions regarding War Diaries and Intelligence Summaries are contained in F. S. Regs. Part II. and the Staff Manual respectively. Title pages will be prepared in manuscript.

Place	Date	Hour	Summary of Events and Information	Remarks and references to Appendices
O.25.C.10 (Sheet 62D)	Aug. 8 (Contd)	12.30 am	VILLERS BRETONNEUX. Arrived at our destination at 12.30 am. Men marched splendidly. MAJOR J.S. LEVIS M.C. reported for temporary duty at 56 CCS.	
CORBIE	9		Got order to move to CORBIE at 10.35 pm. Bivouacking. Left by Bde. Arrived in CORBIE at 3am in rear of 50th Div. Very tiring march in which we were very often held up by troops. Bivouacked. Friendly talked to Transport outside CORBIE. With 5th & 6th CORBIE - BRAY (was not the)	
"	10		Still at CORBIE. A.D.M.S. calls. Men in excellent health & spirits. Lieut. J.N. OURSLER, U.S.M.R.C. posted to 10th Hotts & duty, vice Capt. J.R. JOHN, R.A.M.C. who proceeds to D.R.S. TALMA S.	
"	11		Still at CORBIE. Church parade made in morning. Bathing parade in afternoon. Weather very fine & hot.	

WAR DIARY
or
INTELLIGENCE SUMMARY. 51st Field Ambulance
(Erase heading not required.)

Army Form C. 2118.

Place	Date	Hour	Summary of Events and Information	Remarks and references to Appendices
FOUILLOY (HOSPICE).	AUG. 12.		Got where to move to HOSPICE, FOUILLOY, to where 10th Amo. Field Ambulance are now at M.D.S. One cycle has attached 2 squads. Each of its batallions from the 50th Div. the Ambulance with its now tonight. 17th Division is to attack one April into the PROYART Sector when 3rd Australian Division is to tonight. All motor Ambulance Cars except one large Car were on 3rd Can Sent up to A.D.S. which is being run by 50 & 51 Field Ambulance. Relieved at FOUILLOY at 9 pm.	JAM.
"	13.		listed 53rd Field Ambulance at M.D.S. near AAMEL, & 53rd Field Ambulance at LAMOTTE A.D.S. Took 4 wheeled 53rd Field Ambulance to A.D.S. An hour driven is at Sketch carried in Reserve. The building occupied by the front in very chatty. 6 to kept closed. ment to fouenne thru from gravestones.	JAM.
"	14		Visited 17 D.R.S. at TALMAS & Paid a visit to GROVETOWN area. today from	JAM.

Army Form C. 2118.

WAR DIARY
or
INTELLIGENCE SUMMARY. 51st Field Ambulance
(Erase heading not required.)

Instructions regarding War Diaries and Intelligence Summaries are contained in F. S. Regs., Part II. and the Staff Manual respectively. Title pages will be prepared in manuscript.

Place	Date	Hour	Summary of Events and Information	Remarks and references to Appendices
FOUILLOY (HOSPICE)	AUG. 15.		Medical Board at D.H.Q. on Capt. RHODES, E. YORKS REGT. D.D.M.S. Australian Corps called. Large numbers of marches "gas" casualties brought here today – mostly from 51st Inf. Bde. – 643 cases between 6 a.m. & 12 midnight. Word rec'd re relief 17th Australian Division by 5th Australian Division. Orders rec'd O.C. 15th Australian Field Ambulance to relieve relief to be completed by 12 midnight on 16th inst.	A.A.
"	16.		Unit relieved by 15th Aus. Field Ambulance at Gare Centre FOUILLOY, & moved the forward section some hours later. Came from 17th Division still awaited.	A.A.
VECQUEMONT.	17.		Received orders from 51st Bde. that the Bde. is to move tonight to HERISSART by bus. This orders cancelled on afterwards. Orders received to march to VECQUEMONT. Attd'd Coys of Infantry at 51st Inf. Bde. H.Q. on the occupation of Gp. Casualties. Unit marched to VECQUEMONT at 10.5 p.m. arrived at 11.30 p.m.	A.A.

A7092 Wt. W11128/M1293 750,000. 1/17. D. D. & L. Ltd. Forms/C2118/14.

Army Form C. 2118.

WAR DIARY
or
INTELLIGENCE SUMMARY. 51st Field Ambulance

(Erase heading not required.)

Instructions regarding War Diaries and Intelligence Summaries are contained in F.S. Regs., Part II. and the Staff Manual respectively. Title pages will be prepared in manuscript.

Place	Date	Hour	Summary of Events and Information	Remarks and references to Appendices
VECQUEMONT	AUG 18	10.20 pm	Received orders to move to TALMAS tonight. Marched off at 4.45 am. Arrived in TALMAS. Arrived 2am.	6th A
TALMAS	19		A.D.M.S. calls. Nothing to note.	15th A
"	20		R.D.M.S. called & named me that I serves have to push forward to C.C.S. & Corps troop (N 18 d. central) & prisoner of war Cage at short notice. Gas drive & van inspection. Marked N.18.d. & 5am O.C. time & refreshs. Gambas system. Executor &	15th A
"	21		Received orders from A.D.M.S. to send Major W. BARCLAY, to lent Subdivision to to 38 C.C.S. Capt. A. RANDLE with a Buffalo Sectn to FIENVILLERS. Major J.S. LEVIS with a Buffalo (sheet 57 D) & 1/Lieut. & Capt. W.W.C.P. at N.18. d. Central Cage, CANADAS. D.C. KELLEY U.S.M.O.R.C. to Prisoners from Cage, with 2 days rations.	15th A

Army Form C. 2118.

WAR DIARY
or
INTELLIGENCE SUMMARY. 51st Field Ambulance

(Erase heading not required.)

Instructions regarding War Diaries and Intelligence Summaries are contained in F. S. Regs., Part II. and the Staff Manual respectively. Title pages will be prepared in manuscript.

Place	Date	Hour	Summary of Events and Information	Remarks and references to Appendices
TALMAS.	AUG. 22.		6 Squads of Bearers sent up to D.C. 53rd Field Ambce. Last night. Got orders to send up all Motor Ambces. Except one to 53rd Field Ambce. at AUCHONVILLERS. Can now left to man the DRS. with 16 Ormes.	Noth.
"	23.		R.M.O. & Corp. Gillis Received orders to send up all available bearers to 53rd Field Ambce. at HAMEL.	Noth.
"	24.		Received orders to send 3 horse Ambulance wagons with 24 Data Stretchers to Q.16.d.7.6. (Sheet 57 D). Leaving sick kit practically no away.	Noth.
"	25.		Nothing to note.	Noth
"	26.		Got orders to clear DRS. of all cases that will not be well in 10 days. Sent this morning from TALMAS, to that never in not cart in line Major W. MURDOCH 53rd Field Ambce. Cams down for a rest. Field Ambce, & Capt. FINNEGAN, 53rd Field Ambce.	Noth

Army Form C. 2118.

WAR DIARY
or
INTELLIGENCE SUMMARY. 51st Field Ambulance
(Erase heading not required.)

Instructions regarding War Diaries and Intelligence Summaries are contained in F. S. Regs., Part II. and the Staff Manual respectively. Title pages will be prepared in manuscript.

Place	Date	Hour	Summary of Events and Information	Remarks and references to Appendices
TALMAS	AUG 27.		Visited "C" Section at V Corps W.W.C.P. at N.18.d. Central. Nothing to note.	KMcL
	28		D.D.M.S. I Corps visited the D.R.S. & asked that in the event of him moving forward we should move as much equipment as possible to N.18.d. Central Station to become a Corps Rest Station.	KMcL
"	29.		Capt FINNEGAN orders to proceed to N.I.S.D. for duty. Capt. Q.M. H.B. LEE proceeds on 14 days leave to U.K.	KMcL
"	30.		Major W. MURDOCH, M.C. returns to duty. Nothing to note.	KMcL
"	31.		Have reduced number at D.R.S. to 30 of these the fewer number can be sent at short notice to Divn. if necessary. A.D.M.S. called. This D.R.S. to to move on close of fortnite.	KMcL

KMcLean
Lieut Col RAMC
Commdg. 51st Field Ambulance

MEDICAL

4 Confidential

95/36

16/3451

War Diary

of

51st Field Ambulance

From September 1st 1918 To September 30th 1918

Volume 20

WAR DIARY or INTELLIGENCE SUMMARY

Army Form C. 2118.

MEDICAL — 51st Field Ambulance

Place	Date	Hour	Summary of Events and Information	Remarks and references to Appendices
TALMAS.	SEPT 1		Patch admd at MARTINPUICH & A.D.S. & M.D.S. Brought Major W. MURDOCH M.C., 53rd Field Ambulance to TALMAS, who is suffering from anaphylaxis of antitetanic serum injection	
"	2		Have now arrangements made of patients to 22, most of them till he able to return them into shortly.	
"	3		Patch to 38 C.C.S. & found that "B" Section CCS at VARENNES. is moving today to No 3 Canadian CCS. at Poq W. cage, CANDAS. Saw Lieut. KELLEY U.S.M.O. R.C.	
"	4		Arranges for patients to be admitted to No 3 C.C.S. at GEZAINCOURT if necessary, also to No 38 C.C.S. no moves to BOISLEUX - AU - MONT.	
"	5		Orders received for this unit to move by march route to N.I.O.C. (Sheet 57C) near BEAUVENCOURT. 2 lorries are to report to help to move patients & equipment	

Army Form C. 2118.

WAR DIARY
or
INTELLIGENCE SUMMARY.   51st Field Ambulance
(Erase heading not required.)

Instructions regarding War Diaries and Intelligence Summaries are contained in F. S. Regs., Part II. and the Staff Manual respectively. Title pages will be prepared in manuscript.

Place	Date	Hour	Summary of Events and Information	Remarks and references to Appendices
MILLENCOURT (nr ALBERT)	SEPT 6.		Unit moved by march route from TALMAS to MILLENCOURT at 4.15 pm - arrived at MILLENCOURT at 9.30 - about 19 miles. 2 lorries were not sufficient for the stores & admin. transport to send two more. The stores being left in a open field at TALMAS.	15M
N 10. C. 42 (Sheet 57C)	7		Unit moved by march route for MILLENCOURT to N 10 C. 42. near BEAULENCOURT arriving at 4 pm - about 19 miles. Came near I Corps holding hounds Dressing Station (69th Field Ambulance) ADMS. called & said he was unable to get lorries to move our stores from there.	1/5M
"	8		Went to TALMAS brought the motor lorries from there. Saw B. Lieut. Robinson at hd 3 Cav. C.E.D.	15M
"	9.		Had 1 A.D.M.T. & M.T.L at P. 32. a. 5. 2. & some ambulances to bring 'clean clothing' &c from TALMAS.	15M
"	10		Could not get lorries for stores to TALMAS.	

Army Form C. 2118.

WAR DIARY
or
INTELLIGENCE SUMMARY. 51st Field Ambulance
(Erase heading not required.)

Instructions regarding War Diaries and Intelligence Summaries are contained in F. S. Regs., Part II. and the Staff Manual respectively. Title pages will be prepared in manuscript.

Place	Date	Hour	Summary of Events and Information	Remarks and references to Appendices
N.10.C.4.2. (Sheet 57D)	Sept. 11		Lieut. D.C. KELLEY, U.S. M.O.R.C. returns from temporary duty at 3rd Army P.M. Cage, CANDAS. A.D.M.S. orders No. 75. receives his forecast and to report tonight on relief to 38 F. Division. No. 37249 Sgt. J.C. RATTRAY, M.S. 91 awarded the M.M.	Both
"	12		Nothing to note.	Both
"	13		A.D.M.S. called. Nothing to note. Paid in money for Divisional Man Change Cuttifield to "Q"	Both
"	14		Paid in money returned from home to U.K. Nothing to note.	Both
"	15		Capt. H.B. LEE returned from leave. Lieut. D.C. KELLEY to move Bearer Division under dir. his men. Beam	Both
"	16		Orders received for Bearer Division dais Group to move at 5.30 pm	Both
O.34 Central (Sheet 57c)	17		H.Q. move to new camp near ROCQUIGNY (O. 34 central) at 1.30pm. All cars sent to 52 F. Amb. Very heavy thunderstorm last night.	Both
"	18		had heavy rains. Motors all day at F. Cm.D.S.	Both

Army Form C. 2118.

WAR DIARY
or
INTELLIGENCE SUMMARY. 51st Field Ambulance
(Erase heading not required.)

Instructions regarding War Diaries and Intelligence Summaries are contained in F.S. Regs., Part II. and the Staff Manual respectively. Title pages will be prepared in manuscript.

Place	Date	Hour	Summary of Events and Information	Remarks and references to Appendices
O.34.C.0.5.4 (Sheet 57c)	SEPT. 19.		Visited I.C.M.M. Dressing Station at V.2.b.2.2. arranged for the transport belongings to the next out. Bar HQ tomorrow. Major b/A. J.S. LEWIS to ---- with unit Bart. Bearer.	b/A.
"	20.		Nothing to note. Transports returns from bart. Field Ambulance.	b/A.
"	21.		Capt. M. DOCKRELL, R.A.M.C. joins 51st Field Amb. for duty. 1/Lieut. D.C. KELLEY, U.S.M.O.R.C. reports from 53rd Field Amb.	b/A.
"	22.		1/Lieut D.C. KELLEY sent for duty as M.O. to 17th Div. Wing.	b/A.
"	23.		Sent I Corp orders. Nothing to note.	b/A.
"	24.		Nothing to note.	b/A.
"	25.		Receives orders to join 51st Bde Group at MANANCOURT. Reconnoitred area for site for the Field Amb. Bearer tomorrow.	b/A.
V.13.c.6.2 (Sheet 57c)	26.		Unit moved from O.34. central to V.13.c.6.2 (near MANANCOURT). D.D.M.S. orders Major W. BARCLAY rejoins from 3 Can. CCS on ------- 17th Capt. M. DOCKRELL has sent in his place.	b/A.

W. McLean
Lieut. Col. RAMC

Army Form C. 2118.

WAR DIARY
or
INTELLIGENCE SUMMARY.
(Erase heading not required.)

Instructions regarding War Diaries and Intelligence Summaries are contained in F. S. Regs., Part II. and the Staff Manual respectively. Title pages will be prepared in manuscript.

Place	Date	Hour	Summary of Events and Information	Remarks and references to Appendices
MANAN-COURT	27/10		H.Q.C. worken, nc proceed on leave to United Kingdom.	
do.	28/10		Lt. D.C. KELLY, V.S.M.O.R.Q. returned from funeral Reception Camp and was attached for temporary duty at V Corps P.O.W. Cage. Capt E.V. BEAUMONT, RAMC transferred to 9th Yorks Regt. for duty with this unit. Want entries 8, 52, 80, B.A.Q. (20 O.R.) reported for duty with this unit. Nothing to note.	W.J.Barada Ca W.J.Barada Ca
do.	29/10		Under orders from A.D.M.S. 17th Div. Lt. D.C. KELLY RS motor to Bee R.G.A. for duty.	W.J.Barada Ca
do.	30/10		Proceeded h see R.G.A for duty. 50 war damp earthquake cold.	W.J.Barada Ca Major R.A.M.C. for O.C., 5/5th Field Ambulance.

CONFIDENTIAL

WAR DIARY

OF

51st FIELD AMBULANCE

FROM OCTOBER 1st 1918 TO OCTOBER 31st 1918

VOLUME 21

MEDICAL
Army Form C. 2118.

WAR DIARY
or
INTELLIGENCE SUMMARY.
(Erase heading not required.)

510th Field Ambulance

Instructions regarding War Diaries and Intelligence Summaries are contained in F. S. Regs., Part II. and the Staff Manual respectively. Title pages will be prepared in manuscript.

Place	Date	Hour	Summary of Events and Information	Remarks and references to Appendices
NANANCOURT	1/10/18		Nothing to note	
do	2/10/18		Nothing to note	
do	3/10/18		A working party of 55 O.R. was sent to 3 Cdn C.C.S. at ETRICOURT	C.W. Barclay
do	4/10/18		The same working party was sent to 3 Cdn C.C.S. Capt. E.W. Beaumont detached this Regt. also en route to Valley for a horse.	C.W. Barclay C.W. Barclay
Hqy X.11.6. Sheet 57c.	5/10/18		Unit ordered to move with 57th Inf. Bde Group at 2 p.m. arrived at WILD St 57c at 6.30 p.m. Lt J.I. WISEMAN U.S.M.O.R.C. joined the unit for duty from Base Depot. Capt. E.W. Beaumont was sent to No 3 Cdn C.C.S. for temporary accommodation.	C.W. Barclay
do	6/10/18		[illegible] ad tem dis 55th A group with Major Bain Co. 2/53 Fld Amb to HINDENBURG LINE near BANTOUZELLE & 1/53 Fld Amb to watch Bn Hdts	C.W. Barclay
M33 Central about 57d.	8/10/18	6.30 a.m.	Unit moved en route for BANTEUX, final [illegible]	

Army Form C. 2118.

WAR DIARY
or
INTELLIGENCE SUMMARY.
(Erase heading not required.)

51st Field Ambulance

Instructions regarding War Diaries and Intelligence Summaries are contained in F. S. Regs., Part II. and the Staff Manual respectively. Title pages will be prepared in manuscript.

Place	Date	Hour	Summary of Events and Information	Remarks and references to Appendices
SEVIGNY	9/7/3	11:00	Reached at 8.30 am. Major Rowan Cave & Pickering got on to a unit 51st B.F.B. a.c. got through to relieve 5th Glou.s.	
		3:30am	Lieut Roworth & 2/Lt Wilson & Major G. Lewis H.d. with 4 Orderlies proceeded to get to what 51st B.F.B. had taken over at	
		05:30	MAUASSISE FARM at entrances to A.D.S. at 02:30	
		12:00	Report received from Major Lewis that Post had been established at CHEMIN VERT, and that he was in touch with Battalion R.P's & S.B.P.Os. who a.c. advanced by an.	
		12:30	R.A.P's were being cleared to A.D.S. at SEVIGNY Rd opened a A.D.S. at 13.45.	
		14:30	O.C. got in touch with Maj. Lewis and found the wounded got back to Diedu r and that no men were on the move. Roads during the enemy retirement were very bad. No trucks could be moved. Very heavy casualties among Motor Cars.	

A7092   Wt. W148 9/M1293 750,000 1/17. D. D. & L. Ltd. Forms/C2118/14.

Army Form C. 2118.

WAR DIARY
or
INTELLIGENCE SUMMARY.   51st Field Ambulance

(Erase heading not required.)

Instructions regarding War Diaries and Intelligence Summaries are contained in F.S. Regs., Part II. and the Staff Manual respectively. Title pages will be prepared in manuscript.

Place	Date	Hour	Summary of Events and Information	Remarks and references to Appendices
SELVIGNY	9/10/18	15:30	Our post moved from May Lewis to O.U. Beaumel. No few cases in daylight.	Lt W. Barnesley
AUDENCOURT	10/10/18	07:00	Unit moved to O.U. Cairo and opened A.D.S. at 08:30.	Lt W. Barnesley
		11:00	Report received from Mrs Lewis Post to the effect that his MacCar post in INCHY and Kathy enemy was shelling this area specially NEUVILLY	
		12:00	Early afternoon shelling of NEUVILLY and INCHY dangerous.	
		13:00	A.D.S. was therefore moved to AVDENCOURT and opened at 13:40 hours. Very few cases came in at night. Being situation in NEUVILLY alongside day, our ADS thought it safe for A.D.S.'s here evening.	Lt W. Barnesley
- do -	11/10/18			Lt W. Barnesley
INCHY	12/10/18 05:00		Report received that Sgt P. McKeown M.M. Kathe been killed and that the M.O.s of 7th E.YORKS and 6th DORSETS had been severe cases. INCHY car post having crowded with wounded to A.D.S. was moved to Kathe at 10:00 hrs. Many wounded were dealt with in the evening the day.	
		11:00	Capt Wood (53rd Fd.Amb) and Lt J.I. WISEMAN were sent to 6 & 7 E.YORKS & 6 DORSETS to duty.	

Army Form C. 2118.

WAR DIARY
or
INTELLIGENCE SUMMARY. 57th Field Ambulance

(Erase heading not required.)

Instructions regarding War Diaries and Intelligence Summaries are contained in F. S. Regs., Part II. and the Staff Manual respectively. Title pages will be prepared in manuscript.

Place	Date	Hour	Summary of Events and Information	Remarks and references to Appendices
INCHY	12/10/18	1.00	Capt E.V. BEAUMONT R.A.C. and Capt L.M. TAYLOR U.S.M.C. were posted to the unit for duty. W.P.Barada Col	
AUDENCOURT	13/10/18	09.30	Orders received from A.D.M.S. that the A.D.S. be withdrawn to AUDENCOURT & remain with mobile reserve for #17 "Div. 9". Steps were taken to evacuate the occupants of buildings of A.D.S. and must withdraw at 0930 hrs, leaving INCHY Ad Car and bearer post and A.D.S. as a Rear of a unit. W.P.Barada Col	
			A number of civilians were evacuated and wounded from INCHY. W.P.Barada Col	
AUDENCOURT to	14/10/18 15/10/18	16.20	LieuT. McKEA returned from leave.	
"	16/10/18		Picked an Post at INCHY. As the building is in the centre of the Shelled area & has a lot of glass & very little Shelter, I recommended to BEAUMONT & found a good house with Cellars at the entrance to Linzal BEAUMONT, & advised Major LEVIS to move there in the afternoon took over. A.P.M.D	

Army Form C. 2118.

WAR DIARY
or
INTELLIGENCE SUMMARY. 51st Field Ambulance.

(Erase heading not required.)

Instructions regarding War Diaries and Intelligence Summaries are contained in F.S. Regs., Part II. and the Staff Manual respectively. Title pages will be prepared in manuscript.

Place	Date	Hour	Summary of Events and Information	Remarks and references to Appendices
AUDENCOURT	OCT. 17.		3 men of 53rd Field Ambulance attached to Dorset were killed last night. Visited Car Post at BEAUMONT & H.Q. of 53rd & 52nd Bns. on INCHY. 53rd Fd. Amb. two injured in the line last night by 52nd Fd. Amb.	N/A
"	18.		Visited Car Post at BEAUMONT & R.A.P. of 52nd Fd. Amb. Everything quiet. INCHY heavily shelled in aft afternoon. Reconnaissance for immediate advance lost in to army.	N/A
"	19.		50th Fd. Amb. and 51st Fd. Amb. orders re offensive on 20.10.18 received from M.D.S. of Centre made necessary arrangements. R.A.M.C. Sisters sent Extra sketches to Car Post in NEUVILLY road, & brought up all reserve nurses of 53rd & 53rd Field Ambulance to AUDENCOURT.	N/A
"	20.		Battle commenced at 0200 hours in very thick, drizzling rain. Invited the A.D.M.S. of 50th & 51st Divs. at 0300 knew & found that we had taken the 1st objective. Impossible to collect Stretcher cases as it was very dark. Waited at Bevoir Rd till 0430 & then went out to our A.D.S. of 50th & 51st Divs. home & two German orderlies back as number about 0430 &	N/A

Army Form C. 2118.

WAR DIARY
or
INTELLIGENCE SUMMARY. 51st Field Ambulance
(Erase heading not required.)

Instructions regarding War Diaries and Intelligence Summaries are contained in F. S. Regs., Part II. and the Staff Manual respectively. Title pages will be prepared in manuscript.

Place	Date	Hour	Summary of Events and Information	Remarks and references to Appendices
AUDENCOURT	O.C. 20	(contd)	Sketches taken about 0800 hours. Gas in trees with R.M.O.'s. Had all Bat. Aid posts clear except General case about 1100 hours. Evacuated lightly wounded. Ground very heavy. Got into car into NEUVILLY about 1130 hours & established Car post there. Cars to NEUVILLY Cross Roads bridged by 1200 hours & then large Gas were got into NEUVILLY. Evacuation of wounded was fairly simple. NEUVILLY was heavy shelled all day. A.D.S. at AUDENCOURT kept clear of walking wounded by 3 lorries lent by D.D.M.S. V Corps. Major J.S. LEVIS, M.C. granted a Licence to M.C. and wounded slightly in the face.	[initials]
"	21		Went round R.A.Ps. of 50th & 51st Bdes. Everything quiet & few cases coming in. Call J.S. RENDALL, R.A.M.C. joins for temporary duty. NEUVILLY heavily shelled last night, but few casualties. Capt. E.V. BEAUMONT, R.A.M.C. sent up to relieve Major J.S.LEVIS, M.C. who is to go on leave.	[initials]
"	22		A.D.M.S. called. Bearers ask to be relieved by 2nd Div Field Ambce. Tonight. All Cars belonging to 53rd Field Ambce. were returned today.	

Army Form C. 2118.

WAR DIARY
or
INTELLIGENCE SUMMARY. 51st Field Ambulance
(Erase heading not required.)

Instructions regarding War Diaries and Intelligence Summaries are contained in F.S. Regs., Part II. and the Staff Manual respectively. Title pages will be prepared in manuscript.

Place	Date	Hour	Summary of Events and Information	Remarks and references to Appendices
AUDENCOURT	Oct. 22.	(Contd)	News received from A.D.M.S. for Capt. TAYLOR, RENDALL, & MACGOWAN to join 53rd Field Ambulance, also for Falkirk Benn division of 52nd & 53rd Field Ambulances and to join 53rd Field Ambulance with stretcher carriers and that unit joins AUDENCOURT tomorrow morning.	JJM.
"	23.		Major M. BARCLAY, M.C. & J.S. LEWIS, M.C. proceeded on leave to U.K. Benn division of 52nd & 53rd Field Ambulances joined 53rd Field Ambulance. Capt. Zr. BEAUMONT brought heavy division of 53rd Field Ambulance by the BEAUMONT Change bus marched at NEUVILLY by 63rd Field Ambulance, both to AUDENCOURT and relief of BEAUMONT by 53rd Field Ambulance. Recommendations for immediate award sent in.	JJM.
"	24.		Orders received for unit to move to INCHY tomorrow but these cancelled shortly afterwards.	JJM.
"	25.		Orders received for Beau division to proceed to 52nd Field Amb.	JJM.
"	26.		Beau division joins 52nd Field Amb. at INCHY now in Divl. reserve. Both	JJM.

Army Form C. 2118.

WAR DIARY
or
INTELLIGENCE SUMMARY.   51st Field Ambulance

(Erase heading not required.)

Instructions regarding War Diaries and Intelligence Summaries are contained in F. S. Regs., Part II. and the Staff Manual respectively. Title pages will be prepared in manuscript.

Place	Date	Hour	Summary of Events and Information	Remarks and references to Appendices
AUDENCOURT	OCT. 27		Nothing to note.	51 F.A.
"	28		Visited No 3 Can. C.C.S. to try to get interview with SSgt J.R. MACKENZIE, & L/Cpl H.R. HAYNE awarded M.M. L/Cpl A. HOLDRIDGE M.M. awarded bar. Nothing to note.	51 F.A.
"	29		Reinforcement from 52nd Field Amb.	51 F.A.
"	30		Became divisional	51 F.A.
"	31		Nothing to note. Unit drilling & refitting.	Lieut Col Munro Comdg. 51st Field Amb. 31/10/18.

MEDICAL

No. 38
14/3401

CONFIDENTIAL

WAR DIARY

OF

51st FIELD AMBULANCE

FROM NOVEMBER 1st 1918 TO NOVEMBER 30th 1918

VOLUME 22.

MEDICAL

Army Form C. 2118.

WAR DIARY
or
INTELLIGENCE SUMMARY. 57th Field Ambulance
(Erase heading not required.)

Instructions regarding War Diaries and Intelligence Summaries are contained in F. S. Regs., Part II. and the Staff Manual respectively. Title pages will be prepared in manuscript.

Place	Date	Hour	Summary of Events and Information	Remarks and references to Appendices
AUDENCOURT	Nov 1.		Orders received for this unit to move to INCHY tomorrow.	[initials]
INCHY	2.		Unit marched from AUDENCOURT to INCHY to took over 17 thousand Rest Station. Were joined by 52nd Field Ambulance. - About 150 patients in the Rest Station, which is in a large factory.	MM
"	3.		Became divisional Rest 52nd Field Ambulance. Organised duties in connection with D.R.S.	MM
"	4.		Moved Ambulance wagons & 3 Motor Ambulance Cars to A.D.S. 52nd Field Ambulance at VENDEGIES-AU-BOIS. Capt. P. WALLICE, R.A.M.C. arrived for temporary duty from 10th General.	MM
"	5.		Capt. E. V. BEAUMONT, R.A.M.C. sent for temporary duty to 12th Manchesters in relief of Capt. J. SCOTT, M.C., Evacuates wounded.	MM
"	6.		A.D.M.S. visited unit & orders it to move to FOREST. Very poor place. D.D.M.S. ordered as many sick to site of C.M.D.S. but in a short period to be evacuated. Result do could not be fit in	MM

Army Form C. 2118.

WAR DIARY
or
INTELLIGENCE SUMMARY. 51° Field Ambulance.
(Erase heading not required.)

Instructions regarding War Diaries and Intelligence Summaries are contained in F. S. Regs., Part II. and the Staff Manual respectively. Title pages will be prepared in manuscript.

Place	Date	Hour	Summary of Events and Information	Remarks and references to Appendices
FOREST.	Nov. 7		Evacuated 36 cases to C.C.S. & returned 79 to duty. 20 cases taken with unit which moved to FOREST. Very wet & miserable.	Nil.
"	8.		Visited A.D.M.S. Unit to to move to LOCQUIGNOL tomorrow. Major J.S. LEVIS. M.C. returned from leave to U.K.	Nil.
LOCQUIGNOL	9.		Unit moved from FOREST to LOCQUIGNOL. Took over site of I C.M.D.S. horses for B.R.S. All sick sent to C.C.S. accordingly. Visited A.D.M.S. & had him this int. and.	Nil.
"	10.		Nothing to note. Weather fine.	Nil.
"	11.		Cessation of hostilities at 11 a.m. Bearer division & Ambulance Wagons & Cars rejoined unit. Capt P WALLACE sent to 13 t.h. Manchester to relieve Capt E.V. BEAUMONT who rejoined unit as unit. Warning order received that unit is to join 51st Bde.	Nil.
"	12.		Advance party with Ken to TROISVILLES.	
"			Sgt Polic. sgants arrived at LOCQUIGNOL. Pushing to B.O.E. Paid out.	Nil.
TROISVILLES	13		Unit moved with Bde front to TROISVILLES. Very good site & men very comfortable. Major W. BARCLAY, M.C. returned from leave to U.K.	Nil.

Army Form C. 2118.

WAR DIARY
or
INTELLIGENCE SUMMARY. 57th Field Ambulance
(Erase heading not required.)

Instructions regarding War Diaries and Intelligence Summaries are contained in F.S. Regs., Part II. and the Staff Manual respectively. Title pages will be prepared in manuscript.

Place	Date	Hour	Summary of Events and Information	Remarks and references to Appendices
TROISVILLES	Nov. 14		DDMS & Capt. Giles to by Bath - to visit various battalions. Clothing inspection parade.	
"	15.		Visited Bd H.Q. ADMS called. Capt P McGOWAN returned from temporary duty with 58° Field Ambulance.	
"	16.		Routine parades & fatigues & Kampere being &c. Nothing to note.	
"	17.		Church parade. United Thanksgiving Service at 11 am.	
"	18.		Parade to explain principles of Demobilisation & Reconstruction. Snowing a little.	
"	19.		Nothing to note. Recreational training proceeding well.	
"	20.		Nothing to note.	
"	21.		Route march.	
"	22.		Nothing to note. Field Ambulance.	
"	23.		Route march & nothing to note.	
"	24.		Church parade. Nothing to note.	

Army Form C. 2118.

WAR DIARY
or
INTELLIGENCE SUMMARY. 51st Field Ambulance

(Erase heading not required.)

Instructions regarding War Diaries and Intelligence Summaries are contained in F. S. Regs., Part II. and the Staff Manual respectively. Title pages will be prepared in manuscript.

Place	Date	Hour	Summary of Events and Information	Remarks and references to Appendices
TROIS VILLES	Nov. 25.		Arrived here - Afternoon A/ADMS while on way	NM
"	26.		Inspection of 51st Fd. Amb. by G.O.C. 17th Division. Field Ambce. Congratulated on their turnout.	NM
"	27.		Nothing to note.	NM
"	28.		Visited 53rd Field Ambce. Nothing to note.	NM
"	29.		All mirrors in unit have been manually examined. Transport being thoroughly cleaned preparatory to proceeding to CAMBRAI for interior by Superiors. All Fds. have been	NM
"	30.		Nothing to note. Men very comfortable. Cleaned. Not much sickness.	NM

30/11/18.

W. McKean
Lieut. Colonel.
Comdg. 51st Field Ambulance

CONFIDENTIAL 140/3489

98 39

WAR DIARY (MEDICAL)

OF

51st FIELD AMBULANCE

FROM DECEMBER 1st 1917 TO DECEMBER 31st 1917

VOLUME 23

COMMITTEE FOR THE
MEDICAL HISTORY OF THE WAR
5 MAR 1915
Date

WAR DIARY
or
INTELLIGENCE SUMMARY.

Army Form C. 2118.

MEDICAL 51st Field Ambulance

Place	Date	Hour	Summary of Events and Information	Remarks and references to Appendices
TROISVILLES	DEC 1.		Church Parade. Nothing to note.	nil.
"	2.		15 Coal Miners despatched to Collecting Station, CAMBRAI for release.	nil.
"	3.		Nothing to note. Raining heavily.	nil.
"	4.		H.M. the King inspects the Division informally. Men very enthusiastic in spite of rain.	nil.
"	5.		Capt. H.B. LEE proceeds to U.K. on one months special leave. Capt. P.D. MAGOWAN proceeds to 10th Bttn Sherwood Foresters on relief of Capt. RENDALL to U.K. for duty.	nil.
"	6.		Orders from ABBEVILLE area received. Major J.S. LEVIS, M.O. proceeds to AALLENCOURT to look after R.E. who have gone to prepare the new area.	nil.
MASNIÈRES	7		Left TROISVILLES at 10-15 hrs & marches to MASNIÈRES arriving at 16.30 hrs. Men marched very well.	nil.
HERMIES	8		Left MASNIÈRES at 0900 hrs & arrives at HERMIES at 1300 hrs. Weather very fine.	nil.

Army Form C. 2118.

WAR DIARY
OF
INTELLIGENCE SUMMARY

51st Field Ambulance

(Erase heading not required.)

Instructions regarding War Diaries and Intelligence Summaries are contained in F.S. Regs., Part II. and the Staff Manual respectively. Title pages will be prepared in manuscript.

Place	Date	Hour	Summary of Events and Information	Remarks and references to Appendices
FAVREUIL	DEC. 9		Left HERMIES at 0930 hrs & arrived at FAVREUIL at 1400 hrs. Weather still fine.	nil.
ALBERT	10		Left FAVREUIL at 0930 hrs & arrived at ALBERT at 1600 hrs. Men very cheery. Very fit. Men feverish but fair numbers of men coming in with I.C.T. Put cases up as best possible. B. Sherwood Foresters took ------ Partenberg 10th B. Sherwood Foresters.	nil.
PONT NOYELLES	11		Left ALBERT at 0930 hrs & arrived at PONT NOYELLES at 1400 hrs. Still wet & boisterous weather.	nil.
ST PIERRE A GOUY	12		Left PONT NOYELLES at 0930 hrs & arrived at ST PIERRE A GOUY at 1700 hrs. Very wet & tiring march but men did splendidly.	nil.
HOCQUINCOURT	13		Left ST PIERRE A GOUY at 0845 hrs & arrived at HOCQUINCOURT at 1400 hrs. The latter is a filthy village & the means of keeping men in anyways clean are disgraceful.	nil.
"	14		Sent strong letter of protest in about the village. Visited Lt Col E PAGNE A.A. D.M.S. who promised to move unit as soon as possible.	nil.

HP Forms W4. W1123 9/M1293 750,000. 1/17. D.D & L. Ltd. Forms/C2118/14.

Army Form C.
WAR DIARY
or
INTELLIGENCE SUMMARY. 51st Field Ambulance
(Erase heading not required.)

Instructions regarding War Diaries and Intelligence
Summaries are contained in F.S. Regs., Part II.
and the Staff Manual respectively. Title pages
will be prepared in manuscript.

Place	Date	Hour	Summary of Events and Information	Remarks and references to Appendices
HOCQUINCOURT	DEC 15		Still in HOCQUINCOURT. Personnel Ambulances are very badly billeted in BAILLEUL - BELLIFONTAINE. Garage No 3 Coy A.S.C. at BRONDELLE.	Appx
"	16		Visited FONTAINE - SUR - SOMME which has been allotted to this unit. Much better & cleaner village. Men & O.R. know Commanders.	Appx
FONTAINE-SUR-SOMME	17		Moved to FONTAINE-SUR-SOMME in afternoon. Horses under Cover. This will make a very good billeting area with a little work. People very friendly.	Appx
"	18		Improving billets. Men quite happy.	Appx
"	19		Visited Bde H.Q. Abbvd. visited unit & various workshops. Located a D.R.L. established here.	Appx
"	20		Reconnoitred village to see forward & selected an	Appx

WAR DIARY
or
INTELLIGENCE SUMMARY 51st Field Ambulance

Army Form C. 2118.

(Erase heading not required.)

Place	Date	Hour	Summary of Events and Information	Remarks and references to Appendices
FONTAINE-SUR-SOMME	DEC. 21		1 Hospital Nissen hut, & 6 men from 2/5 Batt. Yorks & Lancs (Pioneers) arrived, but it is impossible to commence erecting it as there are no props for foundations! Indented for them.	nil.
"	22		Props not yet to hand. Nothing to be done!	nil.
"	23		Raining very hard. All arrangements for Xmas dinner for men complete.	nil.
"	24		Major W. BARCLAY, M.C., Major J.S.LEWIS, M.C. proceeded to PARIS on leave.	nil.
"	25		All men of unit had an excellent Xmas dinner & concert in the school.	nil.
"	26		Nothing to note.	nil.
"	27		Erection of Nissen Huts for ORs. proceeding slowly. CRE. inspected billets with a view to improvements	nil. nil.
"	28		Aprons noted unit. Raining heavily	nil.
"	29		Nothing to note.	nil.

Army Form C. 2118.

WAR DIARY
or
INTELLIGENCE SUMMARY.   51st Field Ambulance

(Erase heading not required.)

Place	Date	Hour	Summary of Events and Information	Remarks and references to Appendices
FONTAINE-SUR-SOMME	DEC 30.		Visited 1st Borders & 7th Lincolns. Nothing to note.	
	31.		Nothing to note.	

W H McKean
Lieut Col Name
Commdg 51st Field Ambulance
31/12/18.

4
Jan. 1919

98 49
149 3448

n DIV Bot 1109

CONFIDENTIAL

WAR DIARY

OF

51st FIELD AMBULANCE

From 1.1.19 To 31.1.19

VOLUME 24

COMMITTEE FOR THE
MEDICAL HISTORY OF THE WAR
13 MAR 1919
Date

MEDICAL

Army Form C. 2118.

WAR DIARY
or
INTELLIGENCE SUMMARY.   51st Field Ambulance
(Erase heading not required.)

Instructions regarding War Diaries and Intelligence Summaries are contained in F. S. Regs., Part II. and the Staff Manual respectively. Title pages will be prepared in manuscript.

Place	Date	Hour	Summary of Events and Information	Remarks and references to Appendices
FONTAINE-SUR-SOMME	JAN 1919		Major W. BARCLAY, J.S. LEVIS returned from leave to PARIS.	Initial
	1.		Visited 51st Div. BR HQ.	
"	2.		Visited J. Lincoln & 10th Sherwood Foresters. Failed to draw Medical Stores from Base Depot at ABBEVILLE.	15th
"	3.		Horse parade. Men having a good deal of recreational training.	15th
"	4.		Visited 51st Div. HQ.	15th
"	5.		Nothing to note.	15th
"	6.		3 O.R. proceeded to U.K. for demobilisation. Work at O.R.D is not proceeding very fast. CRE who paid us a visit said additional labour would be better.	15th
"	7.		Supervision. Visited ADMS. hotel. Capts. called re reference to selection.	15th
"	8.		ADMS & DADMS. sick. H.B. LEWIS proceeds on special leave to U.K. Cpl. H.B. LEE	15th
"	9.		Major J.S. LEVIS returned from one months leave to U.K. Work at O.R.D. now proceeding satisfactorily, saw the work of improving min Fillette.	15th
"	10		Nothing to note.	15th

Army Form C. 2118.

WAR DIARY
or
INTELLIGENCE SUMMARY. 5/1st Field Ambulance
(Erase heading not required.)

Place	Date	Hour	Summary of Events and Information	Remarks and references to Appendices
FONTAINE-SUR-SOMME	JANY 11		Nothing to note.	NIL
"	12		Nothing to note.	NIL
"	13		Sent 7 men to U.K. for demobilisation	NIL
"	14		Nothing to note.	NIL
"	15		Nothing to note.	NIL
"	16		Field Ambulance played 78th Bgde RFA in Divisional football competition — Ribands f'm presented to S/Sergt Mackenzie, L/Cpl. Peake 4-1. L/Cpl Stocking. by C.O.E 18th Division on parade.	NIL
"	17		Shayne. 6 Played aband Harlet Barkers Lincoln. Roma voices DCL.	NIL
"	18		Field Ambulance played 7th Lincolns in type competition — drawn, but disgraphics.	NIL
"	19		Lincoln very hard. Nothing to note.	NIL
"	20		Sent 3 men to U.K. for demobilisation. Building at ord. going on slowly.	NIL
"	21		Tug of war competition at 2nd H.Q Field Ambulance won in final by 7/Lincolns.	NIL
"	22			NIL

Army Form C. 2118.

WAR DIARY
or
INTELLIGENCE SUMMARY 51st Field Ambulance

(Erase heading not required.)

Instructions regarding War Diaries and Intelligence Summaries are contained in F. S. Regs., Part II. and the Staff Manual respectively. Title pages will be prepared in manuscript.

Place	Date	Hour	Summary of Events and Information	Remarks and references to Appendices
FONTAINE-SUR-SOMME	JAN 23		Material for new Balk-houses drawn.	km
"	24		Skis- ping very heavy.	Mm
"	25.		Nothing to note.	Mm
"	26.		Capt. A. RANDLE, M.C. & 4.O.R. rejoined from 49 C.C.S.	Mm
"	27.		Nothing to note.	Mm
"	28		Nothing to note.	Mm
"	29.		Nothing to note. Army Act read aloud on parade.	Mm
"	30.		Orders received for Capt & Qr.mr H.B. LEE R.A.M.C. to proceed forthwith to D.M.S. First Army as officer i/c No 1 Advanced Dpot of Medical Stores. Major D.A.D.M.S. visits the Ambulance. 10 O.R. proceed on PARIS leave.	km
"	31		Capt & Qr.Mr H.B. LEE proceeded to report to D.M.S. First Army. Lieut Col. RAMC W.F. McLEAN proceeds on leave to U.K. Army Liais. Co. CW Barnes	

CONFIDENTIAL

WAR DIARY

OF

51st FIELD AMBULANCE

From 1·2·19   To 28·2·19

VOLUME 25

MEDICAL

Army Form C. 2118.

WAR DIARY
or
INTELLIGENCE SUMMARY. 51st Field Ambulance

(Erase heading not required.)

Instructions regarding War Diaries and Intelligence Summaries are contained in F. S. Regs., Part II. and the Staff Manual respectively. Title pages will be prepared in manuscript.

Place	Date	Hour	Summary of Events and Information	Remarks and references to Appendices
FONTAINE-Sur-SOMME	1/1/19		Nothing to report. Owing TS team bus returned for special leave.	W.Bara Co
do	2/1/19		Nothing to report	W.Bara Co
do	3/1/19		Nothing to report	W.Bara Co
do	4/1/19		R.E. material for D.R.S. not yet to hand. Work on D.R.S. at standstill	W.Bara Co
do	5/1/19		Visit of monitor	W.Bara Co
do	6/1/19		Nothing to note	W.Bara Co
do	7/1/19		Capt E.V. Beament proceeded on return to D.D.M.S. ETAPLES for duty	W.Bara Co
do	8/1/19		A supply of R.E. material received for D.R.S. work proceeded with	W.Bara Co
do	9/1/19		Nothing to note	W.Bara Co

Army Form C. 2118.

WAR DIARY
or
INTELLIGENCE SUMMARY. 51st Field Ambulance

(Erase heading not required.)

Instructions regarding War Diaries and Intelligence Summaries are contained in F. S. Regs., Part II. and the Staff Manual respectively. Title pages will be prepared in manuscript.

Place	Date	Hour	Summary of Events and Information	Remarks and references to Appendices
FONTAINE au BOIS	10/11/19		Nothing to report	a/w Base Ca
do	11/11/19		Nothing to report	a/w Base Ca
do	12/11/19		Capt Radler, no proceeded to Engrs HQ for demobilisation	a/w Base Ca
			Capt J.E. Dyke, Relief arrived for 56 Fd Amb for duty. no	
			Capt E.W. Beaumont.	a/w Base Ca
do	13/11/19		Nothing to report	a/w Base Ca
do	14/11/19		Nothing to report. Class instruction for not beginning's Journey.	a/w Base Ca
do	15/11/19		Class resumes in Jnr. from 0700 hrs.	a/w Base Ca
do	16/11/19		Capt J.E. Dyke proceeded to number party with 37th Labour group.	a/w Base Ca

Army Form C. 2118.

WAR DIARY
or
INTELLIGENCE SUMMARY. 51st Field Ambulance
(Erase heading not required.)

Instructions regarding War Diaries and Intelligence Summaries are contained in F. S. Regs., Part II. and the Staff Manual respectively. Title pages will be prepared in manuscript.

Place	Date	Hour	Summary of Events and Information	Remarks and references to Appendices
FONTAINE-SUR-SOMME	FEB 17		Lieut. Col. W. F. McLEAN arrives from France to U.K. Weather in a very bad condition trying to Hanw.	15th M
"	18		Rain out morning. Too much frost to 51st Base H.Q.	15th M
"	19		Nothing to note.	15th M
"	20		6 men proceeds to U.K. for demobilization	15th M
"	21		Lc. 97th field G. R.E. called. Nothing to note.	15th M
"	22		Major W. BARCLAY proceeded on 14 days special leave to U.K.	15th M
"	23		Nothing to note.	15th M
"	24		Nothing to note.	15th M
"	25		ADMS visited D.R.S. 3 H.D. horses demobilized	15th M
"	26		Nothing to note. Roads improving slowly	15th M
"	27		8 mules proceeds for demobilization + 1 mule evacuated sick	15th M
"	28		Nothing to note.	15th M

W. McLean
Lieut Col RAMC

A7092 Wt. W1725 9/M1293 750,000. 1/17. D.D. & L. Ltd. Forms/C2118/14.

CONFIDENTIAL No. 42
160/3551

WAR DIARY

OF

51st FIELD AMBULANCE

From 1.3.19. To 31.3.19

VOLUME 26

MEDICAL

Army Form C. 2118.

WAR DIARY
or
INTELLIGENCE SUMMARY. 51st Field Ambulance

(Erase heading not required.)

Place	Date	Hour	Summary of Events and Information	Remarks and references to Appendices
FONTAINE-SUR-SOMME	MARCH 1		2 H.D. horses & 5 Mules sent for sale.	Nil
"	2		Nothing to note	Nil
"	3		Nothing to note.	Nil
"	4		Nothing to note.	Nil
"	5		Nothing to note.	Nil
"	6		6 mules and 1 H.D. horse sent for sale.	Nil
"	7		Nothing to note.	Nil
"	8		7 men went on Paris leave	Nil
"	9		Nothing to note. 6 M. Carts sent for demobilisation	Nil
"	10		Sergeant Major Dodd & 4 O.R. RAMC proceeded to 1st Army for to China	Nil
"	11		Nothing to note	Nil
"	12		1 O.R. RAMC sent for demobilisation	Nil
"	13		2 M. RADC M.T. sent for demobilisation	Nil
"	14		2 M. Carts H.T. & 1 P.B. between sent for demobilisation	Nil
"	15		4 O.R. RAMC sent to 1st Army for to China	Nil

Army Form C. 2118.

WAR DIARY
or
INTELLIGENCE SUMMARY. 51st Field Ambulance

(Erase heading not required.)

Instructions regarding War Diaries and Intelligence Summaries are contained in F. S. Regs., Part II. and the Staff Manual respectively. Title pages will be prepared in manuscript.

Place	Date	Hour	Summary of Events and Information	Remarks and references to Appendices
FONTAINE-SUR-SOMME	MARCH 16		5 O.M. R.A.M.C. out of demobilisation	clear
"	17		Major W. Barclay R.A.M.C. returned from leave to U.K.	heen
"	18		Major J. S. Lewis R.A.M.C. proceeded to 52nd Field Ambulance for temporary duty vice Lt-Col Boyston R.A.M.C. on leave. Capt. H. Archer, 75 Fd Yorks transferred to 51st Field Ambulance for duty.	heen
"	19		This unit is now doing work of the 51st Inf. Bde. as the Regimental Medical Officers have gone to the Ambulance. Our greater so harassing difficult and the Divl. M.T. Coy are not repairing cars well owing principally to shortage of skilled labour.	heen
"	20		5 O.M. R.A.M.C. out for demobilisation.	heen
"	21		Nothing to note.	heen
"	22		Paid out unit. Capt. H. ARCHER, R.A.M.C. left to report to 2.D.M.S. Eligible for duty T/S.S.M. P.R. WHITE, R.A.S.C. M.T. proceeds to U.K. on furlough.	heen
"	23		Nothing to note.	heen
"	24		Major W. BARCLAY, M.C. proceeds to 52nd Field Ambulance vice Major J.S. LEWIS, M.C., who rejoins 51st Field Ambulance on relief.	heen

Army Form C. 2118.

WAR DIARY
or
INTELLIGENCE SUMMARY.   51st Field Ambulance

(Erase heading not required.)

Instructions regarding War Diaries and Intelligence Summaries are contained in F.S. Regs., Part II. and the Staff Manual respectively. Title pages will be prepared in manuscript.

Place	Date	Hour	Summary of Events and Information	Remarks and references to Appendices
FONTAINE S/R SOMME	MARCH 25.		Nothing to note.	nn
"	26.		Nothing to note.	nn
"	27.		Still very hot weather. Nothing to note.	nn
"	28.		Nothing to note.	nn
"	29.		Nothing to note.	nn
"	30.		Weather very bad. Snowing at times. Demobilisation of 8 O.R.	nn
"	31.		Cancelled owing to storms in Channel. Nothing to note.	nn

31/3/19.

R.W. Lea
Lieut Col. R.A.M.C.
Commdg. 51st Field Ambulance

CONFIDENTIAL

WAR DIARY

OF

51st FIELD AMBULANCE

FROM 1-4-19 TO 30-4-19

VOLUME 27

MEDICAL.

Army Form C. 2118.

WAR DIARY
or
INTELLIGENCE SUMMARY. 51st Field Ambulance

(Erase heading not required.)

Instructions regarding War Diaries and Intelligence Summaries are contained in F.S. Regs., Part II. and the Staff Manual respectively. Title pages will be prepared in manuscript.

Place	Date	Hour	Summary of Events and Information	Remarks and references to Appendices
FONTAINE SUR SOMME	APRIL 1		Went to Cachure, Abbeville for money	
"	2		nothing to note	
"	3		Capt J.S. LEWIS, M.C., left for U.K. for demobilization.	
"	4		nothing to note	
"	5		nothing to note	
"	6		11 OR NCOs & 4 OR NASC HT. left for demobilization. Col Byden spoke	
"	7		Capt. Off. Pkt. called with reference to equipment	
"			Capt. W BARCLAY arrived.	
"	8		nothing to note	
"	9		nothing to note	
"	10		nothing to note	
"	11		nothing to note	
"	12		2 P.B. Unknown & 1 OR NCO MT. left for demobilization	
"	13		4 OR NCOs left for demobilization. 1 OR NCOs sent to Army of Occupation	
"	14		nothing to note	
"	15		nothing to note	

Army Form C. 2118.

WAR DIARY
or
INTELLIGENCE SUMMARY. 51st Field Ambulance.
(Erase heading not required.)

Instructions regarding War Diaries and Intelligence Summaries are contained in F. S. Regs., Part II. and the Staff Manual respectively. Title pages will be prepared in manuscript.

Place	Date	Hour	Summary of Events and Information	Remarks and references to Appendices
FONTAINE-SUR-SOMME	APRIL 16		Col BRYDEN, S.M.O. & Capt Pbt Colson. Paid out amount 7th Bn Bath Regt	mss
"	17		Left for U.K.	mss
"	18		Nothing to note. Col BRYDEN called to Joy Ref. Office of S.M.O. & Capt to be moved to LONGPRÉ	mss
"	19		on 20th. Nothing to note.	mss
"	20		4 O.R. RAMC & 10 M. RAMC N.S. left for Ambulants	mss
"	21		Handed over duties of S.M.O. 17th Div Pkt to Col BRYDEN.	mss
"	22		Arranged with O.C. 3rd Advance Depot Medical Store for take all supplies	mss
"	23		drugs, dressings &c. 7th Bn Lincolns & 10th Bn Sherwoods left for U.K. 7th RAMC N.T. joined to complete Cadre. 10th RAMC N.T. parted ho.1 Coy. Div Train	mss
"	24		Sent all supplies drugs dressings &c to Advance Depot Med Store	mss
"	25		Visited Cadre pubk. to check equipment.	mss
"	26		Visited Cadre pubk. to check equipment.	mss
"	27		2 O.R. RAMC & 2 O.R. RAMC proceeded to U.K. for demobilisation	mss

MEDICAL.

Army Form C. 2118.

WAR DIARY
or
INTELLIGENCE SUMMARY. 57º¹ Field Ambulance.

(Erase heading not required.)

Instructions regarding War Diaries and Intelligence Summaries are contained in F. S. Regs., Part II. and the Staff Manual respectively. Title pages will be prepared in manuscript.

Place	Date	Hour	Summary of Events and Information	Remarks and references to Appendices
FONTAINE-SUR-SOMME	APRIL 28		Voted from Cachie Abbeville & got clearance certificate signed	Somme
"	29		Loaded all equipment wagons ready for move	"
"	30		Entire Unit entrained at LONGPRÉ for U.K. & left at 16.16 hours.	MLR

K.M.Ham
Lieut Col RAMC
Commg. 57ᵗʰ Field Ambulance

No 151 Little ambulance

Nov 19

Army Form C. 2118.

MEDICAL

WAR DIARY
or
INTELLIGENCE SUMMARY

51st Field Ambulance

(Erase heading not required.)

Instructions regarding War Diaries and Intelligence Summaries are contained in F.S. Regs., Part II. and the Staff Manual respectively. Title pages will be prepared in manuscript.

Place	Date	Hour	Summary of Events and Information	Remarks and references to Appendices
HARFLEUR	MAY 1		Unit arrived at Harfleur at 10.30 has & taken over to Embarkation Camp	9/5/44 search
"	2		Unit at Harfleur	hm
"	3		Still at Harfleur 2nd & 3rd men going p.h.S.	hm
"	4		Still at Harfleur	hm
"	5		Still at Harfleur men getting any uniform	hm
"	6		Embarked for U.K. at 18 hrs at Havre	hm

R H McLean Lieut Col
Comdg 51st Fd Amb.

www.ingramcontent.com/pod-product-compliance
Lightning Source LLC
Chambersburg PA
CBHW080853010526
44117CB00014B/2247